A NEW COMPLETE GUIDE
TO THE PRADO GALLERY

ANTONIO J. ONIEVA

A NEW COMPLETE GUIDE
TO THE PRADO GALLERY

Translated by
PATRICIA MAY O'NEILL

A new edition revised by
MYRIAM FINKELMAN

GUIAS DEL MUSEO DEL PRADO
MADRID (España)

Editorial Mayfe, S.A. - Madrid
I.S.B.N.: 84-7105-037-4
Impreso en Artes Gráficas Grijelmo, S.A. - Bilbao
Depósito Legal: BI. 2474-1979
Copyright 1979: Luis Moretón Soriano
Reservados todos los derechos
Printed in Spain - 16.ª Edición (1979)

ORIGIN AND FORMATION
OF THE PRADO GALLERY

In the old San Jerónimo walk, not very far from the church of the same name (belonging to the Monastery of the Order of Saint Jerome), a proud brick and stone building designed by Madrid architect D. Juan de Villanueva, was built by royal foundation in the 18th cent. The chosen location next to the Botanical Garden was the most adequate for presenting the flora, fauna and inorganic matters, studies which at the time of Carlos III were acquiring a singular expansion.

In Spain, in contrast there existed a great art-collecting tradition that was rooted in the Catholic Kings (Reyes Católicos, Isabel y Fernando), especially in Queen Isabel of Castilla who was in love with the Flemish painting. Her successors, Carlos V, the Emperor, Felipe II and III and above all IV, were great protectors of the arts. Felipe IV was well-acquainted with the golden century of Spanish painting, whose principal masterpieces passed through his hands. The number was constantly increased by the acquisitions in England (collections of Carlos I), in Flanders by means of Rubens, and in Italy by the good taste of Velázquez. Some of the King's ambassadors did not have any other mission than the purchase of works of art destined to augment the royal collections. On the other hand, the Spanish churches and monasteries were filled with altar pieces, tablets and canvases, etc., the fruit of acquisitions and donations which frequently adorned the ornaments, chapels and cloisters, at times in excess.

First during the period of the Enlightenmen and later during the Napoleonic invasion, many secularized convents were making themselves depositories of works of art. These were innumerable groups —generally abandoned in foolish places— that some day would attract the attention of experts and cause them to publicly exhibit these masterpieces for the general delight and culture of admirers. The idea that had been already started in the period of Velázquez of forming a museum of art was gaining strength and becoming concrete. And this, oddly enough, in the times of the intruder, Joseph Bonaparte. It was in effect on this occasion when at the decree of Urquijo on December 20, 1809, a museum of painting in Madrid was created. Even before its birth it was baptised with the name of «Museo Josefino»[1].

Doubtless during the same time a fortune of beautiful works to be given to Napoleon, as others had been given to Marshal Soult were separated. After the defeat of Napoleon's troops and the signing of the Treaty of Paris on May 30, 1814, Spain recovered her right to the plundered works, and all were restored to their original places.

Shortly before that date the legitimate King, Fernando VII, enters Spain. One of his principal preoccupations was the maintenance and conservation of the artistic patrimony that mostly belonged to him, and jealously protected the Academies of Bellas Artes of Valladolid and Zaragoza, and principally San Fernando of Madrid.

. The latter sought with growing interest a suitable building where the artistic fortune, unworthily accumulated in various ill conditioned places, could be located. The King granted the Palace of Buenavista which had belonged to the house of the Duke of Alba. Later the Municipality of Madrid gave this house to Godoy, who although the favorite of Carlos IV, never accepted it. In fact the Academy also failed to accept it. But the complaints were so continuous regarding the bad conditions of the paintings that it was necessary to search for a building that would give them truly suitable pro-

---

[1] See *Historia del Museo del Prado* by **Mariano de Madrazo**. Madrid, 1945.

tection. Then the Museum of Natural Sciences, erected by Villanueva in the times of Carlos III, was considered. This building was found so badly deteriorated by the ravages of the War of Independence that Fernando VII and his wife, Isabel of Braganza, took under their protection and the expense of His Majesty the building's restoration. In September of 1818 the Marquis of Santa Cruz, the first aulic director of the museum[2], submitted a two-room design to the King as the building was already repaired for this purpose.

On July 27th of the same year 32 paintings selected by the court's painter, Vicente López, were brought to the museum.

By the end of the same year 1818 more pictures had been added. The following year the total obtained by the inauguration day was 1626 works (not all however being hung). The Museum was inaugurated on November 19, 1819. In the first catalogue of the same year only the following 311 pictures are listed.

Arias, 1; Aparicio, 2; Arellano, 2; Bayeu, 5; Cano, 6; Carnicero, 2; Caxes, 2; Coello, 2; Castelló, 2; Collantes, 3; Carreño, 2; Cerezo, 2; Cruz, 1; Carducci, 7; Espinós, 8; Escalante, 1; Espinosa, 4; Goya, 2; El Greco, 1; School of Herrera el Viejo, 1; Juan de Juanes, 15; Leonardo, 2; López, 1; Madrazo, 1; Maella, 7; Maíz, 6; Mazo, 6; Meléndez, 43; Montalvo, 4; Morales, 2; Muñoz, 1; Murillo, 44; School of Murillo, 3; Orrente, 6; Palomino, 1; Pantoja, 1; Pareja, 1; Paret, 4; Pereda, 1; Pérez (Bartolomé), 2; Pérez (Cristóbal), 1; Prado (Blas del), 1; Ribalta, 4; Ribera, 29; Roelas, 1; Sánchez (Mariano), 6; Sánchez Coello, 1; Toledo, 7; Tobar, 1; Velázquez, 45; School of Velázquez, 1; Villavicencio, 1; Zurbarán, 6.

As one can see, the main lot corresponded to Velázquez with 45 canvases; Murillo following with 44, and then Meléndez with 43. Goya, still alive at the time had only two and Greco one.

In 1820 the Museum was enriched by 87 more pictures and a work by Rubens, entered for the first time. The following year: six by Spanish painters and 195 by Italians. The

---

[2] Ib., **Mariano de Madrazo.**

picture-gallery closed in 1826 due to the amplification of
works, in the same year it was ordered that all the paintings
that had been ceded to the Academy of San Fernando Should
be returned to the royal collections. These pictures were:

Jacob's Blessing, by Ribera.
Adam and Eve, by Van Dyck.
The Annunciation, by Murillo.
Portrait of Felipe IV, by Velázquez.
Portrait of Doña Mariana de Austria, by item.
Portrait of Prince Baltasar Carlos, by item.
Portrait of the Marquis of Pescara, by item.
A Mayor's Portrait, by item.
Samson Tearing a Lion into Pieces, by Lucca Giordano.
Marte, by Velázquez.
Barba Roja, by item.
God the Father, by Mengs.
Two Pastel Portraits, by Tiepolo.
A Fable, by Lucca Giordano.
Two Pictures with Military Trophy, by David Teniers.
Jacob's Dream, by Ribera.
The Saviour, by Juan de Juanes.
The Birth of St. John, by J. Pantoja.
Christ's Birth, by item.
The Vision of Ezequiel, by Collantes.
Sea-side scenes, by Carducho.
Felipe IV's Oath, by Maino.

To this important group was added the collection of the
Academy conserved in the «Special Rooms», whose pictures
were classified by Fernando VII as «indecent» and so he
ordered that they Should not be shown to the public. These
were Venus by Tiziano and the Nudes by Rubens.

During March of 1828, after the installation of the Spanish,
Italian, French and German schools, the museum was reopened to the public. Soon after, the Flemish and Dutch
schools were included.

On September 29, 1833, Fernando VII died. The museum
remained intact for his daughter, Isabel II. Estimated in 39

million *reales*, it was included as part of her heritage «with notorious and unjust prejudice. This fact did not lessen the queen's protection, and the catalogue of 1758 —last of those printed during her reign— lists 2119 pictures»[3].

The governing queen also protected with the greatest zeal the Prado Museum, naming D. José de Madrazo Director on August 20, 1838. The next year on April 26 (incidentally the birthday of Doña María Cristina) six new rooms and a Gallery of sculpture were opened. In 1868 with the fall of Isabel the II the royal museum passed to the national patrimony with the name of «Museo del Prado» (the Prado Museum), to avoid being confused with the Museum of Paintings of the Trinity, an old convent inhabited by Trinitarian monks. The latter museum had served as a depository for the works which for the most part passed over to the Prado proceeding from the secularized religious Orders. To these Orders had come various legacies and donations in order to get bigger the Prado extensively.

During the Civil War (1936-39) the museum remained closed. Some 525 paintings, 180 sketches by Goya and the jewels from the «Tesoro del Delfín» (Treasure of the Dauphin) were taken abroad. The best of these works were exhibited in the Geneva Museum. In July 1939, after the war had ended, the Museum was reopened with every one of the emigrated works.

* * *

The Prado Museum is one of the most beautiful in the world, and if one finds a deficiency it can be accredited to the fact that the Prado was not meant to be a museum. It was formed with private collections, that in our Spanish case were royal. One can easily gather that purely personal preferences have often influenced the choice of works. Our relations with Flanders began in the times of the Catholic

---

[3] *El Museo del Prado* by **F. J. Sánchez Cantón**. Madrid, 1949.

Kings whose daughter, Juana la Loca («the Crazy one»), married Felipe el Hermoso («The Handsome»), son of the Emperor Maximilian of Austria. The catholic Isabel was very enthusiastic about Flemish painting; some of whose triptychs she even carried with her from city to city. Later our presence in Flanders contributed to the demand for frequent export of early Flemish works.

The same thing did not happen with the early Italians, whose indigence is obvious. The Catholic King, interested in Italian affairs as King of Aragon, unfortunately lacked the artistic taste of his eminent wife. So for the entrance into Spain of good canvases of the Italian school it is necessary to wait until the times of the Emperor Carlos V, who admired Tiziano, above all other painters. The lack of good classics of the Dutch school is also obvious. Spain's stay in the territories of Holland was ephemeral and of a war-like character. This of course impeded the development of more elevated interest such as artistic acquisitions. On the other hand if there had been interesting sales or auctions of Dutch paintings in the times of Felipe IV, one could easily say that they passed unobserved by our ambassadors.

Until very recently we had only two primitive Italian works: *The Annuntiation* by Fra Angelico, which belonged to the Ducal House of Lerma, and *The Virgin's Death* by Andrea Mantegna, acquired by Felipe IV in the public auction of property that belonged to the unfortunate Charles I of England. It was only in 1941 that through the splendid generosity of D. Francisco Cambó two paintings by Tadeo Gaddi, one by Giovanni dal Ponte, one by Melozzo da Forli and three by Botticelli were added.

During the epoch of Carlos V and his son Felipe II many famous paintings from the Italian schools began to enter into Spain. In fact, our collection of Tiziano is un-equalled by any gallery in the world, and he who wishes to appreciate the master of Piave di Cadove in all his majesty has to come to Madrid to do so. Next we have the works of Tiziano, Paolo Veronese, Giaccopo Robusti il Tintoretto, Palma il Giovanne, Lorenzo Lotto, Bassano and Giorgione, entered under Felipe II.

The periods of Felipe IV and Carlos III were enriched
by the masterly group of Reffaello, Andrea del Sarto, Sebastiano del Piombo, il Guercino, Gentileschi, Lucas Jordán,
Furini and Giovanni Battista Tiepolo, who painted in the
Palacio de Oriente (Palace of Orient) and died in Madrid.

The Flemish school shows its splendid flowering in our
museum. An exquisite jewel of the collection is the *Descending
from the Cross* by Van der Weyden, sent by Queen Mary
of Hungary, ruler of the Lower Countries. Other works by
Van der Weyden, Memling, Quentin Metsys, Jan Massys,
Gerard David, Thierry Bouts, Petrus Christus, Van Orley,
Roberto Campin and others give us an idea of the early
Flemish paintings which are museum treasures. But all these
grow pale before the collection that we posses of Jerónimo
Bosch (El Bosco), a Flemish-German; the two Brueghels,
the patriarchal Pieter and his son Jan de Velours (surely we
could identify some works by Cornelis Brueghel d'Enfer
another of Pieter's sons); Patinir and David Teniers the
Young. Most of these works were acquired during the reign
of Felipe II and brought by his daughter, Isabel Clara Eugenia, ruler of the Lower Countries.

The aggregations of the Italian-Flemish works continues
with an extensive repertory by Rubens, who visited Spain
twice for diplomatic purposes; of Jacob Jordaens, Van Dyck,
Van Tulden, Pourbus, Vos, Snyders, Fyt and others, bought
mainly by the ambassadors of Felipe IV.

The German works that we possess are not very numerous, but are very well selected. Emperor Carlos V, who was
also emperor of Germany, naturally was painted by German
artists. His son contributed with works by Baldung Green and
his great-grandson the *Self-portrait* of Albrecht Dürer's and
his *Adam and Eve*. As a result we had come to possess the
works of Christopher Amberger, Lucas Cranach the Old,
Holbein and others. In short, Anthony Raphael Mengs worked many years in the Palace of Orient leaving numerous
portraits and allegories.

From Dutch masters we can present originals by Rembrandt, Anthony Moro, Wouverman, Gabriel Metsu, Paulus
Potter, Marinus, Van Ostade, Palamedes, Browver, Cornelius

of Haarlem, Hobbema, Van Scorel, Van Honthorst, Van de
Neer and many others.

The French painters are worthily represented with works
by Poussin, Watteau, Claude Lorrain, Philip de Campaigne,
J. Ranc, Hyacinthe Rigaud, Hubert Robert, Vouet, Vernet,
Meissonnier, Greuze, Mignard, Van Loo, Houasse, etc.,
though we lack Fouquet, Clouet, de la Tour, Fragonard,
Chardin, David, Ingres, etc.

English art is only represented in the Prado by Reynolds,
Hoppner and Romney with one work by Lawrence, another
by Gainsborough and one by Watson.

Other schools such as the Nordic and Portuguese have
very little importance.

We have left to the end the Spanish schools whose value
in quality and quantity are un-excelled by any other nation
or gallery.

If in order to know Tiziano and El Bosco and Rubens
well it is necessary to visit Spain, likewise in order to obtain
a just estimate of our great Spanish painters it is almost unnecessary to leave the Prado museum. If you visit El Escorial,
Toledo, Sevilla, Barcelona or Guadalupe you will complete
the total view, but not one is absolutely necessary. 118 oils,
apart from the sketches by Goya; some 50 by Velázquez,
many others by Ribera; by Murillo, 30; by Greco, 34; by
Zurbarán, 20; by Juan de Juanes, 12; by Carreño, 11; by
Sánchez Coello, 9; by Morales, 8; by Pantoja, 8; by Alonso
Cano, 8 by Mazo, 8; by Pereda, 6; by Valdés Leal, 4; by
Luis Tristán, 4; by Ribalta, 3; by Maino, 3. There are also
represented, with more or less the same number, the Spanish
painters Agüero, Antolínez, Arellano, Arias, both Bayeus,
Becerra, Bermejo, Berruguete, Bocanegra, Cabezalero, Ca-
milo, Cano, Carducho, Carnicero, Castillo, Caxés, Cerezo,
Collantes, Correa, Escalante, Espinosa (Jerónimo and Juan),
Esquivel, Esteve, Ezquerra, Fernández (Alejo), Fernández
Cruzado, Ferro, Fortuny, Gallego, García de Benabarre,
Gilarte, Gómez Pastor, González (Bartolomé), González Ve-
lázquez, Hamen, Herrera (el *Viejo* y el *Mozo*) (The *Old* and
the *Young*), Huguet, Inza, Iriarte, Jiménez Donoso, Juncosa,
Leonardo, López Portaña, López Piquer, Machuca, Madrazo

(José, Federico & Raimundo), Maella, March, Masip, Meléndez (Luis Eugenio & Miguel Jacinto), Mohedano, Muñoz, Navarrete the *Dumb*, Orrente, Pacheco, Palomino, Pareja, Paret, Pérez (Bartolomé), Prado (Blas del), Ramírez, Ribelles, Rico, Rincón, Rizi, Ruiz González, Salmerón, Schut (the *Young*), Sevilla (Juan de), Tobar, Toledo, Vidal, Viladomat, Villafranca, Villandrando, Villavicencio, Ximénez, Yáñez de la Almedina, and the list should be completed with the anonymous masters that are considerable.

★ ★ ★

The structure of the Museum, built by Villanueva, is majestic yet simple, and measures about 200 metres in length and 50 in width. It is composed of three floors with two façades: one to the north with a double perron and terrace. This terrace is in constant use by the public and the western façade is far more sumptuous with its colonnade, niches and statues.

Entering by the northern door we find a spacious rotunda and as we continue we see the grand gallery of the Spanish schools with works by Berruguete, Bartolomé Bermejo, Juan de Juanes, Yáñez de la Almedina, Sánchez Coello, Rizi, Maino, Ribera, Ribalta, Zurbarán, Murillo, Carreño, Claudio Coello, Herrera, Cano, Villavicencio, etc.

In the same rotunda at the entrance, where some historical pictures are hanging, there is a door to the right that leads to rooms XL, XLI, XLII, XLIII and XLIV, where the early Flemish painters may be contemplated. Represented are Roberto Campin (Flemalle's master), Thierry Bouts, Quentin Metsys, Mabuse (Gossaert), Van der Weyden and the school of the Van Eycks. Also included are Memling, Van Orley, Gerard David, Patinir, Brueghel the *Old*, Jerónimo Bosch (El *Bosco*), and the Germans Albretch Dürer, Lucas Cranach, Hans Baldung Green and others.

In front of the same door to the left are rooms II, III, IV, V and VI in which are presented the works of Raffaello, Fra Angelico, Botticelli, Giovanni Bellini, Andrea Mantegna, Tadeo Gaddi, Catena, *il Correggio*, Andrea del Sarto, Bernardino Luini, Sebastiano del Piombo, Tiziano, *Il Giorgione*, Lorenzo Lotto and Palma; Anguisciola, Conte, Carpi, Pontormo, Giulio Romano and Barocci.

And now new rooms have been added to the already existing. They were solemnly inaugurated on June, 1956 and by reason of their vicinity to the old rooms they have been mentioned with the Roman figure followed by the letter A. There are eight such rooms on the first floor and as many on the ground-floor. Room VII is dedicated to the Venetian School; room VII A to Veronese; room VIII to Tiziano; room VIII A to Veronese; Parrasyo and Tintoretto, room IX to Tiziano; room IX A to Tintoretto and room X A to the Bassanos.

Rooms X, XI and XXX are dedicated to El Greco; from room XII to XV to Velázquez and some works by Mazo and Carreño.

The Flemish School is distributed as follows: room XVI to Rubens; XVI to Van Dyck; XVII to Rubens; XVII A to Van Dyck and Jordaens; rooms XVIII, XVIII A, XIX, XX and XXI, to Rubens and some pictures by P. de Vos.

The next two rooms, XXI and XXII, are reserved for Dutch paintings.

From room XXIV to XXXII included we can see Spanish paintings. Room XXXII is the small rotunda of Goya, and the next ones from room XXXIII to room XXXIV are devoted to the French School and some others included in room XXXI (corridor). Rooms XXXVII and XXXVIII are consecrated to Italian painters of the 16th and 17th centuries. Room XXXIX is almost entirely devoted to Spanish painters, and rooms XL to XLIV to the Northern schools.

On the ground-floor we have:

A large amount of rooms that have been devoted to Goya's works. Among the most important of these we can mention room LIII with drawings; rooms LIV and LVII A with paintings; rooms LV, LVI and LVII with «cartoons» for tapestry; rooms LVII A and LV A with paintings, and finally the large room LVI A where we can see all the «black paintings».

Room L contains Spanish altar-pieces.

Room LIX, LX and LX A contain Flemish and Dutch paintings, and rooms from LXI A to LXVIII, with the exception of LXVII and LXVIII, contain Spanish canvases by Ribera, Castillo, Rizi, Cano, Carreño, Murillo, Valdés Leal, Pereda, Leonardo, etc. Next come rooms with the Dama (Lady) of Elche, Medals and the Treasure of the Dauphin.

In the upper floor, rooms ranging from LXXX to XCVIII, some works by great Spanish and Italian masters can be found again, as well as the new and important contribution of Mengs canvases and the beautiful legacy of Fernández Durán. (Vide map of this floor.)

Finally, in the lower floor, semi-basement, next to the Murillo door, new rooms have been thrown open to the public where British and Dutch paintings can be seen, among them those by Reynolds, Gainsborough, Romney, Lawrence, Hoppner, Watson and others.

IMPORTANT NOTE.—It is frequent in all the Museums and Galleries of the world to change the order of paintings' places in one Salon or between distinct Salons. It is not very often that there are changes, and always when they are made, it is for reasonable motives.

In order that the reader of this GUIDE has no difficulty because of a change, we publish at the end of this, a list of the numbers of the paintings and the page in which they are reviewed. So that when a visitor sees the number of any painting (and each number is on the upper part of the painting or in the poster), he will look for it in the list and will find the page of this GUIDE where it is mentioned or described.

Room I.—ROTUNDA

Upon entering into the Museum through the northern door, which we can reach by a staircase, we find ourselves in a rotunda with a bronze group piece in the center, a work by the Italian sculptor **Leone Leoni.** It represents Emperor Carlos V of Germany and I of Spain, dominating the Turkish furor. Embodied is the Turkish figure at the feet of the Emperor.

On the walls are hung as many as eight canvases representing Spanish victories during the epoch of Felipe IV. They are the following:

> **Carducho.** Num. **636,** *Stronghold of Constanza.* Núm. **635,** *Victory of Fleurs.*
> **Caxés.** Num. **653,** *The Recovery os San Juan de Puerto Rico.* Núm. **654,** *The Recovery of the Isle of San Cristóbal.*

(And now please take the door to the left.)

Room II.—RAFFAELLO

This Room is wholly consecrated to **Raffaello,** keeping his first rank jewels, some of which entered into Spain during Felipe IV's reign. He was a skilless King in the political aspect while an enthusiast of the Beautiful Arts. Our ambassadors, knowing the monarch's pleasures, managed to acquire the best pictures whenever they could and sent them to adorn the Alcazar and the Buen Retiro. Some purchases were made at the auction upon the unformate death of Charles I in England. As Prince of Wales he came to Spain considering marrying Felipe IV's sister. Our king showed him his collections enliving the already excellent taste of the young prince, who also finished to form a beautiful Gallery, dispersed upon his execution.

Raffaello Sanzio *was born in Urbino (Italy) in 1483 and died in Rome in 1520. This Italian painter was a disciple of Perugino, and in 1504 went to Florence. The contact with Leonardo da Vinci's works made him lose Perugino's influence. He desired vehemently to paint in Rome, but as he could not for the moment attain his wishes, he remained in the Medici's city during three years painting those charming Virgins exhibited in so many museums. Finally, he arrived in Rome when Michelangelo, protected by Pope Jules II, was at the top of his glory. The Pope had commissioned the latter to do the Sixtine Chapel's decoration, when Raffaello had already begun to paint the Vatican lodges boasting frescoes, such as* The Dispute about the Holy Sacrament, Athene's School, The Parnassus, Heliodore's Punishment, *etc., which Michelangelo did not fail to admire, to the extreme that he apologized before Jules II saying that he ignored the technique of fresco and asked the Pope to transfer the work to Raffaello who dominated it. The Pope did not concede to the change and both of the two genii fulfilled their work.*

Raffaello had broken off many customs; he grouped the figures with a dramatical idea, harmonizing expression and attitude; he gifted his frescoes with an unlimited profurdity, and as a play he resolved the foreshortenings giving them an unknown arrogance. He painted as much as possible in the short life of one who was born to paint. His Transfiguration *in the Vatican Museum;* The Madona Sixtina, *in Dresde; the portraits of Jules II, Leone X, Castiglione and others are unforgetable.*

He lived a beautiful, splendid and short life. Many anecdotes were and are related with the world's famous Fornarina, a Transtevere girl baker, whom he abandoned with a strength that he lacked. The modern criticism does not admit that episode at all, which if it actually happened, could not be more than a temporary love. Today nobody believes these stories because it is hard to believe that the Virgin's portraits could be of the beatiful baker, of whom there are portraits which do not look like one another. These are; one by Sebastiano del Piombo, another the Donna Velata, *and the third, the so well-known of naked bust. Raffaello died on Holy Friday. In the comparison of his work one may say that it was a supermen world created by an adolescent.*

Num. **299,** *The Cardinal.* This wonderful portrait has been the theme of an extended literature: a Renaissance's Cardinal: Bembo's madrigals; Rodrigo Borgia's poison... For some: criminal eyes; for others; a great deal of neo-pagan wisdom and, generally, a sinuous and squint-eyed glance. For Mayer it is an almost demoniacal work and, facing the Gioconda's mysterious smile, he places as partner, this Cardinal's slight malign one. But after all this literature, when we abandon ourselves to the portrait without any preoccupation, we see a face, alive, of an exquisite modelling and enormous interior life. We see a wonderful carnation coloring, fresh and clean; the eyes full of light; a long and aquiline nose and a mouth that although pleated, is about to smile. This warm carnation is enriched with the purpled mozetta and the cardinal's bonnet. The posture of the arm and hand indicates he, the portrayed, was seated. Who was this Cardinal? The first identification with Cardinal Alidosio was eliminated, and later those with Jules of Medici, Scarramuccia Trivulzio and many others. For us Spaniards, it is not the portrait of «a» Cardinal but of «the» Cardinal, the exemplar, unique, unrepeatable. It is a jewel of our Museum acquired by Carlos IV when he was the Prince of Asturias.

Num. **296,** *The Holy Family with the Lamb*, is a delightful composition with the Child upon the lamb. It was painted in 1504 soon after his arrival in Florence and one observes in it that there is no longer an influence of Perugino. Raffaello had appeared to a new world, especially to that of Leonardo, whose *sfumatto* began to preoccupy him letting it enter timidly into his new technique. It is said that in St. Joseph one guesses Fra Bartolomeo's influence. (Kept in the Camerin of El Escorial, and entered the Museum in 1837.)

Num. **302,** *The Virgin of the Rose*, so called because of the rose characterizing the picture, which appears on a little table near the Child's foot. We see another harmonious beauty of four figures grouped in triangle: St. Joseph, the Virgin, the Child and St. John. The young precursor gives Jesus a ribbon with the legend *Ecce agnus Dei* («Here is God's lamb»), with which the Child is about to play. The Virgin is beautiful, and beatiful are the children of a very soft and fresh carnation, perfectly detached from the dark background without being bulky, thanks to an unreproachable *sfumatto* that more than in any other canvas approaches Raffaello to Leonardo da Vinci. In is said that the table, the rose and the Child's left foot are modern additions, made in 1837 when the canvas was brought from El Escorial, adding that it already appeared in an old copy belonging to the Barcelona Cathedral.

Num. **301,** *The Holy Family*, called *The Pearl*, not because it should be Raffaello's pearl, that is to say his best work, neither the pearl of our Museum, the most beautiful; it was so entitled by Felipe IV when it was displayed before his eyes: «Here is the pearl of my pictures!», he exclaimed. It is a happy groupment almost pyramidal, of two aged persons, the Virgin and St. Elizabeth, and the two children Jesus and St. John. In the background, to the left, St. Joseph, the carpenter, works; to the right we see a landscape with a river and a bridge. The harmony of the scene powerfully attracts the viewer. The Child has just left His cradle, with a glad face and, as every child, posed to play with His companion. All this intimacy is augmented with the embrace of Mary and Her cousin Elizabeth, and St. Joseph's presence in his daily work forming a delightful ensemble, magnified with the color's beauty. Raffaello painted it around 1518 (which was his best period), for the Count Luis of Canossa who transferred it to his brother Galeazzo. The Duke of Mantua, of the Gonzaga's family, purchased it for the Monferrato's feud and a title of Marquis. In 1627, with Gonzaga's Gallery belonging to Charles I it passed to England and finally the ambassador D. Alonso Cárdenas acquired the picture for Felipe IV for 2000 pounds. The troops of Napoleon also took off the canvas, which was returned in 1818.

Num. **298,** *Chrit's Fall on the Road to Calvary* or *The Sicilian Spasm* (Pl. 1) as it is popularly entitled. It was previously painted on a tablet and in 1818, in Paris, was transferred to a canvas. The word *spasimo*, erroneously interpreted as astonishment, has contributed to this picture's popular fame though it is not of Raffaello's best works. It was in the convent of St. Mary of the *Spasimo* in Palermo (Sicily) and *spasimo* must be understood as *anguish* and by extent *fall*. The scene corresponds to one of the three falls of Our Lord on the way to Calvary. The composition is perfect, but the sombre and monotonous coloring does not appear to be Raffaello's touch. It is said that Giulio Romano painted a part of the picture. In the composition some note Albrecht Dürer's or Martin Schongauer's influence. It was sent to Spain in 1661 by the vice-roy Count of Ayala for Felipe IV, who was not very enthusiastically satisfied although having paid for it 4000 *ducados* of revenue each year to the convent and 500 more to the prior who brought the picture into Spain. It was stolen by the Napoleonics and returned in 1818.

Num. **303,** *The Holy Family of the Oak* (Pl. 2), is charaterized by the oak appearing in the background. The Holy Family figuring in the Pitti Gallery, in Florence, is similar to this one, and entitled *of the lizard,* because of the lizard, depicted close to the base of the column, substituted in this picture by a fruit. The composition is transversal, ascending from left to right. The Child who also has a foot in the cradle wishes to play with little St. John, who extends a ribbon with the *Ecce agnus Dei.* The Virgin holds Jesus in order to impede Him to slide from her lap; a pensive St. Joseph contemplates the scene. Regarding the composition we can say that it has the charm of all Raffaello's works in which he represents children; this fact always inflamed him with poetry. On the contrary, referring to the coloring, one observes certain tints somewhat strange to Raffaello, causing the thought that the collaboration of his pupils in this picture would be greater than on other occasions. This canvas also made the round trip to Paris. (In the XVIIIth century it already was in the Palace.)

Num. **300,** *The Visitation*, represents the meeting of Mary with her cousin St. Elizabeth, and other life scenes of Jesus. It originally was a tablet later transferred to a canvas, and is not one of Raffaello's most popular pictures. Berenson detects that his disciples, especially Pierino del Vaga, collaborated in the execution. The picture was commissioned by the Cardinal and prothonotary of St. Sylvester of Aquila's Church, in the Abruzzi, about 1519, and Felipe IV bought it for El Escorial. (In 1837 it enhanced the Museum.)

Num. **297,** *The Virgin with the Fish*. The picture represents the Virgin, the Child, St. Jerome, Raphael the archangel and Toby. This tablets, which afterwards was transferred to a canvas, belongs to Raffaello's great period and preceeds the St. Siste's Madonna by one year, in the *Zwinger*, Dresde. The composition is totally harmonious, and definitely wholly due to Raffaello's brush, although many believe to see his disciple Giulio Romano's collaboration. The somewhat serious Virgin contemplates Toby, while the Child in a graceful movement on the book held by St. Jerome seems as, although refrained by the hand of the Virgin, he wishes to approach St. Raphael. The lion placed at the saint's feet induces us to think the latter represents St. Jerome. It figured in St. Dominic, Naples, and was presented to the vice-roy Duke of Medina de las Torres, who ceded it to Felipe IV. Then it was stolen during the War of Independence and returned in 1818. (Proceeding from El Escorial it entered the Museum in 1837.)

Copies. Num. **304,** *Andrea Navagero* is the portrait of a Venetian writer and diplomat. The original belongs to the Doria's Gallery in Rome.

Num. **305,** *Agostino Beazzano* who was a poet from Treviso, a good friend of Cardinal Bembo and his Secretary.

Num. **313,** *The Holy Family «dell'Impannata»* is characterized by the window's name *(finestra impannata)*. It is a copy of the one hanging in the Pitti's Gallery, in Florence. Carlos IV bougt the tablet which came from Aranjuez.

Num. **315,** *The Transfiguration* is a copy of the original belonging to the Vatican's Museum. Many have considered the original as the Raffaello's *pearl*. It seems that this copy was commissioned to Penni by Pope Clemente VII, a contemporary of our Emperor. It belonged to the Duke of Medina de las Torres.

Room III.—FRA ANGELICO
AND BOTTICELLI

This room shelters very few pieces but all of first class. Apart from **Antoniazzo** only two early Italians figure in it: **Fra Angelico** and **Sandro Botticelli,** both of them Florentines and somewhat concurrent in the epoch. The former's picture has been in Spain about three centuries and a half, while at least in the Prado we had nothing by the second. Thanks to the magnificence of the conspicuous politician D. Francisco Cambó, a great lover of the Beautiful Arts, there are in our Museum three excellent pieces, which, if they have been touched by other artists, at least do not lack Botticelli's brush.

Various special circumstances, already exposed in another part of this book, determined an old deviation to the early Italians, with a Flemish predominance. And it happened that while all first-class Museums numbered works by Botticelli, ours had to do without them. Today we are satisfied to display the three hanging together with one by Fra Angelico.

Fra Angelico. *In his century he was named Guido di Pietro, born in Viechio di Muguello, in 1837. He died in Rome in 1455. His brother Benedetto was a miniaturist and it has been said that he influenced our artist's first works. The truth is that from childhood he felt the passion of painting and many argue that he was Starmina's disciple, others Angelo Gaddi's and others finally suggest that he also was Lorenzo Monoco's disciple.*

At twenty, when he was already known as an artist, he and his brother entered the Dominican Convent of Fiesole, near Florence. Since his return to Cortona to exercise the novitiate, his art definitely changed. He suppressed almost completely the golden back grounds, the pompous garments in the angels and Virgin's clothings, and the cresting and Gothic motives which were the frame of his holy figures, to be substituted by the Renaissance archs, extraordinarily simplified as he learnt from Bruneleschi and Michelozzo.

It is said that he was knelt to paint. The colors changed in his hands into heavenly raptures. Only his ardent flame of Divine love should sublimate faces, hands and attitudes arriving to compose figures that evidently are not of this world. His death took place in Rome, soon after the Vatican Chapel's decoration, commissioned by Nicholas V. He is

*buried in the Dominican Convent of St. Mary of Minerva. The Pope
Ordered the engraving of four verses of praise upon his sepulchre.*

Num. **15,** *The Annunciation* (Pl. 3). This tablet is painted with
tempera without oil velaturas. Under the simple porch, adorned with
a slightest border and medals, the scene of the Annunciation is
represented. The Angel with his opened wings, and about to kneel,
pudically retires his body, advancing the head to communicate the
good news to the Virgin. The hands are crossed over his chest and
his very pure profile is well detached on the halo. The Virgin seated
on the platform also retires her delicate body without looking to the
Angel, but hearing him, she imitates the posture of his arms. The
scene is crossed by a symbolic light ray which disappears next to
Mary's breast. It would be useless to speak about coloring delicacies
before the tablet itself: until this very moment everything in it is
an unknown harmony of colors: the blue domes, the subtle tones of
the faces without shades, passing through the habit's transparencies.
Simone Martin himself is far many centuries from this wonderful
tablet. The Annunciation appears before us so simplified as the one
of St. Mark's Museum, in Florence. Fra Angelico, without a pompous
architecture, gold or polished garments in the clothings, has attained
his superior art measure. The expression, the souls of the divine
personages, is what touches our feelings: when the one speaks the
other listens, and each one has his personality alive and his own
character.

Outdoors we see Adam and Eve expelled from Paradise by the
Angel's flamed sword. Both of them went out through a meadow
covered with little enamelled flowers and seldom can we employ
the word *enamelled* better than here, because since 1944 when the
tablet was cleaned, one could astonishingly detect the miniature-sized
and floral riches of the beautiful lawn, warm as an enamel just coming
out from the oven. (A portion of it is indicated by a square to appreciate the difference with the tablet before its cleanness.)

On the bench or *predella* we see five miniature-sized scenes of
the Virgin's Life; from left to right; the Birth and the Betrothal, the
Visitation, the Adoration of the Wise Men, the Purification and the
Death.

The tablet was painted between 1430 and 1445. Fra Angelico's
best epoch, for St. Dominic of Fiesole, and was sold for the construction of a belfry. Farnesio acquired it for the Duke of Lerma; it
entered the Monastery of the Descalzas Reales, in Madrid, and in
1861 in the Prado. It is one of the main jewels.

Botticelli, Sandro, *or Alessandro Filipepi according to his true
Italian name, was born in Florence in 1444 and died in item in 1510.
The critic has denied many of Vasary's data about this painter. According*

to him he was a trifling and gay man, unable of continence, whose father in order to subdue him, made him enter in a silversmith workshop where he was forced to work roughly; when Botticelli became a famous painter he lamentably wasted his fortune and in his old age was forced to move with the help of two crutches; he died in great misery... All this has been contradicted by posterior studies and investigations.

Sandro was a tanner's son, whose father encouraged the boy's fondnesses making him enter the silversmith Botticello's workshop (from whom he took his name), later he went to paint with the Medicis. These, who were touched with the Renaissance neo-paganism, commissioned Botticelli the pictorial expression of the Poliziano's Ode, in which the beatiful Simonetta, Jules Medici's lover, appeared almost divinized, and thus came forth to light The Spring, Venus's birth, Mars and Venus...

It has not yet been found out if Botticelli belonged to Savonarola's party, or to compagnaci; *but after the ultra-radical Dominican's death on the bonfire, his art became deeply changed. He gave up pagan scenes definitely to give entrance exclusively to religious themes, generally gloomy, and even conceived in an insane state (for example* The Descent of Munich*). He died at seventy five, not sventy eight as Vasari says, and he is buried in the All Saints's Church.*

The three tablets exhibited in this Room, and a fourth one belonging to Watney's collection, in London, are the successive illustration of the *Decameron*, a novel by Boccaccio, whose moral maxim is «the punishment of cruelty» and it refers to the Nastagio degli Onesti tale. A beautiful woman does not agree to her noble lover's requirements; the latter commits suicide and the beautiful woman dies without repentance. Every Friday she leaves Hell, and on the earth is pursued by two voracious mastiffs. Her lover, riding on a rapid horse, reaches her, and splitting her body he takes her heart out and throws it to the dogs which devour it. Then the young woman revives in all her integrity, and again escapes, is pursued and mutilated... and so on for ever and ever.

Nastagio, who is also aware of her disdain, one day invites his lady and other friends to a banquet outdoors, not very far from his palace. The disdainful young girl of the novel, completely nude, and the hungry dogs and the gallant persecutor, make their irruption during the feast. The astonished guests stand up, and then Nastagio takes advantage of the opportunity to refer to the story and the meaning of the blood scene. The evading lady considers the punishment reserved for cruelty, she accedes to Nastagio's requirements and the wedding ceremony is celebrated.

Num. **2838**, *Tablet I*. In a forest near Ravena three scenes are represented. In the first one close to the tent raised up out of the town, Nastagio tells his two friends of his misfortune. In the second we see him pensive walking through the forest; and in the third one, occupying the largest part of the picture, the beauty appears followed by the dogs and her lover. It seems that she demands Nastagio's protection while he, astonished by the surprising apparition, cannot help her. The beautiful coloring and magnificent attitudes are maintained in the other tablets. In the background we discover a sea and ships.

Num. **2839,** *Tablet II* with other three scenes, one of them superposed. We see in the first one Nastagio who is terrified at the sight of the breach made by the lover on his lady's back in order to pull out her heart. On a side there is a beautiful horse full of movement which also seems to contemplate the bloody scene. The second one only represents the dogs devouring the woman's heart, and the third, superposed upon the first, is the endless persecution of the revived woman.

Num. **2840,** *Tablet III*. Before us the banquet is displayed with the pursued and persecutor's irruption. The guests express their terror; the dishes and meals fall down. Nastagio once again uses the moment to explain the atrocious meaning of the scene. And then upon this. Nastagio's *enemy* servant goes to fetch him next to the tent to let him know of her mistress's repentance and love. This tablet of a marvellous ornamentation has a stupendous coloring with golden touches cleverly distributed, in order to elude the distraction from the main subject. Seldom can we enjoy such charms in tablets of this size. *Tablet IV*, which as we already have said is in London, represents the wedding ceremony.

The above mentioned four tablets were painted to adorn Lucrecia Pucci's closets on the occasion of her marriage to a member of the Florentine family Bini. The *Catalogue* of the Museum relates briefly the history of its vicissitudes: «Mr. Alexander Banker acquired the tablets in Florence in 1868; upon his death, in 1879 they passed to figure in Mr. J. R. Leyland's Collection: in 1892 they were bought by a Frenchman. M. Aynard, a deputy of the Rhone Department, who sold three of them to Mr. Joseph Spiridon and the fourth to Mr. Vernon Watney. In May 1929, when the Spiridon Collection was dispersed in Berlin, D. Francisco de Asís Cambó purchased the three tablets and gave them to the Prado Museum in December 8, 1941.

Antoniazzo. *An Italian painter of the 16th century, who painted several pictures under Cardinal Caraffa's commission. In his time they had a great success, but at the present their whereabouts is ignored.*

Núm. **577,** *The Virgin with the Child*. D. Elías Tormo believes that it proceeds from Spaniards's St. James in Rome. It is a repetition of a similar fresco existing in that town.

Francia, *brothers, sons of Francesco Raibolini, called «The Francia»; were born in the 15th century and died in the next.*

Num. **143,** *Saint Jerome, Saint Margaret and Saint Francis.* The three figures are standing against a landscape background. Signed on the bracket with the initials of the two brothers who used to paint their orders together.

Room IV.—PRE-RENAISSANCE ITALIANS

This is also a magnificent Room which has not to envy the two previous. The painters are mainly Botticelli's contemporaries, although from different schools. With some exceptions one observes that primitivism disappears and is substituted by Renaissance stimulations, even in what was strictly religious. The color is various and succulent and has its own personality, that is to say, without being mere slave of the sketch, whose outline had to be filled up. The figures have a proper character because they are no longer subdued to preestablished patterns; the compositions are not constrained to strict symmetries and all are in a reasoned atmosphere and light.

Melozzo da Forli. *An early Italian, born in Forli in 1438 and died in item in 1494. He was Piero della Francesca's favourite disciple, and went to Rome with him in 1458. When he was already an eminent painter, Cardinal Richard commissioned him to do one of the most interesting episodes of Pope Sixte IV's life when the latter transfer to Platine the Vatican Library's direction, a fresco terminated completly according to the Pope's wishes. His contempararies named him* The incomparable painter and the glory of Italy.

Num. **2843,** *Angel Musician* (Pl. 5). It is a portion of a fresco with an angel who sings accompanied by a zither, on a lemon-tree branches background. Charming and expressive is the angel, a frequent figure with some variations in the frescoes of this painter. (It also proceeds from the auction of Spiridon, bought by Cambo and given to the Prado.)

Tadeo Gaddi. *An Italian painter born in Florence in 1300 and died in item in 1366. His father Gaddo was his master and he also was his god-father Giotto's disciple, being during twenty four years his assistant. He painted many frescoes in Florence, Pisa and Arezzo.*

Num. **3841,** *St. Eloy before the King Clotaire.* The Merovingian

king who is sitting on a throne surrounded by his counsellors, has
sent for the young Eloy to commission him the gold saddle. To the
right we see another scene with Eloy who has the gold lingots weight.
Although its primitivism, there is expression in the faces and a certain
flexibility in the attitudes. The painter has willed to oppose to the
firm corporeality of the noble men, the almost vaporous subtleness
of the Saint.

Num. **2842**, *St. Eloy in the Silversmith workshop*. The young
saint, with the halo, is working on the chair of gold, while the other
workmen do different things. There are curious spectators looking
at the work and talking but St. Eloy and his assistants do not raise
their eyes. (These two tablets belonged to the Toscanell's Collection
in Pisa, whose auction took place in 1883; then they passed to the
property of Mr. Joseph Spiridon; Cambó acquired them in 1929
and finally were given to the Prado in 1941.)

Ponte, Giovanni Dal. *It is known that he was a Florentine who
lived between the years 1376 and 1437.*

Num. **2844**, *The Seven Liberal Arts*. An horizontal allegorical
composition, resolved with a superior elegance. It may be said that
it is a great procession before Astronomy who is sitting on her throne,
with the wise Ptolemy at her feet. So much the Arts as the men who
cultivated them, are crowned by angels. To the right we see Geometry
with a pair of compasses holding Euclides's hand; behind marches
Aritmetic with the table conducting Pythagoras and finally Music
with the organ matching with its inventor Tubalcain. To the left are
represented Rhetoric with its symbol pairing with Cicero; Dialectic
with the tree branch and Scorpio accompanying Aristotle, and finally
Grammar, holding the scourge and two young pupils preceding near
Prisciano.

The tablet was painted for a closet and one of its panels is conserved in Cambridge. It was owned by Toscanelli, the Prince of Villa-
Franca, Spiridon and Cambó who later gave it to the Museum.

Maineri, J. F. *An Italian painter born in Parma. The dates of
his birth and death are unknown. We know that Hercules de Roberti
was his master and that he worked in Ferrara's and Mantua's palaces.*

Num. **244**, *The Virgin and St. Joseph adoring the Child*. To the
left and on the top we see St. Francis receiving the stigmae. There
are three samples of this composition; the present one, with a landscape's background, another in Berlin's Museum and the one figuring
in the Testa's Collection, in Ferrara. (It belonged to the Elizabeth
Farnesio Collection, Aranjuez.)

Peruzzi, B. *Was an Italian painter and architect, who built the
Villa Farnesia, working with Raffaello. He was born in Siena in 1481
and died in Rome in 1530. Being Raffaello's intimate friend he was*

buried close to the latter's sepulchre. He was Pinturicchio's and Sodomas' disciple.

Num. **524,** *The Abduction of the Sabines*, is a tablet for a wedding trunk and collects a multitude of figures; among them one sees Romula who adjudicates one of the raped women; and to the right the peace between Romans and Sabines. This picture and the following were formerly considered to be by Pinturicchio.

Num. **525,** *Scipion's continence*, represents the *African* who gives back to the conquered Iberian Chief his betrothed, made slave in the Cartagena's conquest. This tablet is the previous companion and had the same destination. Raffaello's influence can be detected in both of the two works. Peruzzi had more merit and renown as architect than as painter.

Andrea Mantegna, *at first he saw the light in the Isola if Cartura, in 1431, and died in Mantua in 1506. Pacchioni referred to him saying that he* was a figure completely carved out of granite; *that is to say, inflexible in his art. He grew up in the workshop of Squarcioni who was an antiquarian. Donatello, Giaccomo Bellini, Paolo Ucello, Fra Filippo Lippi and others used to meet in Squarcioni's shop and the young Mantegna religiously listened to them. Later he moved to Venice in order to work with the Bellinis, father and son, marrying their daughter and sister Nicolasia.*

When he already was a master in the sketching, possessor of color, the fortshortning's conqueror and the triumpher of composition, he accepted the Dukes of Mantua's offer to decorate their palace. Francis Gonzaga and Elizabeth of Este gleefully received him and he began his great work; Julius Caesar Triumphs, *a grand piece, whose frescoes passed to the Carlos I of England collections upon the House of Gonzaga's ruin.*

Mantegna was superb, austere, and did not consent to any observations about his art; instead he always was modest in his exigences and limited himself to take was given to him. After fifty years of work with the only desire of possessing a modest house in which to retire at the end of his days, he could not attain it and so he went to the one he inhabited in Via Unicornio. He left three sons painters; Bernardino, Francesco and Luigi, who could not equal their father's name.

Num. **248,** *Death of our Lady* (Pl. 4). A small yet great tablet, which as the *Cardinal* of Raffaello, has been the theme of an overflowing literature in an imaginative way. Undoubtedly it is one of our Museum's purest jewels. The scene takes place in a sumptuous room on the bank of Mantua's lesser lake, seen through the window. On a modest couch, the Virgin has just died, surrounded by the apostles carrying candles, palms, ointments flasks, perfumingjars or simply a book from which St. Paul reads. The Virgin has an emaciated face, and her pale hands are crossed over her breast. It is not understandable how in such a reduced tablet it has been possible to treat this series of figures that seem giants. They are, as Mantegna, Apostles from top to bottom: strong men, whose strength contrast with the sorrow of their gestures. Among them, St. John's figure in the foreground, has a sculptural attitude and is one of the most beautiful examples of pre-Renaissance.

The composition tends to the quadrangular scheme however its coolness is broken by the apostle's foreshortning inclined over the couch and agitating the incensory before Mary's corpse. The qualities of the clothings and delicate coloring, the detail, the fabric's pleats, the grey light invading the room, the anguishing atmosphere envolving the scene; are incontrovertible successes of a genial painter to whom the small against the great do not exist because everything is great to him. This single tablet, if Mantegna had not left anything more in the world, has been enough to glorify his name for ever.

It seems that it was painted in 1492, when the master returned from Rome (called by Inocencio VII to decorate some chapels in the Vatican) to Mantua where he had a permanent post in the Gonzaga's palace. Charles I of England owned the picture and at his auction it was bought for Felipe IV.

Rossi, Francesco, *called «il Salviati» as well. Was born and died in Florence, 1510-1573.*

Num. **477,** *The Virgin, the Holy Child and two Angels.* One of these is giving the Holy Child a parrokeet. When this canvas was restored in 1946, there appeared in the background groups and traces of a spoiled, covered up figure in the top right-hand corner. Also attributed formely to Vasari. (It belonged to the collection of Elizabeth Farnesio.)

Pontormo, *by name Giaccopo Carrucci, took the name of his birth city where he was born in 1494. He died in Florence in 1557. His first illusion was Leonardo; then Albertinelli and Piero di Cosimo. Finally Andrea del Sarto with whom he ended up arguing and was put out of his workshop because, according to the master, he had been claiming the master's works for his own. Then he became interested in Michelangelo. Soon he perfected his sketch. It is certain that he then practiced a tecniche of firm sketches hardly colored, so that nobody would argue that he had been copying his previos master. The final illusion of Pontormo was Albrecht Dürer, master of the firm sketch, who outlined with a dry point. He is the creator of the portrait of Vittoria Colonna, wife of the Marquis of Pescara, and platonic friend of Michelangelo.*

Núm. **287,** *The Holy Family.* Saint Joseph sleeps; near the Virgin, the Child and Saint John. One cannot deny the influence of Andrea del Sarto, as much in the coloring as in the manner of folding the cloth. (It belonged to the Collection of Isabel Farnesio.)

Giovanni Bellini. *Here is a venerable master from whose workshop* *have come Giorgiones and Tiziano and so many others. The date of his birthday is unknown, and we only know that it was soon after 1429, and that he died in Venice in 1516. He was Gentille's younger brother, who also was a great painter and went to Constantinople to paint Mohamed II's portrait. Andrea Mantegna was his brother-in-law. Some biographer have reasons to believe him to be the painter Giacoppo Bellini's illegitimate son; but it is definite that he always lived in good terms with his brother, Gentille.*

Although being his father's disciple, in many aspects he is considered as Mantegna's imitator, especially in his pictures entitled Christ Dead *and* Sustained by Angels. *However he did not attain his brother-in- law's transparencies. On the contrary, he painted unskilfull* Madonnas *being in his time unimitable as much for their coloring as for their beauty, He also was a great portrayer, but there is only one portrait existing by his hands, that of the Dux Loredano in the National Gallery in London. Apart of his merits as painter, one has to consider that he aids his disciples, without constraining or insisting that they imitate him. The master usually advised;* «consult, but do not copy».

Num. **50,** *The Virgin and the Child between two Saints.* The accustomed rigidity among the earlier has already disappeared; nevertheless a certain hieratism still remains, full of dignity. All the figures, the Child included, are serious, reverent, completing their religious unity. The one to the right, very lovely, which in equal composition represents the Magdalene, in this one is substituted by St. Ursule, carrying in her hand her arrow of martyrdom. The color is pleasant and the pleats of the fabrics masterly treated. Number **576,** *The Saviour,* is a copy which may be Spanish one of the original treasured by the Academy of San Fernando.

Num. **580,** *Ecce Homo,* by an anonymous Italian of the XV century. The canvas is unfinished; in the rear part of same *The Virgin with Child and Saint Juanito,* of Italian authorship.

Room V.—ITALIANS OF THE RENAISSANCE

All this room is dedicated to first class Italian Renaissance painters pertaining to different tendencies or Schools: Venetian, Lombard, Florentine... it is impossible to establish among them other nexus but that they are completely in the Renaissance line, facing not an interior ideal but Nature and Life.

Andrea del Sarto. *An Italian painter born in Florence in 1486 and died in item in 1531. His name was Angiolo (Angel), but he took that of his father's work; «Sarto» or Tailor. He worked in Piero di Cosimo's workshop where he made the acquaintance of Bartolomeo della Porta (who terrified by Savonarola's suplice became a friar) and knew Ghirlandaio's art. He was taken to France by Francis I, who held him in high esteem, and died young at forty five (according to rumors due to family problems). He is one of the great Florentine School painters.*

Num. **332,** *Lucrecia di Baccio del Fede* (Pl. 6), was the painter's wife, a beautiful woman but without common sense who abandoned herself to any kind of triflings while Andrea painted in France. It is a pity to read the letters he sent to her from Paris, believing that she was deeply miserable! The critic has gloated extremely over this woman made by Andrea his idol, to the point of having copied her face in his Virgins and he did so *per averla nell' anima impresa* (because he had her engraved on his mind) as was written by Vasari. But she cannot be reproached for the premature death of her husband, because he died victim of the pest in Florence at the beginning of 1531. It is supposed that this portrait is a little posterior to the wedding.

Num. **334,** *The Virgin, the Child, a Saint and an Angel.* In the background to the left there are two little figures, a woman and a child, walking towards a village. The composition is very harmonious and resolved in a pyramidal desing borrowed from Fra Bartolomeu della Porta. It became during a certain period the Florentine School's canon. The Virgin occupies the eminent place, raising her veil and with the Child superposed to elude the angular outline destruction; at her feet and to complete the triangle are represented the Saint and the Angel. It is believed that the meaning of this scene is the affirmation by Iesus of the authenticity of Toby's book.

Andrea del Sarto's characteristic marks are the beautiful red copied from Ghirlandaio, the softness with which light slips on to the habits and flesh, and the flexible pleating in planes instead of the uniformed and lineal one ill-used by the Florentines, more faithful to sketch than to color. This picture is a masterpiece of our Museum.

Num. **335,** *The Holy Family.* In the Barberini Gallery in Rome, there is a similar picture with little variation. The artist is not interested in the landscape because all his desire is concentrated in the expression of the figures; St. Joseph, with a supercilious look because of the bitterness of the exile; the Virgin overwhelmed by painful misgivings; and the Child who hides His head with fearful face. The whole scene exuding anguish is an excellent pictorial piece. (It was in El Escorial, and Father Sigüenza had already made its description. It entered the Museum in 1839.)

Num. **336,** *The Sacrifice of Abraham, detained by an Angel.* This tablet deserves the same interest as the two previous ones, having a magnificent dramatic expression. In Dresde there is another like it which was painted for Francis I in 1529; but according to Berenson the first original is in our Museum. (The Marquis del Vasto acquired it upon the painter's death and later it was purchased by Carlos IV. From Aranjuez.)

Num. **338,** *The Virgin, the Child, St. John and two Angels.* In the background we see the apparition of an angel musician to St. Francis of Assisi.

Num. **579,** *St. John the Baptist with the Lamb.* It is uncertain whether this picture was painted by Andrea del Sarto. (It was acquired by the Patronage of the Museum in Paris in 1923.)

Il Correggio, *whose name is Antonio Allegri, the most flittering light of Parma's school, was born in Corregio, Emilia's insignificant village, in 1494. The painter's formation always will be an enigma. He travelled only from Correggio to Parma. Where did he learn his unique and different style of art? The authors have carefully investigated his works in order to deduce influences and masters, without being able to definitely affirm anything. In the village of his birth he married Jerome Merline, who gave him three daughters and his son Pomponio who also was a painter.*

Upon his wife's death the painter sank into a bitter melancholy. But Elizabeth of Este, it is said, in order to consolate him, commissioned him to do a pagan series; Antiope, Leda, Io, Danae and Ganimedes. These are the enormous painter's masterpieces which passed to our property being afterwards dispersed. The Leda belonged to Emperor Carlos V and is now in Berlin; the Ganimedes and Io, or Jupiter, were owned by Antonio Pérez, they became confiscated, and upon Felipe II's death passed to Rudolph II (today they are in Vienna's Museum); the Antiope, of the same series, belonged to Felipe IV, who gave it to Charles I of England, and now it figures in the Louvre, and so on.

Soon a widower, with four young orphans, his last years were bitter (his name was Laetus and he called one of his daughters Letizia...). Struck by poverty, he had to make a long trip on foot because he had no money. One day he drank a glass of cold water and died suddenly when he was only forty years old.

Num. **111,** *Noli me tangere* (Pl. 7). «Do not wish to touch me» are the words Christ spoke to the Magdalene upon His resurrection and which inspired this charming tablet (transferred to canvas), in which we see Christ as a gardener and Mary seated at His feet. This is one of the most beautiful figures ever created by brushes: she was kneeling, but so astonished when recognizing Christ that she falls upon her feet, and modestly retires her body and hands but her neck and head advance as if she were imploring an explanation.

Jesus points to Heaven, as His natural home. On the background of rich greens the two figures are prodigiously detached. According to Berenson it is a masterpiece. It belonged to Charles I of England and was acquired by the Duke of Medina de las Torres who presented it to Felipe IV. (Proceeding from El Escorial in 1839.)

Num. **112,** *The Virgin, the Child Jesus and St. John.* The expression of feminine beauty always predominated in Correggio as in this little Virgin in a little cave. When she was represented with the newborn Child, he converted her into a lantern radiating light over the surrounding personages, as in the Adoration entitled *The Night* and others. Exactly as in this tablet in which the light and the figures themselves blend constituting this beautiful composition. (It belonged to Elizabeth Farnesio and came from La Granja.)

Bernardino Luini. *Is one of the painters about whom the most contradictory criticism has flourished. Supposedly he was a disciple of Leonardo, others say of Bravante and some of Scotto. According to some he was in Rome and studied Raffaello's art; and for others (for example Gaudencio Ferrara), he neither saw Raffaello painting nor went to Rome. Vasari makes him but to be a sweet and peaceful character; and to the contrary a modern investigator describes him dissolute and turbulent... But really is known very little about him. It is supposed that he was born in Luino (Great Lake banks), between 1470 and 1480, and that he died in 1553, the location unknown.*

Maybe he was not Leonardo's disciple, but his Lombard origin is accepted without doubt and the woman figuring in almost all his pictures and repeated until annoyance, is more or less his daughter. It is unnecessary to explain her presence and the well-known anecdote of the «Casa de la Pelucca». Luini painted enough in Milan and Lugano; his works are numerous and monotonous; a couple of his pictures are pleasant but when we see them by dozens (they are in almost all European museums) they become tiresome. He lacked inventive, genius and was not a first rank master.

Num. **243,** *Salome receiving the Baptist's Head* is an oft-repeated theme of this painter. The executor gives Salome the Precursor's head. In another version, Salome appears, suffocated, her hair somewhat disveled because of the dance. Here she appears calm, although turning her face away in order to elude the sight of the victim's cut head. (Proceeding from the Alcázar.)

Num. **242,** *The Holy Family.* The Virgin and the children's heads are Leonardian. The whole picture exudes a distant Leonardian paternity. It is said that the composition proceeds from Leonardo, but the same could be said of the subtle and diluted shades of pleats and light. Those who deny any relationship between Leonardo and Luini, would have a great task on their hands to explain this tablet which is one of the most beautiful in this Room. (It proceeds from the Alcázar.)

Parmigianino. Num. **279,** *Pietro Maria Rossi, Count of St. Segundo.* He was a military member of the Medici and Riario Families, who fought at times with our Emperor, and others with his rival Francis I. The statue to his right seems to be that of Perseus. (It proceeds from the Buen Retiro.)

Num. **280,** *A Lady with Three Children,* represents a beautiful Roman matrone with placid and clever face, and not less expressive are the three children who surround her. The composition appears somewhat dispersed, but may be the painter liked its own spontaneity. (In 1794 it figured in the Royal Palace.)

Parmigianino. Num. **283,** *The Holy Family with an Angel.* El Vasari describes a similar one painted by Parmigianino in Parma, before leaving for Rome, and connects it with the *Holy Family* of the Uffizi, Florence.

Bronzino, A. *An Italian painter who was born in Monticelli near Florence in 1503. He was Raffaelino del Garbo's and del Pontormo's disciple, a good friend of Michelangelo and had Cosme de Medici's protection. He predominated in the portrait but more in the sketch than in the coloring. He is the author of two beautiful portraits which merited for him great celebrity; the one of Lucrecia Panciatichi and that of Leonor de Toledo.*

Num. **5,** *Don García de Medici,* was Cosme de Medici and Leonor de Toledo's son, who died when he was only fifteen.

??? Num. **504,** *The Gioconda.* According to most authorities it is the portrait of Madonna Lisa Gherardini, the wife of the Florentine chancellor Francesco di Zanobi del Giocondo, a few suggest that she is Constanza de Avalos, Duchess of Francavilla, Federico del Balzo's widow. Whoever she may be, she appears as a young lady, whose *smile* has inspired realms of prose, verse and music. Vasari tells us that Leonardo worked four years to portray her, and that in order to maintain her pleasant smile he brought excellent musicians to his studio. Painted in Florence around 1504, he brought it to France when he left fatherland under Francis I's protection (who bought it for 4000 gold *florines*). It is in the Louvre in the place of honour, although originally painted on a tablet it was later transferred to canvas.

And this Gioconda of Madrid? For the moment let us say that there are *Giocondas* in different European museums and even in private collections. Apart from Raffaello's sketch, seven at least are mentioned. We have had the opportunity of seeing most of them, and not one, save the Louvre's exception, can be compared to ours, because of its similarity with the original, the coloring beauty and its wonderful conservation. At times it has been attributed to Leonardo's own brushes. Afterwards it has been said that it is a copy by a Flemish or a Spaniard. To our opinion both of these two ideas are undefendable. Historically the first can be refused, not having any trace of truth and the palette itself denies it. Neither do we think that it was a Spanish painter who painted «like this». Yáñez de la Almedina, whose, St. Catherine is marvellous, has never attained such polishing in sketch nor such transparencies of coloring. You have to think of Leonardo or one of his beloved disciples.

Our *Gioconda* is painted on an oak tablet as that of the Louvre. Leonardo painted the original portrait in his Florence studio on his famous «black wall» mentioned in his *Treaty of Painting*, with light in front, as is ours; but never with a landscape background and still less with a clear landscape as is that of Paris. This background of fantastic rocks was added later and it is curious to observe that the landscape's light does not harmonize with the light of the portrayed face, neck and hands. Neither can it be doubted that the same Leonardo da Vinci who was so little interested in painting (see *Leonardo da Vinci* by La Tourette) and yet used four years in portraying Monna Lisa, would have painted but one portrait; because although a present for a lady (leaving apart unreasoned loves) one has to think of someone else. The fact that the Louvre's *Gioconda* has landscape background and ours has not does not allow us to believe in a copy. (The copyist who so faithfully reproduced hair, dress and hands, would never have omited the background.) If Madrid's portrait is a copy, it is of an equal original, and probably a replica of the one made by Leonardo in his studio with a dark background, or a copy of this. But never of the one in the Louvre. Copies were already made in Milan. (Tourette.)

We also ignore how it came to Spain. The fact that the Cardinal of Aragon's Secretary visited Leonardo in his retreat of Cloux, proceeding from Italy, could be the reason.

Is it a copy and not a replica? Then we have to think of one of the best and most beloved master's disciples: Boltraffio or Melzi, because no one else lived with him in greater intimacy. We have seen the *Madonna Litta* of the Ermitage, already and definitely attributed to Francesco Melzi, and in ti we have detected similar transparencies and face's *sfumatto* analogue to our *Gioconda*. But comparing this with the one in the Louvre and omitting the background, it can be affirmed that this is *not* a copy of the other, and not because of the greenish tone which the Paris one is getting, perhaps due to the printing transparency, nor to the defficient transferring from the tablet to the canvas, nor to the illtreatment of its robber. Vicenzo Perugia, during the long months he kept it; but rather because although being the same person portrayed, the portrait is *not* the same; even in the technique, against any opinion, our Gioconda is nearer to the *St. John* in the Louvre, for example, than that of Paris. And regarding the differences we need only add: «Blind is he who does not wish to see».

The Prado's version, replica or copy, is simply wonderfull! The face with its warm and very smoothly *sfumatto* shades; the divine hands have the mellow fleshiness without bones or nerves, characteristic of the naked members of Leonardo. The very subtle and unequalled gold hair slowly treated one strand after one with delight, does not correspond to the hair in other versions: the waist, the mantel, the veil, everything has plenty of very rich transparencies; and concerning the illusive expression in the face, in the eyes, the delicate nose and the smiling and... enigmatic lips, to be literary one needs only to look at the picture.

Our *Gioconda* is only prejudiced by the corner in which it hangs by an understandable and natural prudence; but it actually deserves a place of honor, such as the one that every museum masterpiece has.

The suggestion that it does not represent Monna Lisa but, the Avalos, Duchess of Francavilla, has its origin in a poem by Enea Irpino —Parma's Library manuscript— saying that this lady, defender of Ischia's Island against the French, was portrayed by Leonardo, appearing like the Gioconda, *under the beautiful black veil*, of a widow. (It already figured in the Alcázar of Madrid in 1860.)

Room VI.—VENETIAN MASTERS

Now we are in a Venetian atmosphere and already one «feels» the greatness of the pictures yet un-seen. Once Giovanni Bellini, has been viewed, starts the long theory of his disciples, who honored their venerable master, so much partially because they surpassed him. Florentines accused Venetian that they did not know drawing and the latter argued that Florentines had no idea about color. Eliminating extremes, it is certain that either sketching and coloring characterized each one, but referring to Venetians we shall soon have the opportunity to see it.

El Giorgione. *Zorci, Giorgio, Giorgione, spent all his life in Castelfrancho, his birth place (he was born around 1478 , in Treviso, where* *his protector Catalina Cornaro, ex-queen of Cyprus, celebrated splendid parties and in Venice, in Giovanni Bellini's workshop which became completely revolutioned, to the extreme that the* master *terminated by painting like his disciple. He gained the first battles in the opened air and light, and without any doubt, was the first among his equals. There remain only about cighteen of his authentic works. His* Venus Reclining *(Vienna) was Tiziano's (Florence), Bronzino's (item), Guido Reni's (item), Palma il Viecchio's (Dresde), Poussin's (item) exemplar and the inspirator of almost every lying nudes, from Velázquez to Goya...*

One day in October 1510 he was found dead at thirty three, close to the corpse of his beloved. The pest had seized Venice and all his companion's escaped save him. After the devastating storm they came back finding the two victims. The bodies were burned in a bonfire, and the ashes disseminated, upon the sea.

Num. **288,** *The Virgin and Child with St. Anthony and St. Roch.* The author of *The Rural Concert, The Tempest* and *The Three Philosophers,* is not well defined in this canvas, which, on the other hand, remained unfinished. It has been attributed to different painters, Tiziano included, because he is the most similar painter. In fact he concluded some of other unfinished pictures. Without denying that this tablet could be by Giorgione the palette is surprising. It is certain that the canvas possesses very proper greys of rich tones, but in general his palette was much warmer. The Duke of Medina de las Torres presented it to Felipe IV. (Proceeding from El Escorial, it enters the Museum the year 1839.)

Lorenzo Lotto, *was born in Venice in 1480 and died in Loreto in 1556. Some believe him to be Bellini's disciple and others Vivarini's. He participated equally of the Bergamian and Venetian schools, although the former's works predominated and they correspond to the years between 1518 and 1528. He travelled a great deal ending his sojourns as an Oblate in the Convent of Loreto.*

Num. **240,** *Micer Marsilio and his Wife.* It is a betrothal picture in which we see the betrothed who under the protection of Cupid (with a roguish face), is about to place the ring on his bride's finger. They do not look like lovers; both of the two faces are foolishlooking and very poor in expression. On the contrary the carnations and the pinky tone of the bride are very pleasant. This canvas was in the house of Cassotti, thus it is supposed that Marsilio Casotto is the gentleman portrayed. (In 1666 it decorated Madrid's Alcázar.)

Num. **448,** *St. Jerome, Penitent.* Although the canvas is not signed, as is the previous, undoubtedly it is by Lotto, because in his bills there is a reference to this St. Jerome painted for a Nicholas of Mula who failed to pay it, thus remaining in the workshop. (Delivered by Felipe II to El Escorial in 1593.)

Baroci. Núm. **18,** *The Nativity.* The Lady worships the Child; St. Joseph opens the door of the stable to the shepherds.

Giulio Romano, *painter and architect, whose real name was Giulio Pippi de Gianuzzi, chose Romano because he was born in Rome. Born in 1499, he died in Mantua, 1546. He entered the shop of Raffaello and was his disciple and imitator until the master's death. Some frescoes in the Vatican are combined works of the two artists. When Raffaello died Romano finished them.* The Battle of Constantine *is completely his work. For having illustrated the indecent sonnets of Aretino, he was persecuted by Pope Clement VII, but was able to take refuge in Mantua, protected by the Gonzaga family. In the same city he raised temples, palaces walls and painted a good deal.*

Num. **323,** *Noli me tangere.* Jesus is risen and dressed as a gardener. He appears to Mary Magdalene, who wants to come closer to Him and Jesus says: «Noli me tangere». There is clear influence of Raffaello. It is said that only the drawing is by Giulio Romano, the rest corresponding to Gianfrancesco Penni, called «il Fattore». (Some say that it proceeds from El Paular.)

Girolano de Carpi, *painter from Ferrara, 16th century.*

Num. **69,** *Alphonse II of Este* (?), son of Ercole II, Duke of Ferrara.

Giaccopo del Conte, *painter from Firenze, 16th century.*

Num. **329,** *The Holy Family.*

Pontormo, *by name Giaccopo Carrucci, took the name of his birth city where he was born in 1494. He died in Florence in 1557. His first illusion was Leonardo; then Albertinelli and Piero di Cosimo. Finally Andrea del Sarto with whom he ended up arguing and was put out of his workshop because, according to the master, he had been claiming the master's works for his own. Then he became interested in Michelangelo. Soon he perfected his sketch. It is certain that he then practiced a technique of firm sketches hardly colored, so that nobody would argue that he had been copying his previous master. The final illusion of Pontormo was Albracht Dürer, master of the firm sketch, who outlined with a dry point. He is the creator of the portrait of Vittoria Colonna, wife of the Marquis of Pescara, and platonic friend of Michelangelo.*

Num. **287,** *The Holy Family.* Saint Joseph sleeps; near the Virgin, the Child and Saint John. One cannot deny the influence of Andrea del Sarto, as much in the coloring as in the manner of folding the cloth. (It belonged to the Collection of Isabel Farnesio.)

Lucia Anguisciola *was born at Cremona around 1538. She was a sister of Sofonisba and four other she-painters.*

Num. **16,** *Pietro Maria,* doctor of Cremona. The signature is on the arm of the chair.

Room VII.

Tiziano. Num. **441,** *The Burial of Christ,* a scene with some modifications of the beautiful canvas of the same title, num. **440,** that we shall describe later. Num. **442,** *The Saviour in ortolan dress,* fragment of a painting where the figure of Maria Magdalene is lacking. Num. **443,** *The worship of the Kings.* Inferior to the one of the same title in El Escorial. It has been stated that it may not be a work of Titian. However the great critic and specialist in Italian art, Berenson, ascribes it to Titian and considers it even superior to the canvas of the same title and author in the «Galleria Ambrosiana». (Acquired by Carlos IV.) Num. **444,** *The Virgin of Sorrows.* It is a moving half-body in whose face can be clearly appreciated the sorrow of the Mother without any distorsion in its features. This canvas was directly delivered by Titian to Carlos I in Augsburg. The Emperor took it to Yuste. Num. **437,** *Ecce Homo.* A beautiful half-figure signed by the author. It was also taken to Yuste by the Emperor. Num. **434,** *Mystic Scene,* with halfbody figures, with the exception of the Child. Number **443,** *The Virgin of Sorrows.* Num. **436,** *Christ on the Mount of Olives,* with artificial light effects given by the lantern.

Dosso Dossi, *born in Ferrara in the 16th century. Died in 1542.* Num. **416,** *The Lady of the Green Turbant.* Her right hand lies on the gloves.

Padovanino, Alessandro Varotari, *born and died in Padova (1590-1650).*

Num. **266,** *Orpheus* and four wild beasts, the lion, the unicorn, the dragon, and the serpent peacefully group together before the music of the god. (Isabel Farnesio's Collection.)

Licinio, Bernardino. *This Italian painter was born around 1489 and still lived at the end of 1549.*

Num. **289,** *Agnese, the Painter's Sister-in-law.*

Room VII A.—VERONESE

Save only one picture by Tintoretto, all this Room belongs to **Veronese** (the Museum own forty of his works, acquired in the greatest part during the reign of Felipe IV, who admired **Veronese**). Tintoretto as much as Veronese are in «dii majores», the supreme circle of the art. Both different in various concepts, they coincide especially in the silvered greys which were the «leit motiv» of Verona's palette, and which sometimes Tintoretto cultivated with matchless success.

Veronese, *named Paolo Cagliari, was born in Verona in 1528 and died in Venice in 1588. He was small but plenty of energy and with enough personality to resist the golden paroxism of Venetian school, cultivating instead his own palette with silvered tones without violent contrasts, but in the light scales. At twenty five he already had decorated the Villa Soranza, near Castilfrancho, and had worked for Cardinal Ercole Gonzaga. He was called to Venice for the decoration of the Dodge's Palace. In the ceiling of the College's Hall there are seventeen of his canvases, four more in the Counsel of Ten's Room, and others distributed in various rooms. He represented Venice with beautiful matrons, fair haired, with opulent forms, and arrogant busts dressed with glorious majesty and with crowns of pearls and showing in the right hand the betrothal ring with the Adriatic.*

He also is the instigator of the giant banquets held on those marbled terraces of the Renaissance. Quite careless of historical rigour, he sometimes placed Christ near one of his friends anachronically dressed according to 16th century fashion. He was a happy and very appreciated painter, with the exception of a little vexation caused by the Saint Office due to his historical anachronisms, such as the Banquet at Simon the Leprous House *(painted for the dominics of St. Zinipolo). But he cleverly escaped from these proceedings.*

Num. **491,** *The Dispute with the Doctors in the Temple.* Jesrusalem temple is of strong. Renaissance architecture, in which the painter has composed the scene: Child Jesus sitting on a chain and speaking to the Doctors who listen to Him with noticeable astonishment. Among the Doctors there is a Knight of the Holy Sepulchre Order, who very easily could be he who commissioned the canvas. The Virgin and St. Joseph come in through a door. It is work of Veronese's youth but his style is already defined; nothing about rough contrasts nor golden leaves but a blended middle tone which equally ponders all the composition. (In 1866 it was in the Alcázar of Madrid.)

Num. **501,** *Cain's wandering Family.* In a lonely landscape Cain's wife nurses her son. On foot and close to her is Cain. The canvas produces a disturbing feeling. (In 1686 it figured in the Alcázar of Madrid.)

Num. **492,** *Christ and the Centurion.* This is one of Veronese's best wrought pieces, one which he prepared with previous varying sketches. The composition's scheme is horizontal and divided into two parts; to the left Christ and His proup of disciples, and to the right the Centurion, kneeling, and a group of soldiers and various onlookers. The Centurion, with supplicating face, prays that Jesus might cure his servant. It is the canvas' best figure; Christ appears somewhat dry and rigid. At the background is a Renaissance terrace. The general tone is silver. (Acquired by Alonso de Cárdenas for

Felipe IV at Carles I of England auction and sent to El Escorial.
It entered the Museum in 1839.)

Num. **499,** *Youth choosing between Virtue and Vice*. This canvas,
of lesser proportions than the previous, is a plastic paraphrase of
Heracles myth in which he was tempted by two opposing ways,
reminding in a certain manner the theme of Tiziano's picture *Sacred
Love and Profane Love*. In this one by Veronese, Virtue, modest and
pudic, takes the child by the hand and keeps him away from the
seducing woman who embodies Vice. The background has architectural themes from pagan Rome. Primarily a work of his youth, he
repeated it in his full maturity. Its version figures in the interesting
Frick collection in New York. (It was in the Alcázar.)

Num. **497,** *The Martyrdom of St. Mena*. An egyptian Christian
martyr beheaded the year 296 under Dioclecian's order. (It was presented to Felipe IV by D. Alfonso de Cabrera, a Castille Admiral.)
Núm. **498,** *The Penitent Magdalene*. (Belonged to Elizabeth Farnesio's Collection.)

Num. **486,** *Livia Colonna*. The portrayed married Marzio Colonna
in 1540, and became a widow in 1546, dying assassinated in 1552.

Room VIII.—TIZIANO

This room is dedicated to Tiziano. Those who ascribed
Veronese to Venetian school will observe that they were
mistaken. It is not enough to have painted in Venice, to be
a «Venetian» painter, at least with this school characteristics,
which start with the Bellinis and their disciples, and can be
generalized by a certain family air in the feminine faces
(G. Bellini, Giorgione, Palma *the Old*...), the ambarine and
warm carnations, the lightened leaves which invade the
atmosphere and the «superposition» of color in front of
Veronese «approach». The fact that he did not belong to
the same school does not make him inferior to them; in his
style he too was a genius.

Tiziano, Vecellio, *is one of the most complete painters that mankind has produced. He was born in Piave di Cadore (Italian Tyrol)
in 1447, the son of a renowned lawyer, who gave him a wonderful education. He entered Giovanni Bellini's workshop and very soon became
a master. He presented somewhat the aristocracy of genius and he had
a long, happy and glorious existence. He portrayed our Emperor, Fe-*

lipe II, Alfonso de Este, Gonzaga de Mantua, the Duke of Urbino and all the Dodges of the Venetian most serene Republic, whom he knew during his almost centenary life. He dominated any genre: religious, profane, mythological, warlike or portrait, and died at ninety eight, leaving unfinished his canvas The Pieta, for a picture to be placed upon his tomb.

Num. **420,** *Venus Enjoying Herself with Music.* A subject which Tiziano liked very much. The goddess reclines with a little dog while the musician turns to contemplate her. In the background we see a garden with a fountain, a peacock and a deer. The whole canvas is in musical accordance, from the tepid carnation of the goddess to the landscape's rich greenness. The nude's realistic reprentation is defended by the posture in which she is placed. We already have said that Florentines accused Venetians of not being able to sketch. This Venus with her rythmic plasticity in a reclining posture, would be impossible if standing. In contrast, the opulent forms from the waist to the feet with the narrow bust, insignificant chest and reduced head, are not according to any canon of feminine proportions but nevertheless the nude is splendid with its diluted tints yet without a rudeness of tones. Tiziano was a very complex artist who painted *everything* but moreover everything *well.* It does seem however that in pagan themes of nudes he overflowed his genial inspiration, being as he was a lover of beauty and life. A love which he never renounced. In the magnificent Venice of the Dodges, of rich merchants in contact with oriental sensuality, and fantastic palaces, the Venus and Danaes were very searched though repetition of subjects mattered very little. There is a similar one in this Museum and in the Uffizi of Florence. The present passed to England and Felipe IV acquired it at the Charles I auction. In 1686 it was in the Alcázar; and the intruder King Joseph I who found it in the Academy of San Fernando confiscated the work though in 1818 it was returned to Spain. (It has been in the Museum since 1827.)

Num. **431,** *Felipe II after the Battle of Lepanto Commending his Son to God.* This very clear scene needs no explanation. D. Juan de Austria's victory over the Turks (hence the representation of the chained Turk in the composition) took place in October 1571, two months before the Prince's birth. It seems as if the offer had been accepted because he died prematurely. For this reason this picture figures as one of the most beloved by the Spanish Monarch. Tiziano had already painted Felipe's portrait before the model, twenty years before. He might have requested a sketch, because one was sent to him in Venice, drawn by Sánchez Coello. The canvas is signed on a slip of paper on the third column. The allusion to the naval battle appears in the background. Guzmán de Silva, the Spanish ambassador in Venice, sent the work in 1575. (It proceeds from the Alcázar of Madrid.)

Num. **430,** *The Church upheld by Spain.* Surely it was a commission by Felipe II upon the victory of Lepanto that suggested the theme to Tiziano. The fact is, according to Vasari who witnessed it that in 1556 he visited the painter who had begun a canvas for the Duke of Ferrar, with a similar composition save that it dealt with a mythological subject. It may have happened that the canvas remained abandoned and upon the king's commission he changed the Minerva into the Spain's personification, and Neptune became hooded with the Turkish turban. The canvas was sent to Spain in 1575 and figured in the Alcázar, later in El Pardo, again in the Alcázar, and finally in El Escorial from where it came to the Museum in 1839.

Num. **412,** *The Gentleman with a Watch.* We do not know who he might represent. At one time it was attributed to Tintoretto.

Num. **439,** *Christ and the Cyrene,* is a beautiful canvas, Christ's face of full ideality. Father Sigüenza writes: «It is the best I have seen in my life: it seems to break the heart». So it merits special attention. It is signed on the stone upon which Christ leans. His left hand. The characters I. B. have been interpreted by someones as *Ioannes Bellinus* (John or Giovanni Bellini) and it has been supposed that he had begun the picture and Tiziano had finished it. (It figured in Felipe II's Oratory in El Escorial.)

Num. **414,** *Daniello Barbaro, Patriarch of Aquileya,* writer and ambassador. (In 1666 it was in the Alcázar.) Num. **438,** *Jesus and the Cyrene.* This picture is signed and is inferior to núm. **439.** Num. **413,** *The Man with the Ermine Collar.* Whom he represents is ignored. (It proceeds from the Alcázar.)

Num. **533,** *Portrait of the Elector John Frederick, Duke of Saxony, by Titian.* He is with the sword in the right hand as if he had just taken it out of the scabbard, which he holds with the other hand.

Num. **447,** *Santa Catalina,* Saint Catherine, of Alexandria, with the wheel broken by the angels. Her daughter, Lavinia, the mature, served as model.

Num. **446,** Saint Margaret, *Santa Margarita,* next to the head of the dragon with open gullet. The Saint is also the portrait of Lavinia.

Num. **438,** *Jesus and the Cyrene,* inferior at the núm. **439,** of the same theme.

Room VIII A.—TINTORETTO, VERONESE AND OTHERS

Tintoretto. Num. **374**, *Young man.*

Num. **370**, *A Jesuit.* He is supposed to be Father Lainez. (Proceeding from Leganés' Collection. In 1686 it figured in the Alcázar and was attributed to Tiziano.)

Verones. Num. **500**, *Abraham's sacrifice of Isaac.* Isaac is about to be sacrificed by his father but an angel holds the latter's arm. Obviously it is a work of Verones's good period.

Num. **483**, *Sussana and the Elders.* This theme has been the temptation of all the great painters, because it allows them to contrast the sensual forms of a nude beauty and the impudic heads of the two old men of eager and greedy glance. If we add to this a pool with crystalline water, a garden with an abundance of trees and palace in the background, we can deny only with difficulty the extreme plastic beauty of the ensemble. This canvas of Verones's youthful epoch was repeated by him on different occasions. In 1666 it was in the Alcázar.

Num. **482**, *Venus and Adonis* (Pl. 8). While Adonis sleeps on Venus's lap, the goddess refreshes him with a *ventallo* (fan). One of the dogs howls, wishing to being the hunt and a Cupid holds him. The background is a landscape. This canvas is a divinity in its silvered grey symphony in which Velázquez was so great a master. Justly this great Spanish painter was the purchaser of this picture in Italy for Felipe IV's collections, as he knew quite well the art of selection. Everything in this work is balanced: the faces, attitudes, landscape. One seems to feel a fresh breeze rustling the foliage. It was painted around 1580, and figured in the Alcázar Gallery.

Paris Bordone *was born in Verona in 1500 and died in Venice in 1571. His noble ancestry and excellent education enabled him to enter Tiziano's workshop, and the latter always treated him with great consideration. He was called by Francis II to the Court of France, where he painted for the King. Later he went to Augsbourg where he worked for the Emperor's bankers Függer. In his last works one detects the great influence which Michelangelo had upon him. He was an excellent portrait painter and his jewel is in the Gallery of the Academy of Venice*, The Delivrance of the Dodges' Ring.

Num. **372**, *Self-portrait.* Is a portrait of half length body, and one of his best. The catalogue tells us that this picture was oval shaped in the beginning and that later, in order to make it rectangular, probably in the 18th century, the left hand was added. It was previously believed to be by Tintoretto.

Tintoretto. Num. **484,** *Young woman.* At one time this portrait was attributed to Verones.

Num. **378,** *The gentleman with the gold chain.* It is not known who he might be and he is identified in the said manner; but Allende-Salazar and Sánchez Cantón think that it could be the portrait of Pablo Veronés. Of course, it is a master-piece.

Parrasio, Michele. *He was born about 1516 and died in Venice about 1578. He was the successive disciple of Tiziano and of Veronese.*

Num. **479,** *Allegory; Birth of Prince Don Fernando, Son of Felipe II.* The Virgins surround him and Fame presides over accompanied by Mars and Lucina. In other times it was believed that it dealt with the birth of Carlos V. But Sirs Allende-Salazar and Sánchez Cantón published the letter [1] the original of which is preserved in the Archives of Simancas, written by the painter to Felipe II, calling to his attention the significance of the Allegory. It is a very curious document in which the propitious stars are attributed with the happy event of the royal offspring to whom infinite fortunes are promised. It is known that the offspring did not arrive even for seven years. But the canvas is monumental and interesting, and full of praises for the ill-fortuned prince.

Veronese. Num. **494,** *Wedding in Cana.* Veronese painted various banquet scenes as this one, although larger; in the *Zwinger* of Dresde there are other Cana's Weddings. Always attentive to polychromy and ensemble and the consideration of the figures, he laughed about anachronisms as it happens in this canvas where, close to Christ, and Mary, are various portraits of Venetian gentlemen dressed according to the fashion of the time. The background with columns is also quite frequent in similar themes. All this is such that in the entire composition it seems that the only divine figures and the amphytrion are of the past. It does not belong to the painter's best period. It was acquired by Felipe IV at Charles I of England auction, and came to El Escorial in 1837.

Num. **502,** *The Finding of Moises,* is a small canvas, wich the painter repeated in a larger size. It is very charming and very characteristic of Veronese. The ladies in beautiful garments are very elegant in silvered tones admirably detached from the background verdure. One of them seems to be holding a bow-legged dwarf. We see in the background a bridge leading to a city. Note another anachronism in the representation of the ladies with sumptuous Venetian dresses of the epoch. It seems that the Marquis de la Torre owned it in Venice. It proceeds from the Alcázar.

---

[1] *Retratos del Museo del Prado, identificación y rectificaciones,* by **J. Allende-Salazar** and **F. J. Sánchez Cantón.** Madrid, 1919.

La Tintoretta, *by name Marietta Robusti, daughter of Giaccopo Robusti,* il Tintoretto. *She was born and died in Venice (1560-1590). As a child her father always took her around dressed like a little boy, and thus she was called* il ragazzino. *She learned by the side of her father who was collaborator with her brother, Domenico (so much so that Tintoretto never did want outsider). She died at thirty when her father was about seventy. It was such a shock that he never recovered and died four years after her. The painting of Cogniet,* Tintoretto and His Dead Daughter, *is well known.*

Num. **381,** *Self-Portrait.* One hand covers part of her chest. Due to the transparent aureo-silvery tints, there are some who believe it to be the work of her father. Others have believed that the true Tintoretta was the *Venetian Dame* of the collar of pearls and the knotted handkerchief upon the chest, núm. **383,** and there are others who do not doubt that Marietta is the woman portrayed bi Tintoretto in num. **384** in the room X A.

Num. **480,** *St. Agatha,* showing the sore of her sectioned bosom.

Room IX.—TIZIANO

We enter the olympic room of **Tiziano Vecellio,** which is one of the most august of our Museum, in fact of all the world's museums. He who wishes thoroughly to know such a renowned personality, whose genius filled almost a century, should not omit a visit to this Room which treasures the richest glories to come from his brush, as much regarding religious painting as bellicose, portrait, allegorical, mithological, and every kind of manifestations that can be attained by a multiple temperament.

In this room one realizes that Tiziano loved what was the most beautiful of Nature and Life. His palette did not let enter sufferances, tortures, and the unhappy ghosts of evil. He always looked for what was pleasant, vivid and succulent, and if sometimes he dealt with sorrowful themes, he exalted them with beauty.

We can also observe in this room how the personality of Tiziano was singular and jealously maintained as well in the line as in the color and composition. Between some canvases there is a temporary distance of fifty years and nevertheless in no one work can we detect the natural falls of one who jealously searches his way, nor the hesitations of an uncertain hand. If anything could damage Tiziano it would be the fact that from the very first moment he was perfect. In short, he is the master of a lyrism which did not become decorative, not even in the last years, thanks to the deep classical formation of his youth.

Num. **415,** *The Empress Elizabeth of Portugal* who was a daughter of Don Manuel, king of Portugal, married our Emperor who at the time was twenty six years old when she was twenty two. The Empress died in 1539 and the portrait was painted nine years later, which means that it was made with the aid of a sketch sent from Augsbourg to Tiziano. The portrait was brought to Spain by Doña María of Austria, the widow Queen of Hungary, and it was inherited by Doña Juana la Loca (the Mad); it passed to the Alcázar and later to the Retiro. Through radiography it has been detected that there is a beautiful head under the landscape which reveals that the painter employed a canvas already begun for another subject.

It is a young figure, seated, very beautiful and elegant, with strings of pearls in her hair and two jewels, one of them with a pendant pearl, which could not be the famous *Pilgrim* acquired later by Felipe II. She holds a book in her hand, and through the window a mountainous landscape is displayed. Tiziano painted the portrait when he was sixty years old.

Num. **419,** *The Worship of Venus.* Is one of the most charming pictures in the history of Universal painting. In 1523 under the commission of the Duke of Ferrara Alfonso de Este, Tiziano terminated three pictures for his library, which were the *Bacchanal*, *Bacchus and Ariadne* and this one. When the Duke saw them, he said that he was proud to own the three best works that the genius had ever created. *Bacchus and Ariadne* ended up in the National Gallery; the others were sent by the Count of Monterrey, vice-roy of Naples, for Felipe IV as a gift to the King by Prince Ludovisi. It is related that Domenichino could not refrain the tears when he saw the pictures leaving Italy for ever.

The canvas refers to a theme of the Greek sophist Philostratus when describing one of the sixty four pictures of a Naples Gallery. The cupids are the Nymph's sons, in a merry meadow and underneath the leafy trees shadow they all play, run, spring, fly, and offer the earth's fruits to the goddess of Love. It is difficult to describe such a delightfully happy scene. The variety of postures, gestures and foreshortnings, the graceful faces, the smoothness of the mellow and golden carnation, are all marvellous creations. Some embrace themselves, others kiss one another, a few tell their secrets, one menaces, his friend inducing him, etc... How much Rubens owes his inspiration of his obese angels' garlands to this un-equalled wonder!

Num. **408,** *Federico Gonzaga, First Duke of Mantua*, was the son of Elizabeth of Este and John Francis Gonzaga who married Margarita Paleólogo. He is portrayed with a poodle, and wears a dark blue suit with coat-tails and a braid embroidered in gold. It is a very polished canvas, especially the clothings which originally were black. The noble face one time was believed to be Alfonso de Este's (Lucrecia Borgia's husband), afterwards it was identified with his nephew Gonzaga. It belonged to the Marquis of Leganés and Felipe IV acquired it from his heirs.

Num. **409,** *The Emperor Carlos V*. The sight of this colossal portrait reminds us of others of the Emperor, and some engravings of the period, and one suddenly understands how much Tiziano magnified Carlos V and how he endowed him with an outward majesty which only the natural could approach. He was the son of Felipe el Hermoso (the Handsome) and Doña Juana la Loca (the Mad), born in Gante in 1500 and died in Yuste (Extremadura) in 1558. When the Emperor was in Mantua and saw the beautiful pictorial collection with Tiziano's works owned by Duchess Elizabeth of Este, he expressed his desire to be portrayed by such an eminent painter; a Spanish friend of his, Don Francisco de los Cobos, mediated and Carlos V's wish came true during his second sojourn in Bologna. The Emperor had already had his hair cut because it produced him headache, and so we see him with short hair and the same attire worn when he was crowned King of Lombardy. Close to him his favourite dog, «Sampere», raises its head. The Emperor was then around thirty three years old, and remained so satisfied with the work that he bestowed upon the painter the title of «Count of Lateran Palace». (In 1600 it was in the Alcázar, later Charles I of England owned it probably as a present of Felipe IV, and afterwards it was acquired at the English king's auction for 150 *pounds*.)

Num. **425,** *Danae*, the myth of Jupiter who in order to enter Venus's room and enjoy her charms, changed himself into a golden rain, was several times treated by Tiziano. Apart this *Danae*, which was in the Alcázar and was painted for Felipe II (who was not such a dolt as many believe), we possessed another brought by Velázquez from Italy, which was taken to the Retiro. From there the French confiscated it, later it fell into the hands of Wellington who «made it his own». Today his English successors continue to possess it.

The goddess is lying upon the couch with her legs apart, one hand upon the pillow and the other upon a thigh. It is a nude that only due to the marvel of its form cannot be classified as lewd. At her

side a type of spirit tries to collect rain in his apron. The golden flesh
tones of the goddess are firmly preserved by the painter's eyes who
was sixty seven years old at the time. Still twenty years later he
painted another *Danae*. Although threatened by fire in the times of
Carlos III it was saved by the Academy of San Fernando which
included it in its special rooms.

Num. **410,** *The Emperor Carlos V on Horseback in Mühlberg*.
(Pl. 9). According to Frizzoni this is the world's best portrait. According to Mayer it has a much classic value as the equestrian statue
of Marco Aurelio in the Roman Capitol. Tiziano's portrait is absolutely documented. The polished steel armature garnished with gold
is conserved in the Royal Armory in Madrid; the dark brown Spanish
horse was provided by Monsieur de Rye; the reddish trappings,
are the same which covered the horse and the sky «somewat dark
and reddish seemed to prophecy the blood that would be shed that
day» was faihfully reproduced.

The Emperor appears seated upon a horse with a javelin in his
hand, ready to undertake the famous battle of Elba against the Protestants, in which he obtained an absolute victory with the capture
of the Elector of Saxony, John Frederic. The posture of the Emperor
shows an obvious decision to advance and even the horse is seen in
motion, as the airy tuft wafts between its ears. His face, quite severe,
the helmet and the armature are all impregnated with the reddish
light of the early twilight that pronosticated bloodshed. It could
be that originally the picture was more luminous, in other words,
that it suffered somewhat from the 1734, fire in the Alcázar. Nevertheless, it maintains an irresistible grandeur of one of the best
equestrian portraits in the world, one, that has inspired Rubens and
Velázquez. It was painted in Augsbourg in 1548 and brought to
Spain by Queen Mary of Hungary, sister of the portrayed.

Num. **411,** *Felipe II*, Born in Valladolid in 1527 the son of
Emperor Carlos V and Empress Isabel of Portugal, he died in El
Escorial in 1598. This portrait, in which Felipe was twenty four years
old, was painted in order that his future wife Mary Tudor, the Queen
of England, might know him. She was thirty five then and at thirty
eight was painted by Antonio Moro. Dressed in a well chiseled
armature, and riding a white horse we see him with one hand upon
his sword and the other upon his helmet. The master painted it in
Augsbourg and in a letter from the portrayed gentleman to his aunt
Mary of Hungary he lamented because Tiziano had done the work
hastily. Had the king had more time he probably would have returned
it to be re-done. This circumstance and the fact that the artist had
made some copies of the King's portrait for several Italian Courts,
without the King's knowledge, caused a certain diversion in their

Caída camino del Calvario.—Falling down on the way to Mount-Calvary.
Chute sur le chemin du Calvaire.—Jesus fällt auf dem Weg zum Golgotha.
Caduta durante la Via Crucis.

**La Sagrada Familia del Roble (detalle).—The Holy Family (fragment).
La Sainte Famille (fragment).—Die Heilige Familie mit der Eiche.
La Sacra Famiglia del rovere.**

La Anunciación.—The Annunciation.—L'Annonciation.—Die Verkündigung.
L'Annunciazione.

**El Tránsito de la Virgen.—The Death of the V.
la Vierge.—Der Tod der Heiligen Jungfran.—L'A**

**Angel músico.—Angel musician.—Ange musicien.—Der musizierende
Engel.—Angelo musicista.**

Lucrecia di Baccio del Fede

«Noli me tangere»

Venus y Adonis

relations. Years later Tiziano wrote to the Spanish king suggesting that he painted a series of pictures of his father's victories. Felipe II did not accept the idea (perhaps due to the painter's old age).

In spite of the reservation of Felipe II regarding this portrait, and its dislike by the Queen of Hungary, we can say that it is masterly, and that the armature and the aristocratic head were never represented with more dignity. The same armature was later employed by Velázquez in the portrait of the Count of Benavente, and is conserved in the Royal Armory.

Num. **421**, *Venus Enjoying Herself with Love and Music*, is a similar canvas to num. **420** of the previous room. The little dog has disappeared and is substituted by a Cupid with his face next to the goddess. The expert people say that the face of the little dog is better for its brilliant mother-pearl tone, in contrast to the dullness of the goddess', which induces us to think that it is a copy from Tiziano's workshop. It must be noted that it suffered a good deal during the 1734 fire. On the other hand, it had escaped unharmed from the El Pardo fire in 1608, and it is known that Felipe III asked for it and when told that it had not been damaged contentedly replied: «The rest does not matter because it can be re-done». It is curious that until relatively recent times this picture was more highly evaluated than the Venus with the little dog.

It was one of those pictures destined to be burned by order of Carlos IV but was saved by its entrance into the Academy. His predecesor, Carlos III, had already threatened in the same way as being lewd, but fortunately Mengs persuaded the Monarch that it was not obscene. Carlos III revoked his order to burn it, buj just in case Mengs took it to his studio.

This Venus was given by the Emperor to Cardinal Granvela and a nephew of the latter sold it to Rudolph II, who gave it to Felipe III. Rudolph in exchange received the *Leda* and the *Ganimedes* by Correggio.

Num. **428**, *Salome with the Head of John the Baptist*. For Salome the painter used the portrait of his daughter Lavinia in a beautiful posture almost with her back turned and a profile of her head. Upon the tray the Precursor's head is seen. In the exemplar of Berlín the head is substituted by flowers and fruits. The one in Vienna is a copy from Rubens perhaps taken from the one of Madrid. (It was acquired in the legacy of Marquis of Leganés and came from the Alcázar.)

Num. **418**, *The Bacchanal* (Pl. 10), is one of the three pictures to which we have referred when describing the *Worship of Venus*. It is inspired by the reading of Catullus of whom Tiziano was very fond, and it could be considered as a *chant to wine* not only for the pitcher sustained in the center of the composition, but for the sentence written on the book abandoned on the ground, which translated reads: «He who drinks and does not continue drinking does not know what it is to drink», and even for the satyr that pours the drink to a lady reclining upon the ground.

Certainly it is a fluent composition conductive to stupor. Ariadne, who was always represented dressed, here appears deprived of her clothing and lying in posture full of dismayed languor. The flesh is rosy and undoubtedly treated with supreme pleasure. The bacchant upon whose head the wine is poured is Violante, Tiziano's lover (she also was linked with Palma the Old), who displays two violets on her chest and another one on her ear. Another couple with the girl dressed in a vaporous white vesture dances to the right of the composition. The rest is a conjunct of mythological figures and fauns that do not take part in the dance of Bacchus but drink and cast their happiness in the shadow of the thick-topped trees. The whole subject matter breathes sensuality and an exultant joy. As a pagan expression hardly no other of the Italian Renaissance can excel it. It was given by Nicholas Ludovisi to Felipe IV. (Proceeding from the Alcázar.)

Num. **407**, *Self-Portrait*. The artist has painted himself in profile at eighty nine. Wgen Vasari visited him in is workshop he found this portrait «e le trovó, ancorché vecchissimo fusse, con i pennelli in mano a dipingere» («and found him, although very old, with a brush in his hand ready to paint»). It is a proud portrait with the face resolved in golden tints, black cap, a fur mantel, a golden chain and with brush in hand. His face is pallid and very noble with a long white beard that seems to affix his sharp glance to the model he has in front of him. It is said that it was acquired for 400 *florines* in the auction of Rubens. (Proceeding from the Alcázar.)

Num. **445**, *St. Margaret*. According to the legend St. Margaret was devoured by a dragon but upon making the sign of the cross the monster burst open and the Saint came forth from its flanks. Tiziano has made a free translation of the legend. The expressión of fight and motion is marvellously translated, and the greenness of the skirt in contrast with the very soft flesh tones lends it a true impressionism. The red landscape imposes itself by its eloquent grandeur. In a comment by the painter Pacheco, on one of his trips to the capital, he states that the picture is in San Jerónimo in Madrid. (It never was in El Escorial, and proceeds fron the Alcázar.)

Núm. **440**, *The Burial of Christ*. According to Gronau: *never has human sadness been expressed in a more simple and truly artistic manner*. And one can well add upon seeing this pathetic canvas that nothing beautifies more than pain and sorrow. The dead Christ is held by

Joseph of Arimatea and Nichodemus in order to be placed in the sepulchre. The Virgin raises her Son's as if she wanted to kiss it; St. John is trying to console her, and Mary Magdalene raises her arms in a gesture of affliction and seems to question the beloved disciple.

The color of the composition is golden even in Our Lord's face. The figure of the Magdalene is quite conventional, and serves perhaps to animate the last part with a clear note of light, the same with which the body of Our Lord seems wounded. This canvas was requested by Felipe II and brought to El Escorial in 1574.

Num. **432,** *The Glory,* was commissioned by the Emperor and finished by Tiziano in 1551. It does not represent the Emperor in his Glory but rather his request to enter it through the mediation of Mary. The Emperor, striped off all regal attire, and with his crown at his feet, kneels in a humble posture, evening his hands together in a prayerful attitude. Behind him is his wife Elizabeth of Portugal, his sister Mary of Hungary, his son Felipe II, the Princess Doña Juana, and even the painter. In the center with her back turned is a beautiful woman with bared arms which represents, according to Father Sigüenza, the Church *that appear as though, presenting the princess of the New and Old Testament to God.* Among them Noah appears raising the arch in his hands, Moses carries the Comman- ments while St. John is with the eagle, and Abraham, etc. In the upper part the Trinity comes forth amidst the clouds.

Carlos V held this picture in great esteem and took it with him everywhere, even to his last retreat in the beautiful Monastery of Ex- tremadura. One day he ordered that the portrait of his wife should be brought into his presence and he contemplated it for a long while; then later the lesser known *Prayer in the Orchard,* and finally *The Glory* and when he could no longer resist he said to his doctor, Mathis. «Malo me siento, doctor» («I feel ill, doctor»), and he retired to the bed from which he would never raise again. After the Emperor's death it was taken to El Escorial from where it was brought in 1837.

Num. **422,** *Venus and Adonis.* This subject is inspired in the *Metamorphosis* of Ovidio. In a letter from Felipe II dated London, December 6, 1554, he tells his ambassador Vargas: «The picture of Adonis that Tiziano finished has arrived here and it seems to me just as perfect as you said, although it came mistreated due to a fold that crossed it. We shall see how it can be mended». Today, after four centuries, one still finds the traces of the fold. In 1636 it was in the Alcázar and in 1794 in the house of Rebeque that was the workshop of the Court of Carlos III.

Num. **429,** *Adam and Eve.* Eve has a Venus-like body and the serpent with a child-like body offers her the apple. It is supposed that the composition is inspired in an engraving by Albrecht Dürer.

The picture was painted when the artist was ninety three, and it
suffered quite a lot in the fire of the Alcázar in 1734. When Rubens
was in Spain he made a copy of it in his own style, which we will
find in Room XVI.

Room IX A.—TINTORETTO

Another magnificent room dedicated completely to **Tintoretto,** the only exception being a Self-portrait of **Paris
Bordone.** Tintoretto was the great Venetian figure and rival
of Tiziano, although he owed a great deal to the latter at
the beginning. But their personalities were different. If Tiziano was an amiable painter of sweet calm and the sensuality
of placid paganism, Tintoretto was the passionate, dinamic,
dominating artist who with knowledge alone had to fight
against them all: Tiziano, Veronese, Paris Bordone, Ponchino,
Contarini, Andrea Micheli, Palma *the Young*, Bassano, Salviati and others. Not finding work because it was absorbed
by the others, he exhibited some of his paintings in the
public square offering to do whatever any one else did,
without being paid if his painting did not excel. And finally
he succeeded.

In the rest of his pretensions as a man he was very modest. He always considered himself excessively remunerated
and even returned part of the money given to him for his
works. Nothing mattered to him except to live for his art,
to the extent that although he could have been extremely
rich he always lived modestly.

In order to see the works of Tintoretto it is necessary
to go to Venice, where the series of *St. Roch* and *St. Mark*
and the great decorations of the Palace of the Dodges are
to be enjoyed. The paintings we posses in the Prado were
sent by our king Felipe II.

Tintoretto. *His name was Giaccopo Robusti, son of a dyer, Therefore called «tintoretto» (the dyer's son). He was born in Venice in 1518
and died there in 1594. He was there a short while in the workshop of
Tiziano before learning how to fly with his own wings. He really enjoyed
the great contrasts of light and dark to the extreme that before starting
his compositions he modelled little figures of the themes in clay or wax*

in order to later illuminate them artifically. His study of background was deeply shaded in order to illuminate the models in the same way and thus his golden flesh tones (he liked to paint nudes) were enormously envigorated with the contrast of darkness. After seeing the nudes of Gioccapo Robusti, it seems that the light springs forth from the skin instead of being received.

He painted a good deal through all Northeast Italy and Venice which are full of his works.

Num. **2824,** *The Lavation.* To those who accuse the painter of copying the golden tints of Tiziano he replied with this ample canvas that is a symphony in silver. And to those who reproached him for the excessive crowding of figures which hid many dificulties, he showed them this praise of open spaces, in which the air and even the figures seem to circulate. And he even gifted them with an interminable background of proud architecture and a wide canal with a gondola. The interpretation of the biblical themes is almost vulgar with the independent groupings; here Christ bathing St. Peter, there an apostle in ridiculous posture deprived of his trousers by a companion; others leaning upon the table in a pensive attitude, another adjusting his sandal, who resting against a column in mysterious solitude and a dog in the center... All this is true, and yet nevertheless what pathetic secret has this proud canvas that in spite ot so much dispersion it has a unity of feeling that he who contemplates it immediately observes? Not even Peter himself talks; instead he is limited to a gesture against the Master's humility. Everything is so quiet and in all the faces one discovers the foreboding of an immediate tragedy. This is what Tintoretto has wished to express above all. All the personages are quiet and pensive. Above the priceless plastic values the originality projects itself in the surpassing of the momentary that ceases to be trivial to submerge itself in an emotional and permanent anguish.

The canvas was painted for San Marcuola of Venice and passed to the collection of Charles I of England, later to be acquired by Felipe IV for 250 *pounds.* (It belongs to El Escorial.)

Num. **382,** *Woman baring her breast.* A very Venetian portrait in the sense that there were very few artists in Venice who did not portray beautiful women in a similar way. In the Renaissance similar exhibitions were not surprising, they expressed a natural beauty, as that of the face. One thinks that maybe she is Marietta, the painter's favorite daugther who died at thirty and was very promising in art. The portrait is a delight of color and transparency painted with a cheerful slowness as if he enjoyed himself.

Num. **386,** *Susana and the Elders*, is a youth's sketch (surely for a roof) that had for its center *The Purification of the Booty* which would be completed with the rest of the sketches in the same room. It was acquired by Velázquez in Venice.

Num. **388,** *Esther in the presence of Ahsuerus.* Sketch for the same.

Num. **389,** *Judith and Hollofernes.* Item.

There are for the first time in the same Room, the two paintings on the theme *Judith and Hollofornes* (num. **389,** and num. **391,** splendid in composition and color, with perfect foreshortenings of carnations and rich qualities of silks and brocades. Even though probably the works of youth, the decor and grandeur of the figures are firmly materialised in the temperament of the artist.

Num. **394,** *Queen of Sheba's visit to Solomon.* Item.

Num. **395,** *Joseph and Potiphar's wife.* Item.

Num. **396,** *The Discovery of the Infant Moses.* Item.

Num. **393,** *The Purification of the Booty* (Pl. 11). Upon the victory against the Madianits, among whose booty sixteen thousand virgins figure (of whom only thirty two vere dedicated to our Lord), Moses hears the divine mandate that they be purified. In this canvas in which some nudes figure one can appreciate the nervous drawing of the painter, a trembling profile full of life. *Greco* has been influenced greatly by this detail. It was bought by Velázquez in Venice.

Num. **397,** *Baptism of Christ.* A landscape of Jordan River, falls to the right and the Holy Spirit is seen in a clearness of the sky. Apart from the biblical meaning of the theme we are before two strong and proud masculine nudes. The painter has sacrified the biblical version to the beauty of the forms. The same theme has been repeated in other occasions by the artist. (It proceeds from Aranjuez.)

Num. **398,** *The Paradise,* a precedent with variations of the canvas on the wall of the throne in the huge saloon in the Dodge's Palace of Venice, called *Maglior Consiglio,* a picture of gigantic proportions. One wonders how the original would be. It produces surprise and shock at the same time because more than a celestial paradise it seems to be a human whirl-wind that raises in spiral to God's Throne conquered only by violence. There is a different one in the Louvre. This one in the Prado was bought by Velázquez during his second trip to Italy and it comes from the Palace of the Retiro.

Num. **399,** *Battle between Turks and Christians.* Tintoretto, who painted the naval battle of Lepanto, has represented in this canvas an episode of an abducted woman and a combat between Turks and Christians near the water. It seems that it was painted for Gonzaga de Mantua; later bought by Velázquez.

Num. **387,** *Virtue triumphing over Sin.* This picture painted by Domenico Tintoretto, the great artist's son, represents Virtue embodied in a matron with helmet, caduce and a handfull of grain making Lewdness, Robbery, Treason and Passion flee. His father certainly had a hand in this canvas.

Num. **367,** *Peter of Medici* (?). Son of Cosimo I and Leonor of Toledo came to Spain in 1578 and died in Madrid in 1594. Morelli believed it to be painted by Greco; Berenson does not attribute it to Tintoretto. In 1794 it figured in the Duke of Arco's Villa as by the latter.

Num. **377,** *A Venetian Patrician*. With his right hand he touches a medal hanging from his chest. One might easily ask if the portrait is by Palma the Young.

Num. **369,** *Portrait of the Archbishop Don Pedro*.

Room X A.—THE BASSANO

Palma, the Young, *who was twice* the Old's *nephew and had his same name, was born in Venice in 1544 and died in 1628. He went to Rome very young and there he learned painting and studied the great masters. Returned to Venice he decorated the Royal Palace, boasting his fluency with the brush in large facings. In addition to the two large sized pictures of Room LXXIX, we have this other one.*

Num. **380,** *A Venetian Senator*, which is a beautiful portrait of the purest Venetian school and done during the painter's best period; later he began to lose fluency during the last years of his life and of course his works deteriorated noticeably. This picture was at one time attributed to Tintoretto.

The **Bassano** family and other painters of the Venetian school prevail in this room.

Bassanos, The. *The family name was «da Ponte». Francesco Bassano the Old was born in the 15th century. His son, Giaccopo was born in Bassano between 1510 and 1515, and died in 1592. Giaccopo's son Francesco the Young, was born in 1549 and died in 1592. His other son, Leandro, was born in 1557 and died in 1622. But the most important in the family was Giaccopo, whose Self-portrait hangs in this Room. He has been considered by some to have been Greco's master. He was the master of the workshop (in which he worked together with his sons) fulfilling all the commissions he received. He painted a great deal, especially biblical and rural scenes. His canvases although being somewhat incorrect in the sketch are all of vibrant coloring and almost all of a similar unmistakeable tonality.*

Bassano, Giaccopo. Num. **32,** *Self-Portrait*. It is a very expressive head which some believed painted by his son Leandro. (It belonged to Felipe V, and entered into the Museum in 1827.) Number **21,** *God's reproach to Adam.* Num. **22,** *The animals entering Noah's Ark.*

Bassano, Leandro. Num. **45,** *A Clergyman with a Crucifix.* The coat of armas in the upper part to the left seems to show that he represents a Venetian. Previously it was attributed to Tintoretto and even to Tiziano. (It proceeds from the Alcázar.)

Num. **41,** *The Crowning with Thorns* is painted upon a slate. The scene is meant to be a praise of artificial lights: a torch, a lamp, a small brazier. The resulting effects are hard. (It was in the Alcázar and in the Retiro.)

Num. **29,** *The Rich Avaricious and the Poor Lazarus,* is a version of the well-known parable of Saint Luke. The theme is but a pretext for the rest of the decoration. (It was given to Felipe IV by the Duke of Medina de las Torres.) The same happened with picture num. **39,** *The Return of the Prodigal Son.*

Num. **26,** *The Adoration of the Shepherds.* The author has followed the well-known technique of making the Child resplendent, illuminating those who surround Him.

Num. **22,** *The entrance of the animals in Noah's Ark.* On this painting, Jacob has searched the pretext of the biblical ark in order to show his skill in the representation of all kinds of animals. This painting was bought by Titian for the Emperor Charles V. (It was in the Alcázar from where it went to the Royal Palace.)

Num. **21,** *God's reproach to Adam.* Adam is reproached by God because of his sin and of Eve's, who is also present. But we say the same as said of the previous painting: the pretext for a complete «animal kingdom». This painting was bequeathed to Philip IV by Prince Filiberto of Saboya.

Num. **366,** *Portrait of the Venetian General Sebastian Venero.* He was the General who commanded the Venetian galleys in the naval combat of Lepanto. Magnificent portrait painted by Tintoretto and presented to Philip IV by the Marquis of Leganés.

Num. **384,** *Portrait of Marietta Tintoretto,* painted by her father.

Room X.—EL GRECO

This room is completely occupied by *El Greco* from Crete, who in his way is a forerunner of Velázquez. His masterpiece the *Burial of the Count Orgaz,* which hangs in the church of St. Tomé in Toledo, is not in the museum, not a single complete series of the Apostles (Toledo, Oviedo) nor his last hallucinant pictures (Zuloaga's collection in Zumaya); but we have sufficient and extremely important works to enable us to know his mentality, style and technique.

Although formed in the Bizantine orientalism and the Venetian school, once in Spain he became a complete unadulterated Castilian painter with an august severity and a firm and sure realism. This referring to the portraits, because in mystical subjects he went to the extreme of never denying Byzantine tradition.

Neither the life nor works of *Greco* were of a normal man as those of the genius never are. If *Greco* had not been an exceptional artist he would not have been in Venice but a follower of Tiziano and in Rome a mannerist poisoned by Michelangelo. From these two, as from others, he took that which was convenient and then transubstanciated it by his vigorous, unstable, dreaming and extravagant temperament. His painting was the reproduction of an intimate, austere, lonely, ardent and mystic personality. Careless in his sketch, mislead by his passions in color, which was somewhat the resulting of his spirituality, he left us forms, intonations and lights, that for the first time human eyes were to see.

Nothing of madness, and even less of physical deficiencies nor poor eyesight! He always knew what he was doing and what he did he saw better than anyone else. When he wanted to, he secured his personages with a heaviness and when he so chose he put the center of gravity in the zenith. He adopted two canons: the divine and the human. In the first he changes at will the normal dimensions or converts them into zigzaging blazes. In the second his figures are realistic and natural. In spite of what some say he was understood in Spain from the first. Perhaps he passed posteriorly through an unjustified omission. Today he is considered one of the highest peaks in genius of Art.

El Greco, *with the non pronounceable namè Domenicos Theotocopoulus or Theotocopuli, came into the world in Candia, the capital of the Isle of Crete, which at the time belonged to the Signoria of Venice in 1541, and died in Toledo in 1614. He began to learn about art in his native city and in 1560 he was already in Venice in Tiziano's workshop. Ten years later he went to Rome called for by Julio Clovio to serve Cardinal Farnesio. Finally toward 1576 he came to Spain. In 1577 he*

resided in Toledo where he met Doña Jerónima de las Cuevas and a son,
George, was born. Although his main dream was to paint for El Escorial
he never lacked work. Felipe II entrusted him with an altar picture,
The Martyrdom of St. Maurice and the Theban Legion *which he did*
not like. Greco *returned to Toledo where he painted until his last days.*
His studio was visited by illustrious personalities of the epoch, some
of whom were painted in The burial of the Count of Orgaz *and many*
others passed to canvas. He earned plenty of money and lived well and
it is said that during the banquets which he often gave for his friends
he engaged musicians to enliven the festivity. And when his last moments
arrived he died as a fervent Catholic. It is said that he did not leave a
large fortune but at least sufficient own works and objects of art. He
was buried in a vault of the church of St. Dominic the Antiguo in Toledo,
from where he passed to the church of San Torcuato, which was destroyed.
Finally his remains were lost.

Numbers **806, 810, 811, 813** are portraits of knights to the
moment unidentified.

Num. **2644,** *A Trinitarian* or *Dominican Friar.* Before it was
believed to be a portrait by P. Maino, one of Greco's followers. The
richly modelled head has the simplicity so characteristic of the artist's
last epoch. (Willed by Pablo Bosch.)

Num. **812,** *The Scholar Jerónimo de Cevallos,* is identified by
Allende-Salazar and Sánchez Cantón. He was a governor of Toledo,
a writer of law and politics and a great jurist. The portrait is precious,
contrasting the incomprehensible simplicity of the work with the
intense interior life of the portrayed. (It comes from the Manor-
house of Arco.)

Num. **827,** *The Annunciation.* As all the rest this theme has been
often repeated by the painter with few variations. The Virgin who
prays at her praying-desk turns her eyes to the miraculous apparition
of the young angel upon the cloud. A celestial violation with angels
and the dove of the Holy Ghost is notable, and the background is a
street. The messenger angel is an excellence of beauty and elegance.
(Bought for 150 *escudos* in 1868.)

Num. **808,** *Don Rodrigo Vázquez.* President of the *Consejos de*
Hacienda and Castile and Knight of Alcántara. Although he was not
related to Mateo Vázquez, he coincided with the latter in the persecution of Antonio Pérez, secretary of Felipe II. One appreciates in
this portrait, painted between 1590 and 1600, better than in the
others, the short disorganized brush strokes, with an extreme thin-
ness of color and predominance of the gold gamut. (It proceeds
from the Alcázar and from the Manor-house of the Duke of Arco.)

Num. **809,** *The Knight with his Hand on his Chest* (Pl. 12). This
portrait defines the type of the Castilian gentleman of *Greco.* Highly

distinguished, grave, quiet, dressed in black and wearing a chain around his neck from which a medal hangs. The hand upon the chest, does not only give a feeling to the figure but also it accentuates the plastic beauty. He carries his sword higher than usual, doubtless in order to complete the integrity with the gold hilt. Observe the face and the hand in order not to repeat identical concept in the other portraits. The palette employed is cyanic (the lower half of the iris), with preference for the ochre, dull blues, quiet reds and violets. The hand, as the face, is painted with abrupt brush strokes, that give a weak quality upon contrast or proximity. It is signed in capital Greek characters, and it is believed that the portrayed may be the Knigt of Santiago, Don Juan de Silva, Marquis of Montemayor and Notary of Toledo. (Proceeding from the Manor-house of Duke of Arco.)

Num. **807,** *The Doctor* (Dr. Rodrigo de la Fuente?). The identification has been made by means of the portrait of the National Library. This doctor was a good friend of *Greco* and an illustrious Latin poet.

Num. **817,** *St. Benedict.* Wears black cowl and holds a staff of silver, gold and precious stones in his left hand; the right is held out open with two fingers bent. The face is very hard, with intense dark shadows, though with a gentle expression of meekness. Cloud effects lightly sketched. (Came from the Trinidad Museum in the catalogue of which it was taken for *St. Basil.*)

Num. **824,** *The Trinity.* The Father holds His dead Son in His arms; above them both is the Holy Spirit in the form of a dove and on all sides angels lament the drama of the Son. The scene takes place on a cloud with cherubs. More than a Trinity, it is a study of Piety in which the figure of the Mother has been substituted by that of the Eternal Father as usually interpreted in the workshop of Giovanni Bellini. Some have looked for traces of Michelangelo in this Tizianolike creation with its golden warm and bright light. Both heads of the Father and Son are magnificent. The angels are all feminine and a little too carnal. It was painted when he had recently returned from Italy, for St. Domingo the Antiguo of Toledo. Fernando VII bought it for 15 000 *reales.*

Num. **815,** *Saint Anthony.* He carries a spray of white lillies in the right hand and an open book in the left on which figures a medallion with the Child Jesus. The upper edge of the book is signed with characteres which read: «of the hand of Domingo». (It came from the Trinity Museum, though it is unknown where it arose from.)

Room XI.—EL GRECO

Num. **829**, *The Virgin Mary*. With a precious and charming head almost shy, and full of expression and delicacy. It was painted during the end of the 16th century and is autographed. It is said to be the original of the one in the Strasbourg Museum which is even more beautiful.

Num. **2444, 2889, 2891** and **2892,** *Half-length Figures of the Apostles and the Saviour* shows dispersed figures of the apostleship. Three complete apostleships by Greco are known: two in Toledo and the other in the ducal palace of the Parque in Oviedo, property of Marquis of San Feliz, bought by the Community of San Pelayo in the same city. More or less advanced in technique of the epoch in some cases the lack of facial symmetry of certain figures, and the faulty sketch, especially in the hands, is notable. Also one can appreciate the employment of crude colors and the drawn-out brush strokes of the last period. (They were acquired by the Ministry of National Education in 1946 and from then till now they have been admired by the innumerable visitors who daily crowd the halls of the Museum.)

Num. **826,** *The Holy Family*. A charming canvas for its subject and execution. The Virgin, as well as the Child on her lap, is leaning her hand on St. Anne's shoulders. Facing St. Anne is St. Joseph at whose feet St. John Child appears, entirely naked and bearing a small fruit basket.

With major or minor differences, there are several replicas in Spain and abroad. The one we are examining was painted between 1594 and 1604.

Num. **822,** *Jesus Christ embracing the Cross*. Christ is not shown walking overwhelmed under the burden of the cross as in many similar scenes by other painters. Here, on the contrary, He is walking erect his head raised, his features not showing the burden endured by his shoulders. The signature is written in Greek letters on the lower edge of the cross.

Num. **2645,** *The Coronation of the Virgin* (Pl. 13). The Virgin is seated upon the clouds, her hands on her chest, in an attitude of profound humility and her feet upon a hali moon. At her sides Christ and the Father, who is covered with a snowy mantel, hold the golden crown of the Queen above her head while the Holy Spirit, with his wings among the little heads of the cherubs, looks on. The same theme was dealt by *El Greco* using other figures of the epoch. (Pablo Bosch legacy.)

Room XXX.—EL GRECO

The Adoration of the Shepherds. El Greco shows in this picture the most courageous manifestation of his phosphoric reflexes against a dark background so that they look like enamel. The scene takes place in the stable of a house whose entrance may be perceived through the great porch at the back. The upper part vanishes into a heaven crowded with cherubs and two angels. The angel on the left hand is waving a phylactery on which the words *Gloria in excelsis Deo* are written. The one on the right side is shown in a fervent attitude looking at the New Born. The clouds are dressed in opalescent rainbow colours showing a cotton-like compactness which yields to pressure, as can be seen in the foot of the angel leaning upon the gaseous surface. This almost spherical form of the clouds, used again in the inferior part of the *Coronation of Our Lady*, announces the Greco of the last epoch.

The scene is illuminated by the heavenly light irradiated by the Child Jesus. The Virgin lifting the veil that covers her Son to allow the shepherds to contemplate Him, is bathed in brightness. This same brightness makes the shepherds look like ghosts. The most impressive of the shepherds is the one standing on the right side crossing his arms on his chest and looking at the Child with feverish eyes as in a rapture that, although happy could be taken for painful. The contrast between this corpulent and vigorous figure, as well as the kneeling one, and the insignificant infant that enchants him is one of the most complete successes in the long production of Greco.

Num. **2819,** *St. Andrew and St. Francis*. Each is with his characteristic symbol: the cross and the stigmae. The *Catalogue* tells us: «This very beautiful and well conserved painting was quite unknown until the war. Then it was brought to the Prado by the Attachment of Property and there, lined. When the war ended it figured in the Exposition of paintings recovered by Spain. It was acquired by the Community of the Royal Monastery of the Incarnation of Madrid in January 1942. The canvas does not proceed from the works of art of royal foundation. It was contributed on October 3, 1676 by Mother Ana Agustina of the Child Jesus, daughter of the Dukes of Abrantes».

Num. **2874,** *The Holy Face*, was acquired by the parish of Mostoles in 1944 with funds from the Count of Cartagena legacy.

Num. **823,** *The Crucifixion*. Actually it is more surprising than anguish causing. More than anything it is a symbol of the artist's unquietness. The subject is resolved with a total symmetry of figures and composition. Its lights are strange and phosphorescent. To the side of both arms two angels collect the blood that is shed from His hands and side; at the foot of the Cross, two rigid and lengthened figures are raised, the Mother and St. John are equal in height and size and two others (the Magdalene and another angel) collect the blood from the feet which are contorted in very violent foreshortenings and purposely sought with difficulties in sketch. The two hands of the Magdalene and of the angel upon the beam could not be more miserable. The figure of the repentant woman is more than a little affected and that of the angel cannot be understood and appreciated even with power. Perhaps it is of the same origin as the previous.

Num. **828,** *Pentecost*. The composition is formed with an ascensional plan. The Virgin is seated in the center surrounded by apostles and disciples. Tongues of fire appear above their heads (even Mary's), and above the Holy Ghost in the form of a dove. As usual El Greco has fled from all conventionalism; not even his art of composition has precedent. The poses are agitated and almost convulsive; the hands tell us as much as the faces. The conglomerations seem to indicate that *Greco* was terrified by open spaces. Upon the apostle in the foreground in his dandy blue tunic and yellow cape there are four others. In short, in this jam everything is blazing, as the tongues of fire. It was painted in the last years of the artist and was taken to the museum from the convent of the Trinity.

Num. **821,** *Baptism of Christ*. Is signed on a paper upon a rock where Christ is kneeling. It is hardly interesting as a composition. Next to an inexpressive Christ is a thin and sullen St. John but the most interesting part is the sky where a mellow and radiant God raises His hand to give a blessing and an angelic cohort in pink and blue robes receive the light radiated by the Creator. It was painted for the College of Doña María de Aragón, lady of Doña Ana, the fourth wife of Felipe II. This school or Monastery no longer exists, and in its place the palace of the ancient Senate has been raised.

Num. **825,** *The Resurrection* (Pl. 14). It is a human confusion in which it is difficult to guess just to whom and where each member belongs. We refer to the portion of the guardians which is confusing and active with unjustified nudes in which *Greco* has wished to recall his days in Rome. No one can deny that the fallen guardian on his back who fences with a sword in his right hand is a finished study in foreshortening, form, intonation and line; but the one to his left is a monster converted by michelangelism into caricature. But still something even more unbelieveable awaits us. The third person between the knees of the previous two (he who dreams with his hand upon his face) is against all the laws of impenetrability perhaps with no other mission than to hide whatever he is hiding with his elbow. Some opine that it comes from the College of Doña María de Aragón in Madrid. It was taken to the museum of the Trinity from where it passed to the Prado.

Num. **2445,** *A Knight of Santiago and Saint Louis, King of France.* Supposedly the portrayed is Julián Romero, who died suddenly in Cremona in 1577, the same year in which a Spanish document of Greco already existed with the same date. It is not imprudent to suppose that the portrait was painted in Rome. He is on his knees and covered by a mantel his hands upon his chest in a reverent pose. To his side another Knight with armature and mantel thrown back could be St. Louis according to Cossio, because of the golden lilies that dot the mantel and the *fleuretté* crown at his feet. They correspond to those of *St. Louis* in the Louvre. The inscriptions reads: «Julián Romero of the exploits, from Antequera, Governor of the Order of Santiago, the most famous of the Italian and Flemish armies whose glorious deeds fill history». This last observation and the fact that the heroe was not born in Antequera but rather in Torrejoncillo de Huete or in Huélamo (Cuenca) denote that the inscripción was placed, afterwards without care for identity. (Errazu legacy.)

Num. **832,** *The Spoliation.* A copy of the original which is in the sacristy of Toledo Cathedral, made and signed by the son of El Greco, Jorge Manuel Theotocópuli.

Núm. **1276,** *The Calabrian.* Painted by Luis Tristán. Lippomano, Ambassador of Venice, called this Calabrian «the favourite and almost spy of Philip II».

Room XII.—VELAZQUEZ

> *Instead of going back to the previous room, go out to the Great Central Gallery and with a few steps to the left you will find yourself at the entrance of the Great Rotunda of Velázquez.*

This is obviously a great rotunda, the most beautiful and spacious of the museum destined completely to be a «shrine» of Velázquez's works. In it, with the exception of *The Meninas*, that is in another room apart (XV) one finds what could be called the process of art, or rather the development of the painter, from his first works of Madrid to the last. Thus, for both the professional or the curious visitor this room holds an undeniable historical interest, that permits

one to follow the ascending curve of the artist with his
«repentances» or amendments (because Velázquez always
studied himself), the variation of his palette, the conquest
of space and the simplification of his technique.

The visitor to the museum for the first time ought to
know that his best works are here in The Prado —of course this does not mean to say that there are not excellent
works in other museums (for example, the portrait of Innocent X, in Doria, of Rome) and private collections. Of
course a finished study of this egregious artist can be enjoyed
without leaving these rooms.

Velázquez represents the culmination of Spanish painting
and is at the same time one of the world's best painters.
It is not necessary here to draw comparison because he developed his own style oblivious of the influence in the fundamentals, drawing his art and motives from the most pure
Castilian essences: reality, severity, distinctiveness, impeccable correction of design, cyanic-like tints and something that
was exclusively his... an aerial profoundity and captivation
of the luminosity through the darkness.

Although he cultivated the religious theme, the historical
and that of genre, he dedicated himself mainly to the portrait
in which he had no rival, and even the largest part of his
pictures of composition are actually no more than portraits
with natural backgrounds. There was only one thing that he
did not, or did not wish to understand, Mythology. When
he began it —and Rubens was probably the friend who urged
him to it— he used so much irony that it seems he himself
laughed at his productions. If the world of the gods had
been as bad as Velázquez reproduced it, Mythology would
have lasted only the length of time he utilized in representing
it. And the reason that Velázquez did not actually feel this
chimerical world was not his lack of imagination but rather
his typical Spanish fondness for naked reality. Mythology
deals a lot with decoration and the easy superficial eloquence:
both aspects are completely opposed to his art, whose notes
are austery and profoundity.

Some of his works were burnt in the fire of 1734, while
others are to be found in foreign galleries or private col-

Carlos V

Bacanal.—Bacchanal.—Bacchanale.—Das Bacchanal.—Baccanale

La purificación de las vírgenes madianitas.—Madianite virgins.—Les vierges madianites.—Die Madianitischen Jungfrauen.—La purificazione delle vergini madianite

El Caballero de la mano al pecho.—The gentleman with his hand at his chest.—Le geltilhomme de la main sur sa poitrine.—Der Edelmann mit der Hand auf der Brust.—Il Cavaliere dalla mano sul petto

La Coronación de la Virgen.—The Coronation of Our Lady.—Le Couronnement de la Vierge.—Die Krönung der Heligen Jungfrau.—L'Incoronazione della Madonna

La Resurrección.—The Resurrection.—La Ré-
surrection.—Die Auferstehung.
La Risurrezione.

El Conde-Duque de Olivares.—The Count-Duke of Olivares.—Le Comte-Duc d'Olivares.—Der Herzog Graf von Olivares.—Il Conte-Duca di Olivares

La rendición de Breda.—Surrender of Breda.—Reddition de Bréda.—Die Übergabe von Breda.—La resa di Breda

lections; but his best embellish the walls of our museum, where it is necessary to come if one wishes to study its inexhaustable grandness.

Velázquez, Diego de Silva, *was born in Seville about the middle of 1599 and died in Madrid in August 1660. Because of his fondness of drawing his father sent him to the Old Herrera. But the old gentleman had such a bad temper that the young artist could not tolerate it and thus he changed to Pacheco with whom he remained several years (later marrying Pacheco's daughter). Due to his fried, Juan de Fonseca, he soon moved to Madrid at twenty four, already with the hope of painting the king. Unable to arrange it he returned to Seville and a year later with even greater hopes returned to the Court. He painted a portrait of Felipe IV which was well received and Velázquez became painter of the Chamber and thus was admitted ti the royal service. When Diego was well settled he called his wife and the two resided in Madrid.*

After the visits to Spain of the Prince of Wales (later Charles I of England) and Rubens on a diplomatic mission, Velázquez was advised by the latter to go. to Italy. In 1629 he embarked from Barcelona for Genoa and in 1631 returned after having copied other masters, done some painting on his own and bought several works for Felipe IV. Soon after he painted the equestrian portraits of the king and of Count Duke of Olivares and The Surrender of Breda *or* The Lances. *At the beginning of 1649 he returned to Italy and painted the amazing portrait of Pope Innocent X, which is to be found in the treasury of the Gallery Doria. He bought new works and sculptures before returning one and a half years later to the Peninsula.*

His third and most glorious epoch is that of Venus of the Mirror *(National Gallery).* The Spinner *and* The Meninas. *Desirous of expressing his utmost satisfaction, the king named him Knight of Santiago (in spite of the hostility of the Order who demanded character references).*

When the marriage of the Princess María Teresa with Louis XIV of France was arranged, Velázquez acting as His Majesty's Lodger had to leave for the Island of the Faisanes in order, to decorate the dwelling place in which the interviews of the future couple would be celebrated. His task completed, he returned ill to Madrid. His illness was brief and he died on the indicated date surrounded by his wife, his daughter, Ignacia, who married the painter Mazo, and some friends. His remains rested in the parish of St. Juan Bautista in the crypt of his friend D. Gaspar de Fuensalida, and have not been found after the temple's disappearance.

Begin the visit to the right according to how one enters into the Rotunda.

Velázquez. Núm. **1188,** *The Prince Don Carlos.* The younger brother and follower of Felipe IV, son of Felipe III and Margaret of Austria-Styria. He appears standing with a black suit and gorget, a golden chain and the Toisón. A glove negligently hangs from one of his fingers. It was painted about 1626.

Num. **1182,** *Felipe IV*, was born in 1605, in Valladolid, and died in Madrid, in 1665. Probably the first full length portrait of the King done by Velázquez, about 1628. Carefully observing the canvas, one notes that at first the legs were separated in the portrait, and later connected by Velázquez.

Num. **1171,** *Vulcan's Forge.* It is a mythological episode in which Apollo penetrates Vulcans's forge to reveal the loves of his wife, Venus, with the god Mars, while nearby are four other Cyclops. This canvas, with the *Tunic of Joseph* that is not in the Museum, was painted during his first stay in Italy. (His nude works were particulary excellent.) We have already said that Velázquez did not feel mythology. That fellow with the sunken chest could not be the god Vulcan, nor his companions cyclops. On the other hand Apollo is a good looking young man with a fine physique. But, as a realistic painter, his studies of nudes are impeccable, although they were partly re-painted some years later by their famous creator. The expresión of stupor on Vulcan's face upon learning of his wife's adultery, and the astonishment of the forgers are perfect. It was painted in 1630, and acquired by Felipe IV four years later.

Num. **1170,** *The Drunkards.* When he came to Madrid on a diplomatic mission the Flemish painter, Rubens, saw Velázquez's pictures and recommended him to take a trip to Italy. As much to furnish himself with funds, as to captivate the king, he painted this very beautiful canvas, one of his most popular. And he baptised it with the name of *The Drunkards* wherein we see the triumph of Bacchus. It is another mythological picture without mythology. Not because Velázquez was unaware of it, for Tiziano's mythological pictures han in the palace. But the Spanish artist who never wanted his fantasy to overflow, was once again ironic in laughing at the old gods. Bacchus is an adipose young man who is seated upon a barrel throne crowning a group of tramps brought from the suburs of Madrid. Rich in color, constricted in sketch and plethoric of expression, this painting closes the painter's first epoch. The figures are still strongly silhouetted, they still lack an aerial and luminous surrounding atmosphere, that diffracts the contours, and separates them from the background. But a rich promise is anticipated in this same canvas, because the drunkard in the right background is resolved with four surprisingly simple strokes.

Velázquez received one hundred *ducados* and the king's permission. A few days after collecting his money he embarked from Barcelona with a friend, Spinola, en route to Genoa. (August, 1629.)

Num. **1181**, *Don Gaspar de Guzmán, Count-Duke of Olivares* (Pl. 15). He was Felipe's favorite, son of the second Count of Olivares and Doña María Pimentel, born in Rome (his father was the ambassador) in 1587 and died in Toro deprived even of the court favour in 1645. After having seen the equestrian portrait of the king he wanted to be painted in the same manner. We see him directing a battle (in the background between the horses hoofs) with a general's cane in his hand. The portrait, with the exception of the cloud effect, is a masterpiece superior to that of Felipe IV. The Count-Duke was sufficiently obese and round-shouldered but Velázquez arranged it in the foreshortening from bottom to top in order to dissimulate the defect. It seems that the canvas was always praised not as a pictorial piece but rather for the vanity and pride of the favourite. It produced a very bad impression upon the king and resulted in Don Gaspar's retirement in Toro where he died eleven years later. It was bought by Carlos III for 12 000 reales.

Num. **1178**, *Felipe IV*. Another of the equestrian portraits that the king wanted to own, beginning with that of Emperor Carlos V, by Tiziano. He wears a band across the half armature and clutches the general's cane. The background is a landscape of El Pardo with transparent cloud effects, that are a portent of luminosity. The canvas has been retouched by Velázquez to the extreme that the original painting shows through. Observe that the horse has four hind feet, and that the king's bust has been set back, etc. The canvas is dated 1636 and was sent to the Saloon of Reigns of the Retiro.

Num. **1193**, *Don Juan Francisco Pimentel, X Count of Benavente*, President of the Council of Italy, and Knight of Toison (1584-1652). It is a proud portrait full of Tiziano's influence, in which we see the same armature as in the portrait of Felipe II painted by the Venetian master. It was painted the same year of Velázquez s second trip to Italy in 1648. It figured in the Isabel Farnesio Collection in La Granja.

Num. **1189**, *Prince Don Baltasar Carlos*, is a new portrait of the same prince in hunting dress. He is admirably presented with harquebuse in hand between two dogs, one of which sleeps while the other to the right of the canvas looks at his master. The face is a prodigy of grace and serenity already revealing his character. It was painted for the Tower of the Parada.

Num. **1208**, *The God Mars*. This mythological god is no more than a workshop nude. Rubens represented him with an olympian fantasy, crowned by victorious laurels and surrounded by little cupids and opulent goddesses. But Velázquez has put him seated alone and pensive, with a morion lacking armature and coat of arms, which lay at his feet. Painted for the Tower of the Parada.

Num. **1183** and **1185**, *Felipe IV*. Velázquez painted various epochs of his life. The first is a fragment of a larger picture, perhaps equestrian; the second is smaller and perhaps from the second epoch.

Num. **1198**, *Pablo de Valladolid*. With this portrait begins the series of buffoons, men of pleasure or *vermins* of the Palace who served to amuse the royalty with their sayings and clownish actions. It was the Austrian tradition, because such unfortunates were not considered to be «amusing» in the Castilian tradition. The buffoon appears in the pose of a reciter. Velázquez has valiantly faced a problem of sustentation in this canvas. There is no floor nor walls, nothing but a general atmosphere. Nevertheless the buffoon is firmly maintained, seated, shaped upon the soles of his feet with an absolute gravitorial heaviness. (It passed from the Retiro to the Academy and to the Prado in 1827.)

Num. **1180**, *Prince Baltasar Carlos*, son and heir of the king, who died in Zaragoza at seventeen. (Another equestrian portrait upon a poney.) He is luxuriously dressed in a gold lame doublet, velvet green hose embroidered in gold, a lace walloon and wears a feather hat. It is said that before he finished this portrait in 1636 the poney died and that the Prince, still wanting to be portrayed with the same animal, took it to a taxidermist and it resulted in an excessively round belly and obviously stiff hind legs fastened to the ground. It was also sent to the Saloon of Reigns of the Buen Retiro.

Num. **1200**, *The Buffoon Don Juan de Austria*. Was he thus called to make fun of the buffoon himself or of the original Don Juan de Austria, the Emperor's illegitimate son? The sham naval battle we scrutinize in the background and the armature in the ground lead us to believe that the latter question can be answered in the affirmative. As a pictorial piece it is precious, energically realized in weak hues not even slightly thick. This tecnique belongs to the painter's last years; however, it is attributed to the year 1636. (The same origin as the previous.)

Num. **1172**, *The Lances of The Surrender of Breda* (Pl. 16). The rendition of this Flemish *plaza* is the most brilliant episode of Felipe IV's epoch. The handing over of the keys to the city took place on June 5, 1635. In the center of the composition is the Marquis of Spínola and the conquered, Justinus of Nassau. Instead of looking at the key, Spínola perfers to place his hand upon his enemy's shoulder and to congratulate him for the courage that he displayed in the battle. Groups os Spaniards and Dutch cluster around the two captains. The horse seen in reverse on the right draws the glance to its head and contributes a profoundity to the scenes. In the background a formation of soldiers, a wide and inundated field and bonfire smoke play their parts. The lances that have given popularity to the picture, lend solemnity and balance to the conjunct. Rumor has it that the face behind the horse is our famous Diego Velázquez. Perhaps, because without doubt the warriors that guard Spínola are all portraits.

Our painter excuted this silvered marvel on the ground of the data, furnished him by Spínola during their trip from Barcelona to Genoa. Finished the picture in 1635, the brave soldier was unable to admire it because he died five years before. This composition swollen with creative torrents in which Velázquez exhibits an enviable imagination (replies to those believing him lacking in this quality). He offers us a truly psychological mastery in the personages as in the Dutch background. It is a symphony in silver. Coming from the Saloon of the Reigns of the Buen Retiro.

Num. **1186,** *Cardinal-Prince Don Fernando de Austria.* In 1619 this younger brother of Felipe IV, became Cardinal and Governor of Flanders in 1634 until his death in 1641. Velázquez portrayed him as a hunter with a beautiful hound at his side. It was painted for the Tower of the Parada.

Num. **1191,** *The Queen Doña Mariana de Austria.* The daughter of Emperor Fernando III and of Doña María (Felipe IV's sister), she was a niece and second wife of Felipe IV, thirty years younger than he. She is dressed in a trimmed doublet with a white hand-kerchief to the left. Velázquez has worked marvels with this lean, withered and emaciated face, surrounding her with a decorum unpa-ralleled. She was nineteen at the time.

Num. **1184,** *Felipe IV.* It shows the king in hunter's dress at thirty and accompanied by his favourite dog. It has been corrected by its author, and was originally taken to the Tower of Parada, from where it passed to the new Palace.

Num. **1194,** *Juan Martínez Montañés.* The identification is not definite. This Sevillan sculptor came to Madrid in 1636-37 in order to do an equestrian statue of the King, and Velázquez took advan-vantage of the opportunity to paint this handsome portrait; but other critics, agree that the technique is much more advanced than that which corresponds to those years. He could be Alonso Cano, or perhaps Manuel Pereyra... The dispute continues. The portrayed appears modelling a bust of Felipe IV with a palette-knife in his hand. It is a model of sobriety.

Num. **1173,** *The Spinners.* Velázquez has returned from his second trip to Italy; he has finished his Alcázar works, and has been appoin-ted for Palace charge to decorate with tapestries... This obliged him to pay visits to the Royal Factory of St. Isabel and perhaps in one of them he conceived the idea for this famous canvas, a jewel equalled only by *Las Meninas*. It shows a workshop and five workers and in the background are three ladies contemplating a tapestry. To the left foreground are two women: the young one raises the heavy curtain bidding farewell to the second elder and hooded, the distaff spinning in her hand. To the right are two others, a girl carrying a basket and another seated with her back turned, evidently listening to her, while she disentangles a thread from the spool. In the center a third one beside a cat, collects the wool to be spun on the distaff disseminated on the floor. The hooden woman, with her leg uncovered, has the appearance of a Roman matrone, in the young one we could imagine a beautiful Greek statue. Velázquez with popular models knew how to produce these marvels.

Three lights and two intermediate shades play in the composition: the first light is external falling strongly upon the seated young girl; the second, very tenuous proceeds from the window to the left and penetrates the red curtain; the third one is in the background. In the first penumbra are the two women on the left; the center one is submerged in the second. The luminous background is traced through these two contrasts.

The aereal and luminous perspective places each figure in its respective location. The atmosphere of the workshop is dense and confined as the subtle dust that fills the room. Certain details of sketch and color are very curious and reveal the precursory sagacity of Velázquez. If one looks fixedly during a length of time at the halfed spool to the right and then rapidly turns his eyes to the distaff it seems to spin. This is due to the deformation that the painter has given to the wheel, to the degradation of tones, to the other side of the circle and to the fleshy mass that has substituted for the hand moving the distaff.

In an inventory of 1664 this picture is referred to as *The Fable of Aragne*. Can you imagine Rubens treating the same theme? What a world of gods, of Penelopes, of Onfalias and Ariadnas of disentangled angels in a baroque jumble! Velázquez, on the other hand, wanted to paint only that before his eyes, and with such simple elements as thone of the work room he has realized a work of art that all humanity acknowledges. (The picture was in the Retiro and in the Palace and María Luisa Caturla found it cited in the inventory of works possessed by Don Pedro de Arce in Madrid.)

Num. **889,** *View of the City of Zaragoza*. It is taken from the opposite river bank of the Ebro with a view of the temple of El Pilar. We seem to be on the other side of the river and from our location we see the royal retenue with a coach, etc., thet visited the city in 1646. The master and his disciple and son-in-law Juan Bautista del Mazo collaborated in this work and it is difficult to discriminate «who did what», although it is supposed that the figures in the foreground are by Velázquez. The early painting had a Virgin of El Pilar (the patroness of Zaragoza) with angels in the sky that due to haziness was covered in 1857.

Num. **1192,** *The Princess Doña Margarita de Austria* is the daughter of Felipe IV and Doña Mariana de Austria. Those who believed that Velázquez only painted in cold tones were well answered with this marvel enriched by reds, pinks and silvers. The upper part of the skirt vibrates with fiery tones in which the brush (as in a childish game) has gone its way leaving silvery sparkles that animate the suave pinks. The face and the little hands are enlivened with the reflections from the surrounding, lending heat and life. The execution of the laces and the handkerchief so transparent, suggest the synthetic and sober brush work of his last period. In fact, some authors maintain that the painter left the work unfinished and that Mazo finished it. At any rate the latter's skill is noted in the face, neck and hands.

Num. **1206,** *Æsop* (Pl. 17), is a sarcastical versión of the famous Greek fabulist in a brown smock. His face is very interesting, and far from being a caricature. In fact it is a pity that it had been employed for a mockery.

Num. **1175,** *Mercury and Argos*. Another mythological scene, previously in the Alcázar with two others destroyed in the 1734 fire. Mercury has put Argos to sleep with his flute and taking advantage of the resulting dreams he penetrates the cave cautiously to assassinate him. Io, the cow is in the background. It is one of those valuable paintings of his last epoch. Do not look for gods in the beings represented: they are urchins from the suburbs! The admirable part of this canvas is its silvery tone, the moist sadness of a cold dawn, the refraction of shapes that are enveloped in a weighty atmosphere and the vigorous brush work, more synthetic than ever. Observe the face of the sleeping Argos, who is almost reduced to nothing, or Mercury's whose only trait is a compendium of malice and depravation. It was painted the year 1659 and Velázquez died the following year.

Num. **1207,** *Menippus*, is a risible version of a character from Lucian's *Dialogues*, a satyrical philosopher who flourished in the 3rd century A. D. Velázquez has incarnated a malicious old man wrapped in a worn-out cape. There are several books on the ground and the inevitable pitcher that aids in complementing it.

Num. **1199,** *The Buffoon «Barbarroja»* by name Don Cristóbal de Castañeda and Pernia, emissary of the Cardinal Infante. He was thus nicknamed because he boasted to be a military figure and even liked to dress himself up as a Turk. Once Felipe IV, when seated at

the table, asked if there were any olives and the buffoon replied:
«There are no olives... nor olive trees». This was enough to anger the
Count Duke of Olivares (*olivares* means olive trees) who sent him off
to Seville. He was painted in 1636 but the portrait was never finished.

Room XIII.—VELAZQUEZ AND MAZO

Mazo, Juan Bautista del. *According to some authorities he was
born in Madrid, yet others claim the province of Cuenca, in 1616. He
died fifty-five years later in Madrid and was the disciple and son-in-law
of Velázquez. He married Francisca Velázquez, at whose wedding King
Felipe IV and the Count Duke of Olivares were godfather. The dignity
of being the professor and painter for three years of Prince Baltasar
Carlos, was his and he painted by himself and in collaboration with
his father-in-law. Mazo's last years were bitterly spent because the National Treasury made him responsible for the debts left by Velázquez;
obligation approximating 934 000* maravedises, *without counting the sum
of the Court of Justice. A beautiful work by Mazo is the* Family of
the Artist *(Viena).*

Num. **1216** and **1217,** *The Alcázar of Madrid from Prioress'
garden,* and *Landscape with a temple.* These are two landscapes
painted during Mazo's youth.

Num. **1195** and **1196,** *Don Diego del Corral and Doña Antonia de
Ipeñarrieta,* husband and wife. He was the first Knight of Santiago,
and Judge of the Castilian Supreme Council. His wife is painted with
her son, Luis. Many interpretations have been given to these canvases;
it is said that the heads and the hands of the pair are undoubtedly
by Velázquez but not the robes nor the figure of the child. The
heads are magnificent with an enviable form and colour and if the
blacks are not by Velázquez they are worthy of being so. (Legacy
of the Duchess of Villahermosa, the year 1905.)

Num. **2903,** *Christ on the Cross.* A painting recently discovered
and incorporated in our Museum.

Num. **1167,** *Christ Crucified* is generally known as *Christ by
Velázquez.* The amber carnation is not repeated in any other nude by
the master; it is very dramatic and the face's aspect, semi-hidden
by the falling hair, adds to the effect. This detail, that evidently is not
due to insufficiency of the painter, admirably breaks the excessive
symmetry of the figure affixed with four nails upon an almost invisible
beam. It has not been accepted as a religious symbol because it lacks
maceration and blood. On the other hand erudite literature often
refers to it. It was painted in 1632, for the convent of the nuns of

San Plácido owing to an unproven «sacrilege» of Felipe IV. It was given by the Duke of San Fernando de Quiroga to Fernando VII, and entered the Museum in 1829.

Num. **1223,** *Portrait of Góngora,* a copy by Velázquez. The original is in Boston Museum.

Num. **2873,** *Venerable Mother Jerónima de la Fuente.* A religious of the convent of Santa Isabel de los Reyes and founder of Santa Clara in Manila. The severe traits of the face reveal the early epoch of the life of the artist. The portrait is signed and was acquired for the Community of Santa Isabel of Toledo, by the Ministry of National Education and the Patronage of the Museum, in 1944.

Velázquez. Núm. **1209,** *Francisco Pacheco.* He was father-in-law of the artist and also a painter. J. Allende-Salazar sustains the identification. It was probably painted when Velázquez was twenty.

Num. **1166,** *The Adoration of the Wise Men.* It is believed that there is a Flemish influence but that is not important when one realizes that Velázquez painted it at eighteen or nineteen. It is supposed that the old king is Pacheco, and the young one, kneeling in front, Velázquez and the Virgin, his wife Juana Pacheco.

Velázquez? Núm. **1224,** *Self-portrait?* It is not certain that this is by Velázquez not even his self-portrait.

Room XIV.—VELAZQUEZ AND MAZO

Mazo. Num. **1215,** *A pond of the Retiro.* At one time this was attributed to Velázquez.

Velázquez. Num. **1179,** *The Queen Doña Isabel of France, Felipe IV's wife.* The daughter of Henry IV of Bearn and Mary of Medici. She married by proxy at less than thirteen and joined her husband at eighteen. She died in Madrid in 1644. The equestrian portrait is completely by the great master, even the retouchings added later. It comes from the *Salon de Reinos* in the Buen Retiro.

Num. **1212,** *The arc of Titus in Rome.* It is not certain if it is by Velázquez.

Num. **1204,** *The Child of Vallecas* who was said to have been born with teeth. Francisco Lezcano was born in Biscay and was at the disposition of Prince Baltasar Carlos. The poor fellow's face shows degeneration in its last degree of idiocy and the visitor is unable to contemplate it without being moved to compassion.

Num. **1202,** *The Buffoon Don Sebastián de Morra.* This Don Sebastián was the buffoon of the Cardinal-Infant who took him to Flanders; later he was sent to Prince Baltasar Carlos. He imagined himself a world traveller and a man of the world and was insolent and embittered as one discovers in his hard face and unfortunate lack of friends. He died soon after being painted.

Num. **1201**, *The Buffoon «The Cousin»*. The buffoons described until now, are rascals physically undeformed, ill-spoken parasites who flattered the king much more than the gentlemen of his time (Quevedo, Lope de Vega, Moreto, Tirso de Molina, Mira de Amescua, Góngora, Montalbán, Calderón, Gracián, etc.), pleiad of a new Golden Century without interest for Felipe IV. These other buffoons are deformed beings, defficient, dwarfish, «vermins» for entertainment of whom Velázquez never made fun. Instead, he gave them a compassionate dignity, and a notibility of presence that all men deserve only by having been born.

Num. **1205**, *The Buffoon Calabacillas* until recently called *The Simpleton from Coria*. His name was Don Juan Calabazas and he began serving the Cardinal Infante and later the king. In spite of his cretin aspect he was well esteemed in the Palace, collecting an annual wage of 96 894 *maravedies* and his allowance ascended to 193 785 item, with right to a mule and beasts of burden during his sojourns. He probably died the same year that Velázquez painted him seated between two pumpkins.

Num. **1187**, *Doña María de Austria, Queen of Hungary*. She was Felipe IV's sister, one year younger than him and was courted by the Prince of Wales, later Charles I of England. She married the Emperor of Austria Fernando III and died in 1646. Velázquez painted this portrait of less than half size in Naples on his first trip to Italy in 1630. (It was in the Manor House of Duke of Arco.)

Num. **1197**, *Doña Juana Pacheco, wife of the painter, presented as a Sibyl*. The identification as Pacheco's daughter and Velázquez's wife is supposed at least to be from Isabel Farnesio's epoch, and we see her holding a board with her left hand.

Num. **1210** and **1211**, *Two views of the Garden of Villa Médicis*. Small landscapes of admirable technique painted by Velázquez during the second stay of the painter in Rome.

Num. **1169**, *St. Anthony Abad and St. Paul. First Hermit*. Saint Paul was the hermit who at a hundred and thirteen years lived in the Egyptian desert nourished by a raven who brought him a daily ration of bread. One day St. Anthony went to visit him and that day the raven arrived with a double ration. The two saints are seen, thanking the all-provident God. Like the Primitives, the painter put other miniaturized scenes of St. Antony's life, as the one referring to St. Jerome. We see him led by a beast and resisting a temptation while calling at the gates of St. Paul and aiding the latter in his last moment while two lions open a grave with their claws.

It is a new aspect of Velázquez's inexhaustible art. He could have represented the two hermits saints in natural size in the foreground with a desert background, but nevertheless he preferred to represent them minimized by the rocky greatness of the landscape. If the two figures are masterly, the surrounding atmosphere, an ancient tree, imponent rocks, a river in meander, distant mountains and a cloudy grey sky even surpass in realism and beauty. In respect to the epoch in which the canvas was painted. Allende-Salazar believes it to be around 1634 (the beginning of the second epoch) while D. Aureliano de Beruete prefers the last, or about 1659-60. Of one thing we are certain, it was painted for the hermitage of St. Paul, in the Buen Retiro.

Room XIV A.—VELAZQUEZ

Velázquez. Num. **1168,** *The Coronation of the Virgin.* After Velázquez had returned from his second trip to Italy, the art of Venetians and Florentines still influenced him greatly. In this canvas the lights are Tizian-like and the piramidal scheme is Florentine. In the violet, wine and blue shades and in the air of the composition some have sought reminiscences of Greco. The Virgin's beautiful face is fresh and luxuriant like a blossom, and breathes humility. Less spiritual and more realistic are the heads of the Father and the Son. This canvas was painted for the prayer room of the Queen Doña Mariana de Austria.

Num. **1203,** *The Buffoon called «The Englishman».* Moreno Villa tells us that the Englisman is Nicholas Hodson, brought to Spain by the Duke of Villahermosa, some years after Velázquez's death, so this was probably painted by Carreño. Don Pedro de Madrazo believed it to be Don Antonio *the Englishman* but he had already died before Velázquez went to Madrid. The dog is the same that Mazo painted in picture num. **2571.** Room LXXVIII. Don Aureliano de Beruete attributes it to Velázquez in his last decade. The group with the dwarf and dog is marvellous and *The Englishman* sports a luxury like the one Franz Hals painted when representing haughty persons of his time.

Num. **1219,** *Felipe IV Armed, a Lion at his feet.* The lion is little more than sketched. The canvas has exactly the same dimensions as num. **1191** in the Gran Rotunda and is its mate. Some say that in the latter another painter, in addition to Velázquez, has wielded a brush.

(Numberless): *Prince Baltasar Carlos*, a painting from the studio of Velázquez. The Prince has a bird in his right hand, retained by a cord held by the other hand. A puppy looks attentively at the bird. (Donation of Manuel Gómez Moreno, in 1958.)

Num. **1220,** *Felipe IV at Prayer* painted by a disciple of Velázquez.

Num. **1222,** *Doña Mariana de Austria, second wife of Felipe IV at Prayer*, item.

Room XV.—«THE MENINAS»

You are about to anjoy «the pearl» of Velázquez of which Luca Giordano said «it is the theology of painting»; Lefort, «it is the last word in realistic and textual painting»; Stirling, «he seems to have anticipated Daguerre's discovery by taking a group gathered in a chamber and magically stamping it for ever on the canvas»; Stevenson, «it is unique and absolute in the History of Art»; Teophile Gautier, «but where is the picture?», because it seemed to him to be a continuation of the room». Manet, «after this I don't know why the rest of us paint», etc.

Velázquez. Num. **1174,** *The Meninas* or *The Family of Felipe IV*. (Pl. 18). Why did he paint this picture? It is said Velázquez was painting a portrait of the king and queen and that suddenly Princess Margarita entered the studio with two *meninas* or little ladies from her court, two dwarves of the palace and that they all began to flutter around and at times they formed such graceful groups that Felipe and Mariana suggested that the painter reproduced them in the canvas. The presumption is born from several details, first that Velázquez is behind a canvas, as if he were painting it, second that in the mirror in the background the silhouettes of the parents are reflected and thirdly that the Meninas and the princess frequently entered his studio to watch him work.

We are before an ample sitting room of the Palace that serves as workshop. In the central foreground a group formed by little Princess Doña Margarita, two *meninas*, Doña María Agustina Sarmiento and Doña Isabel de Velasco is formed. The first young lady offers the Princess a vessel with water while the second bows graciously. Also in the foreground to the right is the deformed María Bárbola looking at the spectator while Nicolasito Pertusato places his foot upon the napping dog. The first group betrays composition but the second does not because it is as natural as an instantaneous photograph of surprised people behind an enormous canvas placed on its stretcher. The artist, with palette and brush in hand seems to contemplate the model serving him as the theme for his painting.

In the background to the right we discover in the shadow Doña Marcela de Ulloa, lady of the Palace conversing with an escort dressed in black. In the background an official, Don José Nieto, opens the door and draws a curtain in order that a stream of light might inundate the room. And in short two large pictures and a mirror hang on the wall to complete the background decoration.

One sees a huge room in all its profoundity, populated by persons that maintain their respective distances. All of them are enveloped in an atmosphere and light that naturally corresponds to them. They seem isolated and undetached among themselves with a luminous wrapping and three dimensions. The certainty that we could start walking towards the workshop and that we could move among the figures without stumbling upon them obsesses us. Because evidently we could go around them, and locate ourselves between Velázquez and the canvas stretcher, come closer to Doña Marcela de Ulloa and go out through the door that Don José Nieto opens for us. We look at the floor and it is easy to persuade ourselves that it is a continuation of the one we occupy as spectators and that without doubt we can calculate distances and determine the exact depth of the room.

In order to create the third dimension the artist has not needed a geometric perspective. One may cover with his hand as a screen the line of perspective on the right hand side and still the room continues to manifest itself ample, full, deep and invaded by a slightly thickened atmosphere that one detects in a flood of dust particles settling upon the clearness in the background. The popular saying that Velázquez «painted the air» is a popular guess that accurately responds to the reality of the marvel. Evidently he does not paint air; but without calculating the real existence of the atmosphere, colors and tints cannot be appraised, diffracting and diminuating tones and cualities to place them in a set space. Velázquez did not paint air; but if there had not been atmosphere in the *Meninas* this picture would not be so perfectly realistic.

As in *The Spinners* the lights are three and the dark zones two and the ones can be seen through the others. The first light inundates the foreground from a large window to the right. The following, very tenuous enters from a second window situated behind Doña Marcela de Ulloa; the third very intense is that of the background with which the boldness of the Spinners is repeated. Thus light and atmosphere are persons as real and well-manifested as the humans that serve as the theme. Without them the scene would lack interest; with them Velázquez has arrived at the top of his art and painting.

We observe that the artist is not painting on the canvas which we as spectators are viewing. Since we have before us the whole room we can easily see the groupings. Velázquez is where he can not see them; later, because he chose so or by the choice of the king, he «intercalated» himself among the figures. One might ask what is it that he is painting. At first sight it seems that he is doing the portrait of the king and queen reflected in the mirror in the background. Some, however, do not believe this to be true. In the first place he never painted them as a couple in the same picture; we could easily argue that it could have been so and that the portrait disappeared in the fire of the Alcázar in 1734; nevertheless, in the inventories it does not figure. And in the second place the canvas seems excessively large just for one couple.

We have heard the baseless anecdote that when this famous canvas was finished Velázquez said to Felipe IV: «Sir, it is finished», but Felipe IV denied its termination and taking up the palette and brush painted the red cross of Santiago on his chest because he had been appointed Knight of the Order. No such a thing!: the painting of the cross was not painted at the same time as the picture but rather was added after the artist's death. The picture was finished in 1656 when Diego was fifty seven years old and it was registered in the Alcázar as *La Familia (The Family)*.

In this room a mirror has been hung in the background in order to duplicate the distance of observation. Trying to have its frame coincide in both the visual and the painting the sensation of relief is absolute. Also the same effect is obtained when one looks through a hand telescope.

Room XVI.—RUBENS

This large Room has been consecrated almost completely to **Peter Paul Rubens**. The Prado possesses a very abundant repertory, comparable to the best museums including Antwerp. There are no less than 2000 pictures with his name dispersed around the world which is interesting when one realizes this to be an impossibility for one person even if he painted all day and all night long. His Anrwerp workshop was an art factory. He did not scorn any commission, but generally his followers were left with the work, because the great master contented himself with doing a quick sketch or the finishing touches. His disciples included Van Dyck, Jordaens, Crayer, Snyders, Ceard, Van Thulden, Vos, etc.,

who were all first-class artists. The Prado collection however
is almost completely his work.

Rubens was an exuberant, haughty and imaginative painter,
prodigiously gifted for large decorative themes. He also cultivated the portrait and he has admirable ones; but it is in
the composition where he triumphs whether they are religious
or mythological, even more in the latter where he was per-
mitted all the liberty of expression he needed. He learnt
the nude in Italy and his like for pagan themes. But the
palette is his own. His flesh tones are conventional, although
very beautiful, done in mother of pearl and porcelain with
soft glamorous roses, violets and blues. His second wife
served him as his opulent, mellow and milky white model
whom he portrayed in a thousand ways (naked, semi-naked,
dressed, as a mother, as a Virgin, as a goddess, sometimes
with an exact resemblance, others hinting, but always unmis-
takably Ellen.

His paintings on the whole are not profound nor of great
contrasts and only in a few jewels did he give the limit of
his knowledge, among them *The Elevation of the Cross* and
The Descent, both of the Cathedral of Antwerp which may
be considered as the most eminent.

Rubens, Peter Paul. *He was not born in Flanders but in Siegen
in 1577, as a result of an amorous adventure of his father with Anne
of Saxony, wife of William the Taciturn. This fact obliged his father to
flee to Westphalia. Rubens was ten years old when his family returned
to Flanders and soon after he entered as page of Princess of Ligne,
widow of Count Lalaing. He received a very select education learning
various languages (among them, Spanish) that served him well for his
diplomatic missions. He came to Spain twice; once sent by Vicente
Gonzaga, Duke of Mantua, in the times of Felipe III, and the other
under Felipe IV's reign. He was tall, blond and good looking, blessed
with handsomeness and an undeniable kindness. He was a friend of
Richelieu, Buckingham, Count-Duke of Olivares, all important Euro-
peans. In all Courts that he visited he left elegant proofs of his brush
work as in the Gallery of the Medici, White Hall and the Alcázar
of Madrid.*

*He married Elizabeth Brandt, and, four years after her death, Ellen
Fourment, his sixteen years old cousin with whom he was very happy.
When he died in 1640, his funerals were worthy of a king. He was*

buried behind the Choirloft in the church of Santiago in Antwerp,
and one of his paintings was placed upon the altar; the one showing
him as St. George, Elizabeth Brandt as Mary and Ellen Fourment
as the Magdalene.

Num. **1638,** *The Adoration of the Wise Men.* Is indeed quite
magnificent, painted after a lengthy stay in Italy, in which one notes
influences of Correggio and Michelangelo. The coloring is dazzling
both in the flesh and the fabrics. Although the scene is distinctly
lighted with torches, the Child is like a focus of light that spreads
to all the surroundings. The poor stable of Bethlehem has been
converted into a Renaissance portico. To the right of the composition
an admirable young figure in a violet velvet suit (Rubens) is observed.
During his second stay in Spain he retouched the whole canvas
except his self-portrait although twenty years had already passed.
The burgomaster of Antwerp paid him 1800 *florines* for the work
and later gave it to Don Rodrigo Calderón, at whose auction Felipe IV bought it. (It proceeds from the new Palace.)

Num. **1686,** *Philip II on Horse-back.* The Monarch is armed
and a Victory appears in the act of crowning him with a laurel
wreath. In the background there is a battlefield. It was painted
in Madrid in 1628, thirty years after the death of the King. The
elements that the artist needed to compose the picture were given
him for that purpose.

Num. **1687,** *Cardinal-Infante Don Fernando de Austria in the*
Battle of Nordlingen. In the upper portion the Eagle of the House
of Austria and a Victory are shown. In the background, the battlefield.
Don Fernando was born in 1609, three years after his brother
Philip IV. He was Governor in Flanders and won the battle of
Nordlingen in 1634. Two years after this battle he was painted
in this canvas.

Num. **1643,** *The Supper of Emaus.* The disciples recognize Jesus
in the manner of cutting the bread. It is a canvas of the painter's
last years.

Num. **1695,** *St. Claire among Fathers and Doctors of the Church.*
In the canvas appear St. Ambrose, St. Augustin, St. Gregory,
St. Thomas, St. Norbert and St. Jerome. From the series *Eucharist*
Apotheosis.

Num. **1644,** *St. George struggling with the Dragon.* A large-sized
canvas. St. George is brandishing the sword against the Dragon.
The latter, wounded, is lying down at the feet of the horse. On the
left side, the maid with a lamb. The picture was purchased by
Philip IV from Rubens' testamentary execution.

Num. **1639,** *The Holy Family with St. Anne,* is an extremely
happy group. It is said that the Virgin has the same features as

Elizabeth Brandt, Rubens's first wife. (Bought in the auction of
the Marquis of Carpio.)

Num. **1692**, *Adam and Eve*, is a copy made by Rubens, during
his second stay in Spain, of the same picture by Tiziano somewhat
changed.

Num. **1646** to **1653** included: *Incomplete Apostolate*. Painted for
the Duque of Lerma; they proceed from Aranjuez.

Num. **1642,** *The Piety*. The Virgin, Mary Magdalene and Saint
John surround Christ, dead. The body of Christ is of an extraordinary beauty. It is a work of the last period of the painter.

Room XVI A.—VAN DYCK

Anton Van Dyck might have remained in the workshop
of Rubens, where work was never scarce; but nevertheless
he understood that to be attached to the great master as
were Jordaens, Crayer and others, meant to be always nothing
but a mere follower. He felt that he had a different personality
than that of his master, and noticed that the decorative and
exuberant compositions, whit their opaline and mother-of-
pearl nudes, had reached their full expression in Rubens's
palette. Then, why should he constantly repeat the same?
So he began to consider Italy, the master of masters. And
when he was but twenty one, he undertook the conquest of
an art which would greatly enliven his own temperament.

He found it in Venice, especially in Tiziano and Tintoretto. The elegance of his portraits agreed with the natural
elegance of the young painter. When he was in complete
possession of faculties he went to England, where art was
still in its beginnings. In London he met the types and
seigniory to which his choice was accustomed and we must
avow that the first five years in the court, which were preceded by the works of Holbein, were the epoch of his best
portrait. From this epoch there are some beautiful pieces in
our Prado. On the contrary, in the last period he abandoned
himself to an easy mannerism. For example, he painted several canvases with hands in all kind of postures one can
imagine, and afterwards he applied them to the portraits
according to the way they best fitted in. In the last year it

happened that in a month he painted a portrait each day. For his glory it would have been better that he died five years before, at least in this time he had said his last word.

Van Dyck, Anthony. *This Flemish painter was born in Antwerp in 1599 (the same year as Diego Velázquez) and died near London in 1641. At sixteen he entered Rubens's workshop and appropiated his master's palette and technique to the extent that the two are often confused. At twenty one he went to Italy riding a beautiful white horse given to him by Rubens in proof of his friendship. In contact with the old masters he changed his first style completely. His portraits begin to have a masterly distinction and are paired with those of Tiziano. After having left valuable signs of his skill in various localities, especially in Genoa (Brignole-Sale collection), he left for England, where Charles I was a great protector of Beautiful Arts.*

Van Dyck, aged thirty one, arrived in time. He soon became not only a good friend of Charles but his relative, because the king arranged his marriage to Mary Ruthwen, a lady of the Court, and he also gave them as a present a beautiful residence. The artist lived ten years which were of great activity, and at its end there are not less than three hundred and fifty canvases of this period full of mannerism. This exhausting work of the painter, apart from other irregularities, determined his premature death. Van Dyck is by antonomasia, the painter of Charles I of England and his children.

Num. **1475,** *The Piety* is the reproduction of the famous canvas of Antwerp, with a foreshortening of Christ painted with a model. Mary Magdalene kisses one of His hands. Replicas in other museums.

Num. **1478,** *St. Francis of Assisi.* Painted between 1627 and 1632. Probably acquired in Sevilla by Isabel Farnesio. (Proceeding from Aranjuez.)

Num. **1437,** *The Serpent of Metal.* It refers to a biblical scene during the march of Moses and the Israelites throughout the desert. Although the canvas has the signature of Rubens it is believed to be by Van Dyck. Anyway one observes that some of the heads are the usual models of Rubens's workshop during the stay of his pupil, and therefore it can be as well attributed to Van Dyck or to his master.

Num. **1480,** *The Cardinal-Infant Don Fernando de Austria.* Larger than half body, he is richly dressed such as he entered Brussels in 1634 after the victory of Nordlingen; he boasts a staff of general and wears the sword carried by the Emperor at Mühlberg. Some illustrious critics attribute it to Rubens. It was painted in 1634, and brought by the Marquis of Leganés to Felipe IV.

Numbers **1491** and **1694,** *Heads of Old Men* which evidently were painted in Rubens's workshop, following the master's technique.

Num. **1477,** *The Arrest of Jesus.* Christ looks at Judas Iscariot who approaches to kiss Him. In the foreground to the left, Peter raises his sword to wound Malco. A torch illuminates the scene. The composition in diagonal is very beautiful and the placid face of Jesus breathes dignity. This work of Van Dyck's first epoch and realized in the workshop of Rubens is at the same time a copy of a similar one existing in Bruges. Van Dyck painted like this when he was not yet twenty, thus one cannot be surprised by the fact that he was the favourite disciple of the master. The value is more important under a reference point of view than a pictorial one. Rubens conserved it in the place of honor and at his auction Felipe IV acquired it for 1200 *florines.* (It was in the Alcázar, in the Retiro and in the Palace, passing afterwards to the Museum.)

Num. **1479,** *The one-armed Painter, Martín Rickaert.* It is a beautiful portrait almost full length. The painter appears dressed in the Turkish manner. The characteristic note of the portraits of Van Dyck is the lordshipness which is very expressive in this portrait painted on a tablet. Rickaert, who was armless, was a great painter of landscapes. The present portrait might have been painted around 1630, one year before the death of the portrayed. (In the inventory of the Alcázar.)

Num. **1481,** *Diana Cecil, Countess of Oxford.* Perhaps the wife of the Count Robert de Vere. It is a portrait of the painter's last period. In a landscape with a rocky background, the Countess with an airy glance, boasts the pearls of her jewels and has a flower in her right hand. (In the Duke of Arco manor house.)

Num. **1489,** *Sir Endimion Porter and Van Dyck.* This picture is the jewel of this Room and moreover it has the honor of showing us one of the most joyous selft-portrait of this painter. It is said that Endimion Porter was born in Madrid and was the page of the Count-Duke of Olivares and later the Secretary of Buckingham, with whom he came to the Court of Felipe IV, accompanying the Prince of Wales Charles, son of James I of England. Endimion being an intimate friend of Van Dyck, they are portrayed together in this beautiful oval canvas where they look like two princes. Rubens, who in other concepts was unequalled, never knew how to give such arrogance to his personages. There are two imposing faces, without being haughty. The mother-of pearl grey suit of Sir Endimion possesses unexcelled qualities attained without thickness in the coloring. Only Velázquez could obtain similar marvels. Regarding Van Dyck's black of very rich transparencies, it only would be equalled in the *Banquet of Saint George's Archers*, by Franz Hals. However, Van Dyck does not renounce to some of his themes, full of mannerism, and not because of their easy realization, but in order to please the model; and here we have an example in the left hand of Sir Endimion with the laced cuff;

it is not the virile and vigorous hand which corresponds to the arrogance of the portrayed but a feminine hand more suitable to a lady of the Court, it is one of the hands already «known» by the artist which he used to adapt according to the circumstances. It seems to have been painted during the best epoch of Van Dyck, about 1635. Later Isabel Farnesio acquired it.

Num. **1488,** *The Engraver Paul du Pont* (?). It seems to be well identified, because *Paulus Pontius* (which was his signature) engraved many portraits of Rubens and Van Dyck. The latter represents him with careless curled hair, a lace collar, black doublet and cape. It is a splendid portrait full of expression. Once more we can realize how easily Van Dyck employed the transparent blacks which never held any secret for him. This portrait is also of the painter's best epoch, 1635. (It figured in the inventory of the Manor House of the Duke of Arco.)

Numbers **1487** and **1490,** Two musicians: *Jacobo Gayltier and Enrique Liberti.* The first was a flautist of the Court of England; the second, organist of Antwerp Cathedral. They are two masterful paintings, the first some ten years before the other.

Num. **1486,** *The Count Henry de Berg* was a nephew of Maurice de Nassau, at first a good friend of Spain and later its enemy until his death in 1638.

Numbers **1482** and **1483,** *Frederic and Amelie, Princess of Orange.* Frederic Henry de Nassau was the son of William the Taciturn, and Amelie de Sols-Braunfels, married him. It is said that both of the two portraits were painted in the Hague in 1628. They belonged to the collection of Isabel Farnesio.

Num. **1484,** *Charles I of England.* The son of James I who came to Spain when he was Prince of Wales, to be engaged to Doña María de Austria, Felipe IV's sister. The marriage stipulations were broken due to a religious matter (Charles was a Protestant) apart from other reasons, and the Prince returned to his country where he reigned upon the death of his father. He was beheaded by order of Cromwell, erected dictator in 1649. Van Dyck has portrayed him with armature on horse-back. (From the collection of Isabel Farnesio.)

Num. **1492,** *Diana and Endimion Surprised by Satyr.* According to Homeric tradition, Jupiter was the father of Endimion. He lead the life of a shepherd and one day being tired of walking he remained to sleep in a cave. Diana (the Moon) seized by his beauty, came down to embrace him. When taken to the Olympus, he offended Juno, Jupiter's wife, and then he was thrown to the earth and condemned to sleep perpetually. Diana visited him every night and sometimes she remained placidly sleeping close to him. A satyr discovered them one day and Jupiter knew that they had a son called Ætolus. Since then they were separated forever. Endimion is the personification of sleep. In everything we can detect Rubens's influence. (It was preserved in the Academy as all the nude pictures.)

Num. **1474,** *The crouwning of thorns.* Christ is crowned by a soldier and an executioner. They are two curious figures which appear as portraits situated at the back. This work was a gift of Van Dyck to his master Rubens. Van Dyck was inspired by an *Ecce Homo* of Titian.

Room XVII.—RUBENS

Num. **1685,** *Mary of Medici* (Pl. 19), was the daughter of Francis I Great Duke of Tuscany, and the wife of Henry IV the Bearnais. Rubens painted the magnificent Louvre series for her marriage. It is a masterpiece of the Flemish painter in which he glories an elegantly contained sobriety; beautiful in the attire and expression, by its own right it is placed at the height of the best portraits by Van Dyck. (Acquired at Rubens's estate.)

Num. **1689,** *Anne of Austria, Queen of France,* the dauhter of Felipe III and thus sister of Felipe IV, married Louis XIII, the King of France. She was born in Valladolid in 1601 and died at the Louvre in 1666. This portrait is less spontaneous than the previous, although it is less beautiful in its ensemble. (In the inventory of the Alcázar.)

Num. **1688,** *St. Thomas Moore, Grand Chancellor of England.* Henry the VIIIth ordered him decapitated and he was canonized four centuries later. Being a friend of Erasmus of Rotterdam upon his request Holbein painted him. This is a later copy made by Rubens in London. (From the collection of Isabel Farnesio.)

Num. **1645,** *Act of Devotion of Rodolph I of Habsbourg.* He was the 16th century German Emperor who, when hunting saw a priest carrying the Holy Viaticum to a nearby village, he immediately dismounted and not only gave his horse to the priest but led it by the rains. The Emperor's page gave his to the sacristan who carried the lantern. Some critics suspect that the picture is not by Rubens. (It was in Felipe IV's bedroom.)

Num. **1662,** *Atalanta and Meleagrus.* The scene refers to the wild boar of Calidonia. Meleagrus was the legendary Heroe, son of Mars and Altea. A great hunter he was extremely expert in javelin throwing. Artemis in order to revenge Æneas, sent the beast to the forest to cause a famous massacre and although Meleagrus killed it, Atalanta was the first to wound the wild boar. She is in the center shooting an arrow. (Proceeding from the Alcázar.)

Num. **1684,** *Portrait of the Infanta Isabel Clara Eugenia*, daughter of Philip II and wife of Albert of Austria. In the background, a view of Mariemont.

Num. **1683,** *Portrait of the Archiduke Albert of Austria*. View of Tervueren.

The Virgin and the Child, by Rubens, with garland by Brueghel; *Cybelle and the Seasons*, by Bruegheland Van Balen; *Garlands*, by Christian Lukx and Catharine Ykens.

Num. **1418,** *The Virgin and the Child in a Picture Surrounded by Flowers and Fruits*. For this garlands of fresh flowers traced with brush point, Rubens sought the collaboration of John Brueghel de Velours, son of Pieter. The animals which embellish the background are by the same collaborator. Similar replicas exist in other museums.

Room XVII A.—VAN DYCK AND JORDAENS

In this room we meet a new Flemish painter: **Jacob Jordaens.** What does this artist represent in the Antwerp School? Jordaens is rough scoring but splendid in the luminosity, with incendiary reds learned from Rubens and the darknesses of the caves inspired by Caravaggio. He represents the orgiastic gaiety, the good mood of the Flemish peasant, the heavy meals, the foamy wine, the cornemuse and the popular noise. His best canvases are more motley than those of Rubens but they are also truer. When he was liberated from his influence and became himself, barbarous and rough but exceptional, he created his definite works, which are those inspired by popular themes —*The King Drinks*, *The Satyr and the Peasant, the Kermesses*— somewhat Dutch, of great style in red tones and a free brush play. Without such an overflowed imagination as that of his master, he will resort to the amusing and traditional fables, which he will surround with a glittering decoration and a series of domestic contributions such as meals, furniture, table-service, a kettle and brazier... which today are as worthy as actual documents.

Jordanes, Jacob, *was born in Antwerp, in 1593, the son of a fabric merchant. He entered the painting workshop of Adrian van Noort young (at the time the latter was the master of Rubens). He remained there until he was twenty three then marrying Catherine, his master's daughter.*

Rubens soon excelled the old Van Noort, drawing Jordaens behind him; the same palette, the similar conception of beauty and an equal model. Jacob was aware of his failures which he attributed to his unableness and constantly studied the Italians and Dutch. When Rubens died Jordaens's glory started and his workshop became the most esteemed in Flanders. His best work is Fecundity (Brussels). The influence of his father-in-law and his frequent trips to Holland determined his conversion to Protestantism. He died in 1678 at eighty five and was buried with his daughter Elizabeth (who also died the same day) in the Protestant church of Putte, in the same tomb where the remains of his wife, Catherine are kept.

Num. **1544,** *The Mystic Betrothal of St. Catherine.* Some critics appoint this canvas to be one by Van Dyck, a fact that can be true or not because the first works of this painter as well as those of Jordaens are in such a manner confused with the first paintings of Rubens that any discrimination is useless. The master used to correct some of his disciples' works and they also helped one another. Thus, only in cases where we have documentation of the epoch, would it be possible to determine the legitimate paternity of doubtful canvases. This one to whomever it may belong, is beautiful. The head of the Virgin, lacking ideality, is neither Dyckian nor Rubenslike and the same happens with the angel carrying the palm. On the contrary, these of the two elder, one of them St. Francis of Assissi, and the general coloring are of Rubens's workshop. (From the colletion of Isabel Farnesio.)

Num. **1549,** *The Artist and His Family in Garden* (Pl. 20). Jacob carries a lute in his left hand; his wife, Catherine, appears seated with her daughter Elizabeth; in counter-light and standing is a servant with a basket full of fruits and flowers and a dog is behind the master's chair. This wonderful picture is one of Jordaens's jewels. Very rich in coloring and very gay in the conception, it is very «His own», because here all traces of Rubens have disappeared. Every face looks to the spectator and all are expressive and, let us add, charming. It would be easy to speak about some roughness in the hands and laces and make mention of Van Dyck, but the fact is that everything in this canvas is truly without mannerisms, and all is joyful without orgies of color. (Proceeding from Aranjuez.)

Num. **1550,** *Three Roving Musicians.* The same happens as in número **1544.** Hymans believes that this tablet is painted by Van Dyck; but the reality is that Jordaens has painted half-length *Apostles* with the same free techniques and similar models, which claim the fraternity with the musicians of this tablet. The expression of the one playing the clarinet and of the two singers adopting the same attitude, is so like Jordaens and so far from Van Dyck, that it is hard to attribute the paternity to the latter. (Proceeding from the Moncloa Palace, it entered the Museum in 1827.)

Num. **1546,** *Meleagrus and Atalanta.* The episode of this canvas reveals the moment in which the wild boar of Calidonia, already killed, is about to be distributed. The hunters wish to exclude Atalanta who first wounded it. Meleagrus defended her, and during the fight has to kill his mother's brothers who opposed him. The mother damned him and the Furies drew him to hell. To the right in the foreground appear Meleagrus and Atalanta with their dogs; to the left, is the group of hunters who ask the distribution of the beast which one of them points out with the hand: to the right are Meleagrus's uncles, who later will perish in the fight. Rubens's influence is evident but without the master's precision and firmness of coloring in this sketch. (Proceeding from Aranjuez.)

Num. **1548,** *Goddesses and Nymphs after the Bath.* It is a very pompous composition with the figure of Venus who is combed by a negro servant, nymphs who are dressing after their bath, little cupids with presents, and little spirits throwing flowers... Previously it was attributed to Rubens. (It proceeds from the Retiro.)

Num. **1547,** *Offerings to Pomona.* He has taken advantage of the theme to exceed in the painting of animals, still-lives, etc., apart from the figure of Pomona, very arrogant with Amalthea's horn, but who in reality has very little of a goddess. It is a youthful work.

Num. **1545,** *Child Jesus and St. John.* Once attributed to Rubens.

Van Dyck, Anthony. Num. **1495,** *Mary Ruthwen.* We have said that Charles I of England was friendly with Van Dyck and suggested him to marry a Scottish noble who was called, Mary Ruthwen. The marriage took place in 1639 and eight days after the birth of a girl, Justina Anne, the painter died. Mary married again but soon died. The painter has portrayed her dressed in blue and adorned with pearls. (From the collection of Isabel Farnesio.)

Num. **1493,** *Portrait of the Marquis of Leganés.* Doña Policena Spinola was the daughter of Ambrosio Spinola (portrayed in *The Lances* by Velázquez) and wife of the Marquis of Leganés. It may have been painted in Antwerp in 1621 or 1922. The white gullet and the beautiful black dress detach magnificently from the pale face and the beautiful and delicate hands.

Num. **1494,** *St. Rosalie,* This picture has old restored parts. (Proceeding from El Escorial.)

Rubens and **Van Dyck.** Num. **1661,** *Achilles,* Calchas, the prophet, said that Troy would be conquered only with Achilles's mediation, but that he would die in the fight. Then Thetis, the mother of the heroe, dressed him like a woman and sent him with Lycomedes's daughters, but Calchas knew it and communicated the fact to Ulysses and Diomede. Both went to the Court of Lycomedes disguised as merchants in order to discover him. While the daughters of the king admired the fabrics and perfumes, Achilles took the coat of arms and grasped the sword which was among the other goods. Then he was discovered and taken to the conquest of Troy, where he died due to an arrow which wounded him in the heel. Rooses's references indicate that Van Dyck collaborated in this canvas when he was but nineteen. (It proceeds from the Alcázar.)

Room XVIII.—RUBENS

Num. **1640**, *Rest during the Flight to Egypt*. Whenever he can do so the artist leans to the decorative even in the themes of desolation austerely treated by other artists. The Virgin's face is that of Ellen Fourment.

Num. **1691**, *Dance of the Villagers*, is the contribution of the painter to popular «fiestas». It also was acquired in the aforesaid estate.

Num. **2455**, *Achilles discovered by Odysseus*. Van Thulden collaborated in this canvas which has less importance than that of the same title in Room XVII A.

Num. **2456**, *The death of Decie*, and has also been called «The defeat of Senacherib» which is a confused mass of soldiers; knights and corpses.

Num. **1710**, *Hércules killing the Hydra*, a copy by Mazo.

Num. **1725**, *Huntress Diana*, of the school of Rubens.

Num. **1420**, *Festoon of fruits with little Cupids*.

Num. **1853**, *Festoon of fruits and vegetables*, by Van Utrech.

Num. **1665**, *Diana and Her Nymphs Surprised by the Fauns*. Diana, the huntress, had gone to the forest with the nymphs in order to practice her venatic arts and while resting, is suprised by a group of fauns who try to seize them. The fight between the nymphs and the persecutors is the theme of this composition developed in frieze and it is one of the hundred commissioned by Cardinal-Infante for Felipe IV. The effect of motion and flight is admirably attained, as is the play upon the white and tanned carnations. In the midst of the battle Diana sleeps laying between a wild boar and a dead deer. (This picture also, as many of his others, had to be taken to the Academy to save it from the fire.)

Num. **1666**, *Nymphs and Satyrs*, by Rubens. A beautiful painting with color, design and animation. The Horn of Plenty is in the central group. According to Rooses, this picture was painted between 1637 and 1640 and was acquired in the estate of Rubens for 800 florins. It had to be on «quarentine» in the private Rooms of the Academy.

Num. **1690,** *The Garden of Love*. Several women amuse themselves with lute music near a baroque pagan temple. A couple arrives,
another dances, others converse and dozens of scattered cupids,
with flowers, doves or torches, fill the space and accompany the
bystanders. It is a delicious union, harmonic, full of grace, joy and
color. The general tones attain a golden green. Nevertheless each
lace, damasc and silk has its own particular qualities. Such parties
were quite frequent in his mansion, which has served as decoration
for this one in which we see Ellen Fourment queen of beauty and
elegance. This prominent work of Rubens has a replica with variations
that belonged to the Duke of Pastrana and today figures in the
Rothschild's Collection (inferior of course to ours). It was sold in
Rubens's estate and acquired by our King Felipe IV.

Room XVIII A.—RUBENS

Num. **1680,** *Heraclitus the weeping Philosopher*. Num. **1681,** *De-
mocritus the laughing Philosopher*. Num. **1682,** *Archimedes*. The previous two pictures were painted in Valladolid for the Duke of Lerma,
during Rubens's first trip to Spain under the reign of Felipe III.
The third, of the same epoch, was destined for the Torre de la Parada.

Num. **1676,** *Vulcan Forging Jupiter's Rays*. Vulcan was the great
armsmith of Jupiter, Achilles, etc.

Num. **1678,** *Saturn devouring his sons*. Saturn, or Chronos, represents time who devours his sons (the days).

Num. **1669,** *The Judgment of Paris*. In 1639 the Cardinal-Infante
wrote to his brother Felipe IV: «*The Judgment of Paris* is finished...
and according to all the painters it is the best that Rubens has done,
it only has one fault... and this being that the three goddesses are
too naked... Venus is a portrait resembling his own wife that without
doubt is the best of what we have here».

The scene results from the marriage of Peleus and Thetis which
caused a dispute among Juno. Minerva and Venus, regarding who
was the most beautiful of the three and the winner would receive
the apple of Eris. They sought Paris as Judge (son of Priam and
Hecuba) King and queen of Troy. Paris was a shepherd on the mountains of Ida. Juno, to be selected, offered him power Minerva wisdom
and Venus love. Paris ordered them to disrobe and chose Venus. At
the shepherd's right Mercury appears presenting an apple. Venus
is the grace situated between the other two and in effect, face and
body are the portrait of Ellen Fourment. The artist painted the theme
quite often and the version in Madrid excells those of Dresden and
London. (A masterpiece, one of the most beautiful in the Museum.)

Num. **1679,** *The Abduction of Ganymedes.* Ganymedes, the Troyan Prince, famous for his beauty, excited Jupiter's desire of keeping him at his side. The god, in order to attain his purpose, adopted the shape of an eagle and carried him off to the Olympus to substitute Hebe in his functions of god's cup-bearer in pouring them the ambrosia or the liquor of immortality. Ganymedes is represented as a child too obese and effeminate. (Painted for the Torre de la Parada.)

Rubens. Num. **1670,** *The Three Graces* (Pl. 21). They were three Greek divinities of whom Hesiod is the first to give us notice. One was named Eufrosine, which means the Joyous; another Aglaia, signifying Dazzling and the third one Thalia that is to say, the Flourishing. If the Muses were the protectors of poets, the Graces were those of philosophers. In the Hellenistic epoch they were already represented, as the Roman writer tells us, *nudae et connexae,* naked and joined, and so they are represented by Rubens in this magnificent tablet, bound, joined and chaste. She to the left is Ellen Fourment, the painter's wife. And all three are according to the Flemish type of woman, more fat than robust. It is a work of the master's last epoch. He does without the mother-of-pearl and opaline carnations. But of course something still remains although somewhat stilled by more realistic and pale notes. Most of the enchantment produced by these nudes proceeds from the contrast with the dark tone of the landscape. The work was acquired by Felipe IV at Rubens's estate and escaped fire thanks to the protection of the Academy of San Fernando.

Num. **1674,** *The Fortune,* is another nude of the eternal model. On a sphere as if it were a ship and with her mantel employed as a sail, she navigates to an unknown course. (It was painted for the Torre de la Parada and came to the Museum proceeding from the Academy.)

Num. **1663,** *Andromede Liberated by Perseus.* Cassiopeia, mother of Andromede boasted that her daughter was more beautiful than all the Nereids. They complained to Neptune, who to punish them poured torrents of water which inundated the country, at the same time as a monster appeared destroying the last remains. In order to liberate herself from the monster it was necessary that Andromede abandon herself to him, the father of the young girl consented fastening her to a rock. There the valiant Perseus found her and killed the monster. He untied and married her. In this canvas Rubens has enjoyed the contrast between the naked beauty and the coarse armature of the liberator. The dragon lurks in the sea depths. Also Pegasus the horse is seen. Felipe IV commissioned him to paint it and it was the last one left unfinished (finished by Jordaens). From the Retiro it passed to the Academy and from there to the Museum.

Num. **1677,** *Mercury.* On foot, with skull at his side, as with the helmet and staff in the left hand. A work of a pupil from a sketch by Rubens and retouched by him. Painted for the Torre de la Parada.

Room XIX.—SKETCHES OF RUBENS

Num. **1697,** *Triumph of the Catholic Truth.* Num. **1698,** *Triumph of the Church.* Num. **1699,** *Triumph of Eucharist Over Idolatry.* So you see that Rubens's commissions were not always of pagan themes. Isabel Clara Eugenia. daughter of Felipe II, requested seventeen paintings (Tormo calls the series Apotheosis Eucharistic) in order to weave the same number of tapestries destined for the Royal Discalces of Madrid. Rubens did the paintings on tables in 1628 and charged 30 000 *florins.* The above three belong to the series and are but slightly more than sketched because from them the «cartoons» or models would be painted in the established sizes. They all show the explanatory and baroque fecundity of this great painter of allegories.

Num. **1700,** *The Triumph of Divine Love.* From the same series. Num. **1701,** *The Triumph of Eucharist over Philosophy.* Item. Number **1702,** *The Four Evangelists.* Each one appears with his symbol. Item.

Room XX.—RUBENS AND OTHER CONTEMPORARIES

Num. **1693,** *The Rape of Europe.* The nymph Europe was snatched by Jupiter, who changed himself into a bull, and is seen riding and escorted by little cupids. On the bank the other nymphs cannot hide their anguish. It is also a copy of a work by Tiziano painted for Felipe II and given by him to the Duke of Grammont; today found in the Gardner museum of Boston.

Num. **1671,** *Diana and Calixte.* Calixte, a Greek name of a woman, was the daughter of the king of Arcadia Licion, and friend of Artemis (Diana among the Romans symbolises the moon). Gifted with a great beauty, she excited Jupiter's cupidity who loved her and left her pregnant. Diana's companions were bathing and when Calixte refused to disrobe, the goddess obliged her to do so and her pregnancy was revealed. The nymph is expelled from Diana's company. She had been led by a negro to the pool. All the figures are by Rubens the landscape is by Lucas van Uden. Diana is again the portrait of Ellen Fourment. (It passed to the Academy and later to the museum in 1837.)

Num. **1727**, *Hunting Diana*. A lively scene full of mobility. Diana appears leaning upon her spear and walking together with four nymphs, one of whom is blowing a horn. Six graceful dogs, painted by Paul de Vos, join the huntresses.

Num. **1628**, *Europa abducted by Jupiter*. The same theme treated by Erasmo Quellyn.

Num. **1463**, *Jupiter and Licaon*, by J. Cossiers.

Room XXI.—PAUL DE VOS

Paul de Vos (1596-1678), cultivated the choice of the epoch with these themes and painted canvases with animals, sometimes of large size, for the decoration of the hunter's residences, at times animales in flight, others as in what were later called «still lives», or fighting among themselves. They tried the greater realism because it could not be the greater faithfulness to the natural. Our museum is rich in this kind of paintings.

Num. **1870**, *Deer pursued by a pack of Hounds*. Num. **1869**, *Roedeer Hunting*. Two large-sized pictures representing hunting scenes. The movements and foreshortening of the beast are very realistic, as if taken with a camera. The animal pictures by Paul de Vos were hung in the hunting pavillions of kings and princes.

Num. **1673**, *Mercury and Argos* by **Rubens** is a mythological theme very frequent in the Renaissance painting and during the following-centuries, Mercury, the son of Jupiter and Maja, was born so precocious that the same day of his birth he sprang up from his cradle and went to Pieria in order to steal the oxen of Apollo. One day, when just a lad, he received orders from his father to steal Io, the calf, from the giant Argos, Mercury with his flute caused Argos to fall asleep and then killed him and the robbery was thus executed. The landscape is the work of painter **Luke van Uden.** (Painted for the Torre de la Parada.)

Cossiers. Num. **1485**, *Narcissus contemplating himself in the fountain*. He was so much in love with himself that one day he fell to the water and drowned, changing into the flower named «narciso» (daffodil).

Rubens School. Num. **1718**, *Sleeping Eros*.

Room XXII.—REMBRANDT AND OTHER DUTCH PAINTERS

Wholly covered by Duth painters, among them Rembrandt excells with one work, and we also see the names of Potter, Van Ostade, Gabriel Metsu, Palamedes, Hobbema, etc.

Rembrandt, Harmensz, *was born in Leyden in 1606, the son of a miller, and he received the first lesson in Elsheimer. Moving to Amsterdam he perfected his art and painted at twenty six* Lesson of Anatomy. *Two years later, already famous, he married Saskia van Uijlenbourgh, who brought to the marriage 40 000* florins *(a great deal of money in that epoch). Rembrandt began to purchase artistic objetc and antiquities to the point that he could form a real museum. Saskia soon died leaving a son, Tito. The same year —1642— Rembrandt gave the mayor of the city the prodigious canvas wrongly entitled* Night Watch, *which is neither a watch nor night time. This canvas did not please and then the commissions diminished. Rembrandt had to turn to the money-lenders and the bankrupt began. His last great work is* The Syndics.

He died at sixty three in 1669; one year after his son Tito. His last desperate years were supported by two women Geerthghe Dirhx and Henrickje Stoffels. When the artist died he left a debt of 12 000 florins, *which could not be cancelled wholly at his auctions in which 67 canvases figured of his own hand.*

The Mill, *Rembrandt's native house was sold by himself before his death for 250* florins *and it is the same landscape purchased in 1811 for two and a half millions francs, by Lord Landsdowne for America. Rembrandt's funeral was paid for by his friends.*

Num. **2808,** *Self-Portrait.* We do not know of any painter who portrayed himself as many times as Rembrandt did. This was not due to any kind of narcisism which would have been indefensible, but because he was his own model in order to resolve problems about light, and even more about penumbra which he dominated more than any other painter. The penumbra was constantly his preocupation and above all the luminous penumbra, the one which remains under the hat before the harsh light shines upon the other half of the face. The fabric which remains in the outline when a luminous blow inundates a prominent portion, and the figure of a second plan coming forth from inside when it has not yet reached the lightened zone.

His peasant's sinuous face, wrinkled as the furrows of the ploughed ground where he grew up, offered itself admirably for the play of lights, shades and penumbras and he did not omit any occasion for illumination himself artificially before the mirror in order to seize the minutest difractions of light which he afterwards brought to so many faces of Jews who formed his repertory of portraits. He painted these self-portraits and portraits with much thickness of color, as adding relief to the realism which was a very free technique of his last epoch in contrats with his first period to which belongs the *Lesson of Anatomy* and so many portraits of the beautiful Saskia full of his first love. To his last epoch belong *The Knight of the Gold Helmet* (a portrait of his brother) which is a marvel of sensitive qualities, and this beautiful *Self-Portrait*, which has enhanced our Museum since 1941. (It was acquired with funds proceeding from the Exhibition of Geneva and the contribution of the Ministry of National Education in 1944.) The diplomat. Mr. Alexander Muns, owned the picture and it was sold by his heirs.

Potter, Paul, *was a Dutch painter, born in Eukhuizen in 1625 and died in Amsterdam in 1654. He was his father's disciple and distinguished himself in the painting of animals, especially the bobine, to the point that his picture* The Calf *(«De Jonge Stier») in the Museum of The Hague, is considered as one of the most eminent works of the Dutch School. He died young when he was only twenty six leaving a hundred canvases.*

Num. **2131,** *In the Pasture-ground.* It is a tablet with two cows and a goat in the foreground excellently treated. (Donation of the Marquise widow of Cabriñana.)

Honthorst, Gerard. *Utrecht 1590-1656. He was known in his country by «Gerard of night», because of his fondness in the representation of figures lightened by a torch or a candle. Blocmart was his moster; he travelled throughout Italy and lived in London. Finally he established himself in The Hague and became Painter of the Chamber of the Dutch Courts. His work was influenced by Rembrandt.*

Num. **2094,** *The Incredulity of Saint Thomas.* We see Jesus, the incredulous apostle, another disciple and an old woman. It has been attributed to Stomer and to Guercino. (In the Palace of Madrid.)

Van Ostade, Adrian. *Haarlem (1610-84). He was Franz Hals's disciple and codisciple of Brower who influenced him greatly. He is the gay painter of jumbled interiors, audacious and rough scenes.*

Num. **2121,** *Rural Concert.* Num. **2122,** *Peasant Kitchen* and number **2123,** *Villagers Singing.* These are three small-sized tablets common to this painter, which show popular scenes of his period with its picturesque vulgarity. They are very well painted, with cold notes and successive penumbras apart the exact feeling of movement.

Metsu, Gabriel, *was born in Leyden in 1630 and died in Amsterdam in 1667. Gerard Dou's disciple; he was greatly influenced by Rembrandt and very renowned for his lovely interiors.*

Num. **2103**, *Dead Fowl.* This white cock hanging from a leg is not a proverbial theme of this painter but it reveals the polishness of his brush. (Acquired by Carlos IV.)

Wouwerman, Philip. *Haarlem (1614-68). He was his father's disciple and he fled from the workshop after snatching a young girl whom he took to Hamburg to get married. He worked in this town and in 1640 he returned to Haarlem. He painted a good deal and earned as much. His principal scenes represent soldiers on horse-back in the meadows near the channels with settlements in the background, or themes of hunting of which he was very fond.*

See numbers **2148**, **2149** and **2150**.

Van Goyen. Leyden, 1596-1666. *Landscape.* **Coosema.** Número **2572**, *Fruiterer.* **Schaleken.** Num. **2587**, *A Gentleman.*

Greber. Num. **2097**, *Offering*, masterly in light and color.

Room XXIII.—REMBRANDT AND OTHER DUTCH PAINTERS

Rembrandt. Num. **2132**, *Artemis* (Pl. 22) is the Queen of Pergamun, receiving the ashes of her husband presented by a servant. In the background is an old woman. It is a wonder of the painter's first epoch, signed in 1634. And as in that time he had married Sachia, it has been supposed that she might have been the model for the personage. But it does not seem so, although we cannot say that she does not look like his young wife, as it is frequent in many painters in love to transfer to the faces they paint something of what they love. Artemis appears very beautiful, with jewels pearls adorning hair, ears, neck and a pendent chain of gold with precious stones. She is dressed in yellowish white, with an ermine collar and wide embroidered sleeves, in which the artist shows his ability with the brush, with a very characteristic luminosity which is his *leit motiv* in all the pungent forms emerging from the penumbra. (In 1772 it was registered in the Palace of Madrid: tribune and back room piece. It was acquired for 2500 *reales* in 1769, among the twenty nine paintings owned by the Marquis de la Ensenada. Mengs mediated in the operation.)

Palamedes, Anthony. *He was born in Delft in 1601 and died in Amsterdam in 1673. He had the same tendency of Van Ostade, equal choice and perhaps still more freedom.*

Num. **2586**, *Soldiery Scene.* A Dutch interior in which we see a soldier nearby the fireplace flirting with a woman. (Legacy of the Duke of Arcos, 1935.)

Hobbema. *Amsterdam (1638-1709). He undoubtedly was a disciple of Ruysdael, and after him the best landscape painter of Holland. He died in a great misery and as misunderstood as Ruysdael.*

Num. **2860**, *Landscape.* One of the most beautiful of this Dutch painter, it is magnificent, with its intense greens and beautiful background. In a little bald sport in the oaks forest, a man on horseback, followed by a dog, is speaking to a woman. (Acquired in 1944 with funds of the Cartagena's legacy.)

Roos. Núm. **2208**, *Shepherd with Cattle.*

Solomon Köninck. Amsterdam, 1609-1664. *The Philosopher.* Splendid master-piece with influence of Rembrandt.

Ruysdael, Jacob, Haarlem (1619-1682). *Landscape.* **Van Brekelencan,** num. **2136**, *An old woman.* **Van Mierevelt,** *A gentleman* **Cornelius Jansen van Ceulen,** num. **2588**, *A Young Man.* **Goddfried Schaleken,** num. **2135**, *Light's effect.*

Room XXIV.—EARLY SPANIARDS

This room is the vestibule of the great central gallery dedicated to the early Spaniards: **Berruguete, Bermejo, Gallegos, Jiménez** and some anonymous of great interest. Room L, in the lower part of the museum, contains good tablets by fifteenth-century Spanish painters.

P. Berruguete. *Born in Paredes de Nava (Palencia) about 1450, he died in Madrid in 1503, and was the painter of the Catholic Kings. He went to Italy where he painted for Frederich of Montelfeltro, a gentleman of Urbino. Upon returning to Spain he was sent by Torquemada to decorate the King's cloister in Avila. He also painted the main altar in the Church of St. Thomas. These pictures from the tablet passed to the Prado Museum, and represent life scenes of the saints belonging to the Order of Saint Dominic of Guzmán. Pedro was the father of the famous sculpturer of religious themes, Alonso Berruguete.*

Num. **618**, *Auto de Fe presided ower by St. Dominic of Guzmán.* The place where the Act took place is not definitely known, but it could be Avila. St. Dominic presides over the scene from his canopied seat of honor between the judges and examiners. To the left in the tribune are the condemned, one of them in penitent attire. To the right two naked heretics suffer the pains of fire. Others in penitent garments wear hoods symbolizing infamy. The strangest figure of all is that of the examiner, who seated below the saint, sleeps tranquilly while the «Auto de Fe» takes place. (It was bought for 3000 *escudos* in 1867.)

Num. **125,** *The Adoration of the Wise Men.* It is a Renaissance temple in the outdoors. The Child takes some coins offered by the kneeling King.

Num. **126,** *Two Wise Men.* In the right part of the preceeding canvas.

Num. **609,** *St. Dominic and the Albigenses.* This is a sort of a Judgement by God: heretical books are thrown to the flames while the holy books remain unharmed. St. Dominic is present during the marvel and we see a group of Albigenses to the right.

Num. **610,** *St. Dominic's Miraculous Cure of a Young Man.* The persons revived is Napoleón, nephew of Cardinal Esteban, who is on the right of the miracle in the picture. Through an arch we see a scene with a horse dragging the body of young Napoleón.

Num. **611,** *St. Peter, and the Martyr's Sermon.* It is a curious figure of Dominic who is either meditating or sleeping on the stairway.

Num. **612,** *The Martyr St. Peter at Prayer.* The most pathetic and impressive tablet, and as a result the best of the series.

Num. **613,** *The Martyrdom of St. Peter.* An assassin sinks a dagger in him, and in the background we note a city and a river.

Num. **614,** *The Sepulchre of the Martyr St. Peter.* We see a blind man with his guide among various persons before the Saint's sepulchre.

Num. **615,** *Apparition of the Virgin.*

Num. **616,** *St. Dominic of Guzmán.* It is supposed that this was the central pannel of the altar-piece. The Saint dominates the devil with the cross and the halo reads: «St. Dominic the examiner».

Num. **617,** *St. Peter the Martyr.* We see a knife in his head and his breast woundeb by a dagger.

B. Bermejo. *Born in Cordoba about 1442 he lived his whole life ignored. Most of the time he lived in Barcelona, where one of his best works,* Pietá, *is to be found in the Cathedral. Others are located in London, Paris and Vichy. The «Bartolomeus Rubens (Red)» of the Ludlow collection is no other than our Bermejo or «Vermeio» as it is written in Latin. The date of his death is unknown. Tormo, among many others, considers, him, «the most vigorous of the early Spaniards».*

Num. **1323,** *St. Dominic of Silos.* It belonged to a tablet terminated in 1477 painted for Daroca and is the central panel. It has something of the grandeur and yet is miniature-like thus reminding us of the early Flemish. St. Dominic is in a frontal position seated on a carved throne. He betrays a very solemn expression with an intense and interior glance and he holds an open book in his hands. His face indicates his strong traits and he seems to live and breath.

His cape, mitre and staff, which have been minutely created, and above all the Gothic altar, with the many colored figures of the seven virtues, prove the patience and good taste of the artist. He is in love with his labor and works with the golds without loosing the external richness. There is harmony in his play upon colors and in the decorated symmetry which he has deliberately sought. (This tablet came from the Archaelogical Art Museum and entered the Prado in 1922.)

Fernando Gallegos. *Born in Salamanca in 1440 and died in the same city about 1507. According to Passavant he was a disciple of P. Christus; Lafuente Ferrari finds similarities in Both; one sees his Hispanic-Flemish lineage. He painted altar-pieces for Zamora, Toro, Salamanca, and Ciudad Rodrigo; the twenty five tablets of this cathedral are to be found completely in the Cook Collection in Richmond (England).*

Num. **2647,** *Christ Blessing*. It is the main tablet of an altar-piece, perhaps that of Toro. From his Gothic throne the Saviour, who holds the world in one of His hands, blesses mankind. Two miniature figures of the saints and their symbols with phylacteries of the four gospels complete the composition. Many have wished to see the influence of Van Eyck in this tablet but it is not evident. His style is obviously more advanced in the facial expression, the movement of the limbs and the folds of the clothes.

M. Ximénez. *He was a resident of Zaragoza known between 1466 and 1503.*

Num. **2519,** *The Resurrection*. It is a frame of the altar piece with five panels which are: *Gargano Shooting his Arrow at the Bull, The Procession and Apparition of St. Michael above the Castle, The Resurrection of Our Lord, The Seizure of Saint Catherine and St. Catherine in the Moment in which She is Going to be Beheaded.* They are very severe figures richly dressed in religious vestments with a genuinely Flemish urban background. It belonged to the altar-piece of Egea de los Caballeros. (Acquired by the museum in 1930.)

Num. **1260,** *Virgin of the Catholic Monarchs.* **Anonymous Spaniard** (Pl. 23): The Virgin with the Child appears seated on an exquisite throne. St. Thomas and St. Dominic are standing on the sides each with a phylactery and kneeling before them are the Catholic Kings, Fernando and Isabel with their children, Prince Don Juan and Princess Doña Isabel. We also see Thomas of Torquemada and Peter of Angleria. The picture's colors are very graceful and probably the portraits have been drawn from memory. The illuminated perspective has been better attained than that of the geometric, and the panel comes from St. Thomas in Avila, with evident Flemish influence. (It belonged to the Duke of Arco.)

Bartolomeus (B. Bermejo?). Num. **1322,** *The Virgin.*

Anonymous Spaniards. Num. **2575,** *The Annunciation.* In this we see the influence of Van der Weyden.

Num. **2576,** *The First Marquis of Santillana at prayer.* Behind the poet Marquis we see a page. Observe the unusual altar.

Num. **2577,** *The Nativity.*

Num. **2578,** *Death of the Virgin.*

Num. **1326,** *St. Michael the Archangel.* Regarding this panel on canvas Pantorba tells us: «The war-like figure of the young Archangel, surrounded by the good and bad angels is presented with vivid and fluent lines. The coloring is dense and sharp as much so in the viscous qualities of the devils that cover the lower part —qualities well attained—, as in the mantel, armature, and the coat-of-arms that the protagonist displays». (A work bought by the Museum in 1925 from the Hospital of St. Michael of Zafra.)

Num. **1329,** *St. Gregory,* from the school of Gallegos.

Num. **1331,** *St. James the Elder.* (Willed, as the previous one, by Don Luis de Castro Solís.)

Num. **705,** *The Visitation.*

Num. **706,** *The Birth of John the Baptist.*

Num. **707,** *The Preaching of St. John the Baptist.*

Num. **708,** *Baptism of Christ.*

Num. **709,** *The Prison of St. John the Baptist.*

Num. **710,** *The Beheading of the Baptist.* The last six panels come from the Cartuja of Miraflores (Burgos) and were previously attributed to Petrus Christus. However, today they are believed to be by a Flemish-Hispanic painter of the last 16th century.

On one side and the other of the Virgin and Catlolic Kings, four splendid paintings by Juan de Flandes have been placarded, which are: *The Prayer in the Garden, The Resurrection of Lazarus, The Ascension of Christ* and *The Pentecost.* Juan de Flandes was the painter to Queen Isabel.

THE CENTRAL GALLERY

This gallery has been dedicated to Spanish paintings, and includes works by **Maino, Ribalta, Zurbarán, Pantoja, Pereda, Rizi, Murillo, Claudio Coello, Herrera** *the Young*, **Alonso Cano, Villavicencio,** etc., and terminates in the room representing Goya. Greco and Velázquez have separate rooms. It is a gallery in which there is far from little to see and it reflects that which was Spanish painting during the 16th and 17th centuries. It was a style of painting indeed eminently religious to the extreme that apart from some portraits and still-lives, each work contains images and Catholic religious scenes. It was the tradition of the Council of Trent that completely incorporated itself in the Spanish soil, and impregnated the sensibility of our artists, completely remote from the slightly felt pagan painting.

The Spanish characteristic was the full realism of the most purified spirituality. These are not antagonistic terms, for the Spanish painter is well aware of each brush stroke. He takes his subject matter from the same nature but simultaneously anoints his bodies with the oil of Divine Grace which glistens and shines in the ecstasies, in the honey-like mouths and in the attitudes ennobled by an unearthly emotion.

Room XXV.—SPANIARDS OF THE 16th AND 17th CENTURIES

The painters that figure in this room are: **Ribalta, Jusepe Leonardo, Pereda, Maino, Rizi, Zurbarán** and some who are anonymous.

Ribalta, Francisco. *It is believed that he was born in Castellón de la Plana in 1555, but according to recent investigations Solsona (Lérida) has the honor and he died in Valencia in 1628. His son, who showed great promise, died young. In spite of the fact that he was believed to be Juan de Juanes's disciple they have nothing in common. At first he* *worked with Navarrete el Mudo (Dumb) in El Escorial and later went to Italy where he studied and copied the Florentine, Roman and Napolitan masters. Most believe him to be a follower of Caravaggio because he, like Ribera, copied what is commonly known as «tenebrismo» a gloomy darkness, which is the accentuation of light and dark contrast purposely sought and prepared. But it seems that he did not even know the other painter nor seen his works. Ribalta had sufficient creative intellect to develop new forms and tones during an epoch in which the Italian painting presented its arguments in a well-exhausted pictorial language.*

Curberland has written that when on one occasion a Ribalta picture arrived in Rome from Spain it was triumphantly received because it was considered to be like «a Rafaello»; possibly Ribalta is more advanced than the painter of Umbria. He was a lavish sketcher, a constrained colorist and his color never discomposes the firm outline with which he stereotypes his figure. Neither does his well-accentuated sketch break the color harmony. Francisco Ribalta is one of the great Spanish painters whose value is augmented with the passing of time and study. Most of his works are to be found in the College of the patriach and Museum in Valencia where, as in Algemesí, he painted a complete Altar-piece. He made several replicas of his famous Last Supper *and one of them became the property of Marshall Soult.*

Num. **2804,** *Christ embracing St. Bernard.* What a marvellous work! This creation even excells the previous and will always be a masterpiece. What need had Ribalta of the Caravaggio-like darkness in order to represent these massive figures by dint of separating them from the backgrounf with a fascinating luminosity? Christ's arms are un-nailed from the cross but although confined by the nails on his feet he bends to receive and embrace St. Bernard. What else could we wish for in the saint's face? A face drowsy in soft ecstasy while he enjoys the indescribable heavenly delights. The dry and emaciated flesh of the saint caused by his fasting is enlivened by contact with the Redemptor. His mouth smiles sweetly as his hand falls effortlessly upon the divine arms. His figure results enlarged by the amply pleated habit so masterly outlined. Christ's ample and robust chest and shoulders remind one of Michelangelo Buonarrotti's nudes copied by Ribalta in Rome and Florence. The shaded and noble head is succesfully represented in order to detach the vigorous head of St. Bernard. For some time this work was attributed to Ribera. (It probably belonged to the Cartuja of Porta Coeli and was obtained for the Museum with the Count of Cartagena's legacy.)

Maino, Fray Juan Bautista. *Born in Pastrana (Guadalajara), and died in Madrid, in 1649. A disciple of Greco, he entered the Order of St. Dominic. He was the art professor of the Prince of Asturias,*

D. Felipe, later Felipe IV. Maino's painting lacks depth because he does not play with lights, shades and darknesses. His silvery lighting is equally disseminated upon the canvas, leaving his figures superficial or lamellated. Many modern studies employ similar lighting effects.

Num. **886,** *The Adoration of the Wise Men* (Pl. 24). Although it is less original than the previous, the colors are beautiful. One sees a slight Flemish influence similar to Rubens's style in the placement of the characters. But in our opinion the Virgin lacks ideality. The Child un-impressed by the gifts offered to Him raises His right hand as He prepares to bless. The vertical position of the three kings is very curious as is the presence of the little negro valet, a character not unknown to Rubens. This signed work formed part of the altar-piece of San Pedro Mártir, in Toledo with those of Villanueva y Geltrú.

Num. **885,** *The Recovery of Bahia in Brazil.* A huge canvas representing an episode in the reconquest of Bahia against the Dutch led by Don Fadrique de Toledo during Felipe IV's reign. Fadrique shows a tapestry portraying the King, the Count Duke of Olivares, Gaspar of Guzmán and a figure representing the victory. The corpses of Heresy, Passion and War are at his feet. The episodial groups are very interesting, for example; the curing of a wounded man, mothers with their sons, the groups of people talking, etc., are all endowed with an impressive realism and seem to be actually taken from daily life. This apparently flavourless painting has the modern savour typical of those painted by «impressionists». (Taken to France by Joseph Bonaparte, it was returned in 1815.)

Carducho or *Carducci, Vicente was born in Florence in the year 1578. He was a disciple of his brother Bartholomew with whom he came to Spain in the year 1585. He was made painter to Philip II and Philip III and decorated the gallery of the Carthusian Monastery of the Paular. He was the author of the book «Dialogue of the Painting» (Madrid, 1633) and, some of his works can be found in Paris, Dresden, etc.*

Num. **2502,** *St. Bruno renounces the archbishopric of Reggio.* Pope Urban II offers him the miter and the bishop's crosier and, St. Bruno's gesture who refuses them is appreciated. It is signed on the right: V. C. P. R. F. (Vicente Carducci Pintor del Rey Felipe).

Num. **3018,** *The Pentecost.* The apostles, the Virgin and a Saint willing to receive the donations of the Holy Spirit.

Jusepe Leonardo *was born in Calatayud about 1605 and died in Zaragoza in 1656. An unlucky artist, he was a disciple of Pedro de las Cuevas, and stopped painting eight years before his death.*

Num. **858,** *The rendition of Julliers.* This Rhemish place was surrendered to Ambrosio Spinola in February 1622, Marquis of the Balbases, the same one who received the keys of Brest in Holland, an episode being painted by Velázquez in his famous work *The*

Lances. Spinola is accompanied by Diego Messía de Guzmán (who at a later date became the Marquis of Leganés). The two warriors have an escort of victorius soldiers behind them. The conquered Governor is giving up the keys of the town with a tired gesture. Behind the Governor are his servants with the horse of their chief. The walls of the town can be seen in the background. The conquered soldiers leave over the drawbridge, while the Spanish soldiers are paying honours to them with their greatest gentility.

The Museum has the sketch which served the artist to complete this painting and which figures in the legacy carried out by Pedro Fernández Durán.

Num. **859,** *The seizure of Brisach.* Brisach is a town in the Rhineland where an episode of the thirty year war took place. This episode was the conquest of the place by the Duke of Feria, also called Gómez Suárez de Figueroa who was born in 1587 and died in the year 1634. On the right hand side of the composition, you can see the Duke on horseback who turns his face towards a soldier and, it seems that he is going to tell him something important. In the background, the Rhenish town can be seen with its moat flooded and, of which the defensors are escaping. There is a burning fortlet in the surroundings. The country seems to be occupied by the Spanish soldiers. This war scene took place in the year 1633 under the kingdom of Philip IV.

Rizi, Francisco. *Greatly influenced by Carducho some say he was a pupil. Was born in Madrid, 1606, and died in El Escorial, 1685.*

He was made painter to Philip IV, Carles II and the Chapter of Toledo. Favoured by all the courtiers, who liked his style of painting, he succeeded in amassing a large fortune.

Num. **1127,** *Portrait of a General of the Artillery.* The identity of this cavalier who wears the star of the Order of Calatrava is not known. He is standing, in a good pose, with cape, vandyke collar, riding boots, plumed hat in one hand in the other his general's cane. The cannon shows the division to which he belonged.

Carducho. Num. **639,** *The miracle of the water.* St. Bruno and his first six disciples thank God for the abundancy of water coming out of a rock. In the background, there are some temples under construction. The work is signed under the spring of the water: VINC. CAR. P. R. F.

Rizi, Fray Juan Andrés. *He was born in Madrid in 1600 and died in Monte Cassino (Italy) in 1681. Juan, the son of Antonio Rizi from Bologna, began painting with Maino. When he was thirty two years old he professed in the Benedictine Order. He painted a good deal for churches and monasteries of Montserrat, Burgos, Salamanca and Madrid, and although one of Velázquez's contemporaries, his work* *was also held in high esteem. He decided to spend the last years of his life in Monte Cassino where he retired to forget the life of a painter.*

Num. **887,** *Portrait of Don Tiburcio Redin.* Redin was born in Pamplona in 1597, and was Knight of the Order of Santiago and the holder of many other titles. Due to a difference of opinion that he had with the viceroy of Pamplona he retired from the world at forty and put on the Capucin habit dying as a missionary in Caracas. This portrait has the appearance and distinction of works by Velázquez. The legend appearing in the portrait is a brief resumé of his life.

Pereda, Antonio de. *Born in Valladolid about 1608, died in Madrid in 1678. He is considered to be a disciple of a mediocre painter, Pedro de las Cuevas, although we see the influence of his contemporary, Velázquez. Upon request of the Count Duke of Olivares he adorned some of the rooms in the Palace of Buen Retiro in Madrid.*

Num. **1317,** *Relief of Genoa by the Marquis of Santa Cruz.* This scene represents the arrival of the Spanish ships in the Genoese port which was besieged by the French. Don Alvaro de Bazán, second Marquis of Santa Cruz, commanded the fleet and he is shown reverently receiving the Dodge of Genoa, who is followed by some of his senators. Behind the Marquis are four Spanish gentlemen and a valet. The latter, while looking at the spectator, carries a helmet with a tuft of feathers. Probably the picture was painted with the aid or references, because the city in the background is more Flemish than Italian! However it has many good qualities, for example the liberator's armature and the display and dignity of the Spanish gentlemen.

Num. **1340,** *St. Peter Delivered by an Angel.* The Saint, with broken chains upon his feet, is helped to escape by the angel. (Signed; acquired from the Count of Leyva in 1931.)

Num. **1046,** *St. Jerome Listening to the Trumpets of the Last Judgement,* nude of half length. The Saint holding a wooden cross turns his ear in order to hear better. An interesting note is that the open book facing the viewer displays an engraving by A. Durer, with his monogram. (It comes from Aranjuez.)

Room XXV A.—ITALIANS

Tiziano. Num. **436,** *The prayer in the Orchard.* In the upper part, the countenance of Jesus can indistinctly be discovered. The work was promised to Philip II in a letter of June 19th 1559 and the painter tells him that he will send him the picture on April 26th 1562. Said work was handed over to the El Escorial in the year 1574.

It suffered very much during the fire at the Alcazar in the year 1734 and, it was taken to the Museum in 1837.

Sebastiano del Piombo, *Born in Venice 1485 and died in Rome in 1547. His name was Sebastiano Luciani, and in his last years he was nicknamed del Piombo due to his office in the stamping on the lead («piombo») seals, pending from the papal bulls. He was the rival of Raffaello, and painted with him in Farnesio's Palace, accusing the latter of copying from him his manner of painting which he learnt with Tiziano and Giorgione. It is related that both had a great discussion about the supremacy between the color and the sketch, which was the same as a discussion of Michelangelo against Raffaello, because the first was Sebastiano's protector who had a blind admiration for the great decorator of the Sixtine Chapel. In any case there actually was a certain similarity between Sebastiano's and Raffaello's art. Thus, the Uffizzi Gallery in Florence treasures the famous* Fornarina's *portrait so long attribuited to Raffaello's genius although being by Sebastiano del Piombo, whose paternity posteriorly has been returned to the latter.*

Finally he also estranged Michelangelo, surely because of their equal unbearable characters. His last days were sad, and almost forgotten by his contemporaries, he died in 1547.

Num. **346,** *The Descent of Christ to Limbo.* To the right and kneeling appear Adam and Eve. It is also a beautiful canvas. Cruzada Villamil has written that the picture is not by Sebastiano del Piombo, but Navarrete *the Dumb,* whose signature intentionally was rubbed off by the Madrazos; but the truth is that the canvas already figured in El Escorial, where Velázquez placed it as a work of the mentioned Venetian artist, and so it has been posteriorly repeated without being denied by anybody nor attributed to Navarrete.

Num. **345,** *Jesus Carrying the Cross.* This canvas defines Piombo well. The sketch fails: the short and lustry figure of Christ, with His arms heavier than the cross itself, lacks grandeur. Instead, the color is beautiful and typically Venetian, as well in Jesus as in the Cyrene and the Roman soldier in the third plan. The coloring of the landscape and figures is also a success. A replica of this picture hangs in the Ermitage Museum in St. Petersbourg and it is stated that it was painted for the Count of Cifuentes, Carlos V's ambassador. The previous was painted around 1520 and Felipe IV sent it to El Escorial in 1656 (see Room V).

Cima da Conegliano, *was born in Conegliano around 1460 and died around 1518. This Italian painter was disciple of Mantegna and in a way of Giovanni Bellini, whose influence seems noticeable since the artist's establishment in Venice. His placid while majestatic compositions of a beautiful coloring deserved him a great predicament. One of his most brilliant works is the* Virgin's Presentation in the Temple, *in Dresde. Paolo de Sassoferrato and the Boccaccino were his disciples.*

Num. **2638,** *The Virgin and the Child* is not very excelling work. (It proceeds from Pablo Bosch's legacy.)

Tiziano. Num. **417,** *The Marquis del Vasto haranguing his Troops.* He was named don Alonso de Avalos, Marquis del Vasto and of Pescara. Following our Emperor's orders he went to Venice in 1539 to greet the new Dodge, Peter Lando. In the occasion he commissioned this picture to Tiziano. The Marquis appears with his son, Ferrante Francesco, the elder, who holds the helmet in his hands. The general with the staff of command in one of his hands, raises the other to speak to his soldiers who form an extensive crowd with lances in the background.

We see a very tall noble figure with a wide forehead, placid glance and thick beard, who is dressed in a rich damaskeened armcoat, whose lustre is enriched by the red of the cape. The figure of the valet is not less beautiful in his dress and short hose. The twilight's purples form a very pleasant accord with the golden tones of the carnation and clean reflections of coats and helmets. The Marquis could very well have chosen an isolated portrait which was all the rage in that period, but he preferred this one of compositive character which produces a breathing and vibrant expression of reality itself. It passed to England and was adquired by Felipe IV at Charles I's auction for 250 *pounds*. It escaped miraculously from the Alcázar fire in 1734, although slightly deteriorated.

Dosso Dossi, *born in Ferrara in the 16th century. Died in 1542.*

Num. **416,** *The Lady of the Green Turbant.* Her right hand lies on the gloves.

Tiziano. Num. **441,** *The Burial of Christ,* a scene with some modifications of the beautiful canvas of the same title, num. **440,** that we shall describe later.

Num. **433,** *The worship of the Kings.* Inferior to the one of the same title in El Escorial. It has been stated that it may not be a work of Titian. However the great critic and specialist in Italian art, Berenson, ascribes it to Titian and considers it even superior to the canvas of the same title and author in the «Galleria Ambrosiana». (Acquired by Carlos IV.)

N.º **42,** *Ecce Homo.*

Licinio, Bernardino. *This Italian painter was born around 1489 and still lived at the end of 1549.*

Num. **289,** *Agnese,* the painter's Sister-in-law.

Palma il Vecchio *(the Old), named Giaccopo. One of his nephews, Antonio, was the father of Palma* il Giovane *(the Young). We know very little about «the Old». He wad born in Serinalta (Bergamo) around 1480 and died in 1528. He worked in Giovanni Bellini's workshop,* *however his art was more Bergamian than Venetian, as it is realized in his types, especially the feminine, which are more representative of his native country than of opulent and aristocratic Venice. His women are unmistakable; beautiful, blond, somewhat common with their thick and short necks and wide busts. On the contrary, the carnations are succulent and exuberant, with an ambar tint reminiscent of Bellini's workshop.*

A great deal of fantasy has been created about Giaccopo Palma, even accrediting him with a daughter, Violante, who was Tiziano's lover and inspiration. Recent documents have proved that Palma never married nor had descendents. His wealth passed wholly to his nephews.

Num. **269,** *The Shepherds' Adoration.* We could say that this tablet does not seem very much like those of Palma the Old, so it is not surprising that it is attributed to Veronese. The composition appears somewhat hasty, although with beautiful coloring. Some herds are definitely Tiziano like as that of the second shepherd to the right and that of the Virgin. The landscape's background has a natural freshness. (Proceeding from the Alcázar of Madrid.)

Moroni, Giovanni Battista *was born near Albino (Bergamo) in 1525 and died in Bergamo in 1578. He was Alessandro Bonvicinos's disciple, but he surpassed his master especially in the portraits. The lack of idealism has been reproached for he was only interested in reproducing what was strictly material. Nevertheless we must say that Titian held him in high esteem.*

Num. **262,** *A Military.* (In 1666 it was in the Alcazar of Madrid and in 1794 in The Retiro.)

Room XXVI.—RIBERA

Ribera, El Españoleto. *We are before one of the most renowned personalities of Spanish painting who was provided with the limitless mean of expression of the Spanish and Italian 17th century. Yes, we can definitely classify him as a genius in regard to his vocational aptitudes. As well as Ribalta, who is claimed to have been his disciple, Ribera is accused to have copied the darkness of Michael Angel Amerighi, il Caravaggio. But these same accusers have overlooked that this artist adapted himself instead to the evolution of the Italian art. An art that in order to rejuvenate itself had to adopt a language of lights and darks previously unexpressed.*

Játiva (Valencia) 1591-Naples 1652. He left Spain as a young man and in Naples married Catherine Azzolino. Being of small stature he was soon nicknamed by the Italians «El Españoleto» (or the little

*Spaniard). His fascinating interest in darkness lasted until 1630 more
or less. During this epoch his art was free and vigorous, strong and
atrociously realistic. He used brushes with metalic bristles treating his
paste with great resolution and energy in such a manner that his ample
brush strokes, colored, lighted, and formed at the same time. Later when
his talent was matured he began to lighten his palette and to gain in light
that which he lost in the mysterious tecniques of his colors. Almost no
one or nothing escaped his palette and brush and among his works are
mythological scenes, religious and non-religious, painting of genre, etc...
However he did not paint historical personages and gentlemen of his
period. Today his works are honoured in all the galleries of the world.*

Almost a complete «Apostleship» figures in this room with apostles that have more than one version, proceeding from the Casino
of the Principe, El Escorial. The roughness of some faces obeys to
the atrocious realism that the Levantine painter attaches. He visited
the isolated districts of Posilipo in search for well-characterized types,
black eyes, energetic features and hirsute faces, that later he converted into apostles or into classical personages, that could bee
Homer, Archimedes, Diogenes, or Æsop. He always expressed them
with thick brush-strokes, decided, strong and without replica. In his
Saint Jeromes or Pauls Hermits he praised the bodies of the statues,
macerated and sculptured, painted with horsehair brushes that were
almost chisel-like. In his *Saint Tais, Magdalenes* or *Egyptian Mary*,
he arrived at the impressive delirium of dry flesh provided that he
did not recall his ill-fortuned daughter, Anne, his model, who for
him was ultimate perfection.

Num. **1083,** *St. James the Elder.*

Num. **1075,** *St. Paul, first hermit.*

Num. **1100,** *Saint Bartholomew,* just one more of the many painted by Ribera in the course of his life. A marvellous light golden torso
against the background of the cave. So is, too, the white mantle
with beautiful foldings. His hand is holding a knife, instrument of
his martyrdom.

Num. **1118,** *Jacob receiving the blessing of Isaac.* A canvas broader
than it is high and very long, almost as a panoramic view. The blind
Isaac is feeling the skin that covers the arm of Jacob, led by his
mother. Esau, in the background and foreign to the scene, is coming
back from his work. The delightfull still life on the table near the
bed is worthy of notice.

Num. **1106,** *Egyptian Mary,* older in appearance than in age,
is shown in the background of the cave. Her breast and arms are
skeleton-like. There is a skull on the stone.

Num. **1105,** *The pénitent Magdalene.*

Num. **1109,** *St. Roque.*

Num. **1069,** *The Trinity*. Once again we see a total and absolute realism. The Father's head is too human, too obviously a «workshop model». The Holy Ghost is between the Father and the Son, who leaning upon his Father's legs is not the Saviour glorified by the resurrection, but the recently un-nailed Martyr of Golgotha. The burial garments held by the angels, receive the Divine and dead body. The attention is concentrated more in the beaufitul model of Christ with the excessively contrasted shades, than in the rigor of the composition. (It was bought for 20 000 *reales* by Fernando VII from Agustín Esteve, the painter.)

Num. **1108,** *St. John the Baptist*. Ribera, friend of asceticisms and macerations, has painted a youthful and graceful Baptist that, although without wishing to, evokes a remembrance of Leonardo da Vinci in the Louvre.

Num. **1078,** *The apostle St. Andrew* (Pl. 26).

Num. **1117,** *The Dream of Jacob*. It may be a canvas lacking in subject but it is full of grandeur. Jacob is sleeping during the day with his head and hand resting upon a stone «pillow». His is not a face with merely closed eyes, nor even one of a sleeping person but rather a realistic portrayal of a man who is dreaming. Note the calm serenity of his noble features, the slightly-opened mouth. There is an un-definable «something» in this half-shaded face that indicates that not only is he sleeping but also in vigil at the same time. Although prostrate on the ground it is an exalted and higly dignified figure. One hardly notices the scale of angels («Genesis», Chapter XXVIII): only a gilded vapor that obliquely ascends. In the contemplative glance one sees that which he wishes. Neither does the landscape have concessions of any kind; an uprooted half tree by the sea winds and a few barren rocks. (Although signed on one of the rocks, this work was once considered to be by Murillo, and from the Farnesio collection in La Granja it was removed to the Academy of San Fernando.)

Num. **1072,** *The apostle St. Peter*. Two keys in the right hand a book in the left. Wears a thick ochre mantle. The head is venerable and highly contrasted on a dark grey background.

Num. **1103,** *Mary Magdalene*. Once again the model is Ana, the painter's daughter (previously, St. Agnes for Dresde). At sixteen she was seduced by Don Juan José de Austria, the illegitimate son of Felipe IV and «The Calderona». Carried away from her home and later abandoned, she soon gave birth to a baby girl who later became sister Margarita de la Cruz and Austria, of the Order of the Royal Discalced of Madrid. The vexation of her escape and the consequences greatly embittered the last years of the artist's life. He represented his daughter as the Magdalene but without the disfiguration of penance, without eclipsing her natural beauty nor her sweet glance. The very conventional composition is reduced to a beautiful portrait. Some believe that she is Thais not Mary Magdalene. (Coming from the collection of the Marquis of Llanos the canvas was acquired to enhance the royal collections in 1772.)

Num. **1101**, *The Martyrdom of St. Batholomew* was painted in 1639, during his second and last phase. It could very easily, for its coloring, figure among the best works of the Venetian school. We say for his coloring, because the tremendous realism of the composition is Spanish from frame to frame. The spectator's eyes are drawn to the nude and colossal figure of St. Bartholomew which is molded with a richness of light and an ambar coloring that almost convert it to a sculpture. Observe the brush work that very simply arrives at an absolute expression of the corporality. The painter has deliberately chosen a common head so as to be the most distant as possible from the heavenly beautiful. And to this head only the sad gesture lends a sense of nobility. Without doubt any other painter lacking self confidence and of lesser stature would have fled from this problem without looking backwards. The Saint is about to be raised on the cross for his skinning. (That is to say, the painter did not wish to describe the actual martyrdom but rather the preparation.) The personifications of the executioners (one of them carrying a knife in his pocket) are exerting super-human efforts in trying to hoist the martyr. The two on the left who are particularly twisting and bending, reveal two of the left who are particularly twisting and bending, reveal tense muscles whose expansion is in proportion to the heavy body which they are trying to raise. To the right of the group one of the on-lookers remains stupefied as if he is refusing lending his aid to the task. In the lower part another group to the left is a true representation of the popular reaction of those curiously watching the action, since a matyrdom without spectators seems incomplete. The blue sky is broken by a floating cloud which in crossing the composition gives it a doubly pathetic character. The painter's signature can be detected on one of the rocks. (In 1666 it was in Madrid's Alcázar.)

Room XXVI A.—ZURBARAN

Zurbarán, Francisco. *Born in Fuente de Cantos (Badajoz) in 1598 and died in 1644 in an unknown place. In Sevilla he was the pupil of Pedro Díaz de Villafranca and a strict imitator of nature. Ribera's works, which arrived from Italy, had a considerable effect on him. Zurbarán painted many works for convents in Cordoba, Sevilla, Jerez and Guadalupe. It has been said that Velázquez commissioned him with*

*Felipe IV's consent, to decorate some rooms in the Palace of Buen Retiro
and to that purpose he painted* The Hercules Works. *He completed an
extremely comprehensive cicle of St. Bonaventura's life and at present
some of the components of the latter are in Paris, Berlin and Dresde.
However, his pearl is the* Apotheosis of St. Thomas *(Sevilla)*

*Absolutely no one except Zurbarán has painted praying and medi-
tating friars with their almost tactile white habits so well projected upon
the blackness of the backgrounds. Doña Leonor de Jordera or Tordera
became his second wife and by her had many children. He was commissioned as the king's painter and as a result we have the following
uncertain anecdote. One time Zurbarán, upon finishing one of his canvases, was autographing it with his title of «The king's painter» and
Felipe IV quietly came up behind him and dubbed him; «the king's
painter and king of the painters». Lafuente Ferrari states; «Zurbarán
is one of the most coherent and profound of the seventeenth century Spanish masters, because he raises the world about him to a higher spiritual
level without violating the Spaniard's attachment to, and respect for,
the surrounding world. The firmness and religious exactness of his art
reflects the culture and mentality of the early seventeenth-century
Spaniard».*

*Zurbarán, the sincere and deeply religious «painter of monks» spent
almost all his life in contact with convents, among those who lived only
for divine love and studious monks who meditated with pen in hand.
His best works are in Guadalupe, Grenoble, Cádiz and Sevilla.*

Num. **1237**, *Apparition of St. Peter the Apostle to S. Peter Nolascus.* The Apostle appears as he was martyred with his head in
reverse position. We see a mournful and aesthetic painting in which
almost transparently white religious habits are definitely admirable.
The folds and pleats cause a desire to touch and gather them. No
Spanish nor foreign painter has described, as has Zurbarán, these
solitary religious persons who have actually, through their austere
lives, converted their habits into premature burial garments. «Fran-
ciscvs de Zurbarán faciebat 1629» is in the center of the lower part.
(This canvas belongs to the same series as the previous one, which
were all bought by a Dean of the Order of Mercy and ceded to Fernando VII in exchange for Velázquez's portrait of Doña Mariana
de Austria.)

Num. **1250**, *Hercules tortured by the gown of Nessus.* The hero
is tortured by the burning gown which Deyanira had sent him and,
which had belonged to the centaur Nessus; this centaur had been
the victim of Hercules in person.

This canvas, as well as other nine, have been painted for the
Hall of the Kings at the Palace of Buen Retiro. Properly speaking,
they do not represent the 12 works of the hero; as, at least, two

Esopo.—Aesop.—Esope.—Aesop.—Esopo

Las Meninas (detalle).—The Meninas.—Les Menines.—Las Meninas (Teilbild).—Le «Meninas»

La Reina María de Médicis.—The Queen Mary of Medicis.—La Reine Marie de Médicis.—Die Königin Maria von Medici.—La Regina Maria de Medici

**La familia del pintor.—The Painter's Family.—La famille du Peintre.
Die Familie des Malers.—La Famiglia del Pittore**

Las tres Gracias.—The Three Graces.—Les trois Grâces.—Die Drei Gratien.—Le tre grazie.

La Reina Artemisa.—Queen Artemis.—La Reine Artémise.—Die Königin Artemisia.—La Regina Artemisa

**La Virgen de los Reyes Católicos.—The Virgin of the Catholic Sovereigns.
La Vierge des Rois Catholiques.—Die Jungfrau der Katholischen Könige.
La Madonna dei Re Cattolici**

La Adoración de los Magos.—The Adoration of the Magi.—L'Adoration des Mages.—Die Anbetung der Könige.—L'Adorazione dei Re Magi

would be missing. Those are paintings which represent diverse episodes of the life of Hercules. However, some real works of his are
the 1ist, 2nd, 3rd, 8th, 10th and 12th.

In the year 1701, these works on canvas were put on the inventory
of the Palace without the name of their author. In 1794, they were
classified by Lanfranco. Ponz attributed them to Zurbarán and
praises them. Cea Bermúdez wrote these strange words: «The works
of Hercules in four paintings», as if he would have believed that the
rest of them was painted by another painter. Elias Tormo attributed
the numbers **1245, 1247** and **1249** to Zurbarán and, he considered
that the probable author of the rest of them was Angelo Nardi.
But the receipt signed by Zurbarán and discovered by Mrs. Caturla
made all these doubts disappear: the ten works were painted by
the hand of Zurbarán.

Num. **656,** *The Defense of Cadiz against the English.* Although previously this historical painting was considered to be by the painter
Eugenio Caxés, and was displayed in the Rotunda at the entrance
(Hall, Room I), wit others of a similar theme, to-day it is recognised
as the work of Zurbarán and is displayed amongst others by him
in this Room.

Num. **1248,** *Hercules deviates the course of the river Alphée.* The
hero constructed a dam to deviate the river and he looks at the
spectator so that he would admire his prowess.

Zurbarán. Num. **1236,** *Visions of St. Peter Nolascus.* This canvas gains one's attention because of the natural qualities of the clothes
contrasted upon the background. Obviously the celestial angel who
is showing Jerusalem to the saint is far from celestial. In fact he
seems to be merely a model, and unfortunately the saint's expression
is also impersonal. However, the study of fabrics and folds upon
the models reveal him to be a painter with strong qualities.

Num. **2992,** *The Immaculate Conception.* It lacks the enchanting
baroque style of the Murillo, though it is very noble in its so short
and severe form.

Num. **2803,** *Still life.* There is a sharp contrast upon the dark
background of various bronze, clay, and porcelain pots. This almost
perfect study of the natural was one of his early works. (A gift of
Cambó in 1940.)

Num. **1239,** *St. Casilda.* She is the moorish saint who while
carrying provisions in her skirt to her father's Christian captives,
discovered that the food miraculously had changed to flowers. More
than one of his saints is in reality a portrait of an elegantly dressed
seventeenth-century woman; St. Casilda is probably his first wife
Doña Beatriz de Morales.

There has been a great deal of confusion regarding his saints

8

because many are his while others are mere imitations. As a result these «saints» are to be found in almost every European museum.

Num. **2888**, *Flower-pot*. Acquired by the Ministry of National Education in 1946.

Num. **2594**, *St. Luke in front of the Crucified Jesus*. This is one of the most pathetic painting by the artist. A Christ with a wasted away face, his feet crossed and united to the cross by four nails serve as a model to a painter who sure knows how to use his palette and brushes. Following a patristic tradition, St. Luke was a painter; but it seems certain that it is a self-portrait of Zurbarán. His face could not be more attentive and expressive. It is one of the canvas with the greatest contrasts of light and shadow, perhaps, one of the most characteristic light-dark ones which had been obtained by this artist. (It was bought from Mr. Cristobal Colón in the year 1936 with funds of the legacy of the Count of Cartagena.)

Num. **1249**, *Hercules hunting the wild boar of Eeymanthe*. We see the hero swinging his war club and fighting against the wild boar, called «the hog of Calydon». It is the third work.

Num. **1010**, *St. Anthony of Padua*. There is more richness in the quality of the clothes than there is in the countenances.

Num. **1246**, *Hercules and Anteo*. The hero has lifted up Anteo so taht he would not touch the ground and recover new forces because of its contact. The scene does not represent any work done by Hercules.

Num. **1245**, *Hercules dominating the bull of Creta*. The hero is caught in action when he just took off his formidable war club to fight the bull. In the background, a scenery with a lake can be seen. It is the 8th work.

Num. **2442**, *St. Diego of Alcalá*. This new version of the miracle of St. Casilda presents the saint admiring and showing the flowers that have been transformed from food. (Acquired from Don Emilio de Sola in 1932.)

Num. **1242**, *Hercules victorious against Gerrion*. Gerrion was one of the Greek giants of their mythology who was of triple height and, who was supposed to be the strongest man on earth. Here, we see him knocked down and conquerred by the hero. It is the 10th work.

Num. **1247**, *Hercules and Cerberus*. The hero attacks the monster with three heads who id found to be in the door to Hell, as he wants to free Alceste. It is the 12th work.

Num. **2472**, *St. Jacob de la Marca*. In the background we see him liberating a child from death. (It proceeds from the beautiful chapel of San Diego in Alcalá de Henares.)

Room XXVII.—VELAZQUEZ AND MAZO

This room is actually but a small space between the two large naves of the Central Gallery. **Velázquez** appears once more but not his most representative works, rather two «in wich he had a hand». So please remember that they are not to be considered totally as his works.

Therefore we will limit ourselves to state and review them.

Velázquez, Don Diego. Num. **1176,** *Felipe III on Horse-back.* Mounted on his white horse we see him half in armature with gorgeret, a plumed black hat, red sash and cane in hand. The backgroung is foggy and populated. When Velázquez went to Madrid from Sevilla, Felipe III and his wife were already dead. The portraits are therefore by another, possibly Bartolomé González. Most of the horse, the right arm, the leg, foot and spur, and ornaments that fall upon the group and part of the coast in the background, have been attributed to Velázquez. (It was previously located in the Salon of the Kings in the Palace of Buen Retiro.)

Num. **1177,** *Queen Doña Margarita of Austria, Wife of Felipe III.* Consult the previous description. She is attired in full black embroidered skirt, white waist, gorgeret and a hat decorated with plumes and pearls. Upon a garden-background we see the small chestnut and white horse decorated with richly-wrougt trappings. Note the famous «Jewel of the Austrias», formed by an exquisite diamond —the most pure and beautiful known in that period— and a pear-shaped pearl. These gems were bought at a high price by Felipe II and you will see them adorning several other queens in Prado pictures. In this work Velázquez aided only in the lower part of the forelegs and some finishing touches to enliven the adornments of the trappings. (It was in the Salon of the Kings in the Palace of Buen Retiro.)

Mazo. Num. **1214,** *The Queen's Street in Aranjuez* is a somewhat colorless painting coming to us from Aranjuez.

Velázquez, Diego de. Num. **1213,** *The Triton's Fountain.* (For several years this canvas was attributed to him.) His rather dark-toned work is vivified with little figures that could easily be by his son-in-law, Mazo. And if we are to believe Allende-Salazar this work coming from Aranjuez is by Velázquez.

Room XXVIII.—MURILLO

This room, which is the first portion of the Central Gallery's second nave, is devoted entirely to **Murillo** and includes his best works in the Prado. The master from Sevilla, definitely merits an ample rotunda as that of Velázquez for both his quality and quantity (numbering 44 according to Pantorba). But unfortunately the museum has insufficient space. Nevertheless the Gallery is sumptuous and well-illuminated so the works have been wellplaced. During the last five years the criticism of Murillo has been far from benevolent. But if one realizes that he never left Sevilla and Cádiz, and was selftaught in the fundamentals, benevolency is far from necessary. Upon viewing his paintings we have to admit taht he is a great and amiable painter full of charm, and the most popular of all the Spanish masters. Lafuente Ferrari tells us: «Murillo is an artist deeply original in relation to the Spanish painting of his time; his paintings represent that amiable aspect of Catholicism that was one of the shades of the Counterreformation, and Murillo was without doubt one of the best interpreters of this tendency, not only in Spain but in all European art». Later he continues: «But if he had not been an exquisite painter his choice of the most apt themes for the popular religious spirit of his time would not have been worth while. The very personal discovery of his models, a vaporous and delicate technique selection and good taste in color, an extremely fine sense of lighting, is what you will find in Murillo for all time one of the best painters of the 17th century» Lafuente Ferrari terminates this part of his capable study of Murillo by saying: «We should always insist upon his positive aspects, so delicate and sentimental, so distant from the exasperated and rigorous sensibility of present-day man. Murillo's is an art that ventures into an already lengthy epoch of discredit and of inactuality perfectly justifiable from the point of view of our epoch's taste, a taste whose exaggeration causes us to utter historically unjust judgements against the artist and to ignore his positive and excellent qualities».

Murillo, Bartolomé Esteban. *Born in Sevilla at the end of 1617, died in April 1682. He was the last of fourteen descendants of a surgeon father who died when Bartolomé was in adolescence. He married Beatriz de Cabrera and they had nine children, the larger part of whom were priests or entered the convent. Juan del Castillo was his master. He painted and sold many works, had houses in Sevilla, founded an Academy of Drawing and Painting and died as a result of a scaffold fall in Cádiz while painting a huge canvas (Palomino describing the accident tells us that his intestines could be seen, meaning probably that it was a hernia.) He was taken to Sevilla where he died due to the blow suffered.*

Murillo has been called «the painter of the Conceptions». His pearl is St. Thomas of Villanueva Alms Giving to the Poor. (In a Sevilla Museum). His canvases are in all the museums of the world, with beautiful collections honoring St. Petersbourg, Munich and Budapest. The largest part of those in The Prado were bouth in Sevilla by Queen Elizabeth Farnesio, the wife of Felipe V, on a trip to the city of Betis in 1729.

Num. **2809**, *The Immaculate Conception of Soult*. Murillo represented the dogma of the Immaculate Conception of the Virgin Mary many times, a dogma which the Spaniards vigorously supported. In reality he does not deal with Conceptions —a conception does not have tangible reality—, but instead with Assumptions an expression of the dogma that the Blessed Virgin was «assumpted», or carried by the angels to heaven. It deals with an adolescent girl sometimes blond, other times dark-haired, and generally in a white tunic and sky blue mantel. Upon the background of golden hues she stands on half moon floating upon a vaporous cloud supported by the angels. In the upper part a group of cherubs is never lacking. The most beautiful and perfect of the three Conceptions in this room is the one called «of Soult». It is thus called because it was stolen by this French Marshall in Sevilla, from where it was taken to Paris in 1813. It has a general ambar tone that is a true delight to contemplate. The hands of the Virgin are crossed upon her chest, the head is graciously inclined and the eyes are raised to the heavens. She rises above the globe aided by little angels in the most varied placements and bizarre postures. Another angelical cohort accompanies her in the ascension. We could ask for nothing else in this supremely charming canvas enveloped in golden light from which the little hands of the cherubs emerge, and on occasions blend with the same light. Only in a few paintings by Rembrandt does one find similar profoundity of light. (When Soult died this work was sold in an 1852 public auction, and bought by the Louvre for 615 000 *francs*. Later it was returned to Spain in 1940 through an agreement with the French Government.)

Num. **972,** *The Conception of El Escorial.* We see an extremely beautiful and resplendent face as the Virgin is raised by four angels who carry lilies, palms and roses. (Carlos V acquired it for the «little house» in El Escorial.)

Num. **974,** *The Conception of Aranjuez.* (It was in the chapel of St. Antonio in Aranjuez from where it came in 1918.)

Num. **994,** *The Dream of the Patrician.* This refers to the pious legend of the Virgin's apparition to John, the Roman patrician, inspiring him to erect the church on Esquilino Hill. The patrician and his wife sleep tranquilly oblivious and distant from the couch that the spectator discovers in the shadows. The Virgin, with the Child in her arms, shows them the mountain where she wants the temple to be consecrated. While the painter searches for the popular note he has not omited a clothes basket and a sleeping puppy. It is not a Roman arch, but rather a reduced arch in which the composition harmonious in lighting and perfectly balanced in content, is successfully included. (This painting, also plundered by Marshall Soult, was given to the Napoleonic museum. General Don Miguel of Alava's Assistant brought it and the following to Spain in 1816. It was originally painted for Sta. María la Blanca of Sevilla.)

Num. **995,** *The Patrician Reveals his Dream to the Pope.* Pope Liberio receives the patrician and his wife as they describe their dream. To the right a procession wends its way to the Esquilino, covered by an August snow, where the temple of St. María Maggiore of Rome will be erected.

Num. **962,** *The Good Shepherd.* The child, as he sits upon a rock, fixes an intense gaze on the spectator. He holds a staff in his right hand and his left one rests upon a lamb. Classic ruins and a flock of sheep are in the background. This classical expression of beautiful painting is from the of Isabel Farnesio. Collection.

Num. **963,** *St. John the Baptist,* as a child. It is of the same style as the preceeding one.

Num. **964,** *The Children of the Shell,* is one of the most popular works by Murillo in which he employs a very vaporous technique with enveloping light. The Sevillan artist was an inimitable painter of children. (The Elizabeth Farnesio Collection.)

Num. **978,** *St. Bernard's vision of the Virgin Mary.* In this painting of intranquil realism the Virgin rewards St. Bernard for his eloquence. (Elisabeth Farnesio Collection.)

Num. **979,** *The Descent of the Virgin to Reward St. Ildefonso.* A subject matter already dealt with by *El Greco.* The Virgin offers St. Ildefonso a chasuble as a reward. The devout old lady who appears with a candle in the right of the composition is noteworthy, and according to antecedents of our classic literature, refused to give it to an angel preferring to keep it until the hour of her death. (Elizabeth Farnesio Collection.)

Num. **984,** *The Conversion of St. Paul*, represents St. Paul's fall and the apparition of Jesus asking him: «Why do you follow me?». (Acquired by Carlos IV.)

Num. **989,** *St. James the Apostle*, was acquired from the Marquis of the Ensenada.

Num. **1005,** *Landscape*. Num. **1006,** *Landscape*.

Num. **2845,** *The Khingt of the Collar*. Dressed in black, white horse, and with hat and gloves in his left hand. We do not know whom Murillo painted in this, his last portrait. (Bought by the Ministry of National Education in 1941 from the descendants of Don Tomás Veri.)

Room XXIX.—DISCIPLES OF THE GREAT MASTERS

This, is a prolongation of the previous room, which displays the creations of the generation following the great masters. **Carreño, Antolínez, Cabezalero, Mateo Cerezo, Villavicencio, Claudio Coello, Herrera** the *Young*, **Mazo,** etc., are represented. Of course they do not reach the loftiness of their masters but they do display dignity and quite frequently a magnificent plastic exuberance. But unfortunately the outstanding qualities of their art are not sufficient to enliven it. From here on Spain becomes populated with foreing painters brought by the early Bourbons, and until the marvellous genius of Goya she will not raise her head again with pride.

Cabezalero, Juan Martín, *was born in Almadén (Ciudad Real) in 1633 and died in Madrid in 1673. Thanks to the correction of his sketches and their color properties this disciple of Carreño de Miranda almost equalled his master.*

Although not quite of equal value he was definitely one of the best second-class painters and his works are conserved in the Chapel of the Thira Order in Madrid and frescoes in the Chapel of the Sepulchre of San Plàcido.

Num. **621,** *Scene from the life of St. Francis*. The saint receives a young man in black suit and gorget led by Jesus upon the surface of the water. For some interpreters it refers to an episode in the life of Count Orlando of Cattani, of Chiusi; according to others to a vision of St. Francis dealing with a priest not wanting to receive the habit. Proceeding from San Hermenegildo in Madrid, it is the companion work of *San Pedro of Alcántara*, of Munich, and was one of the fifty paintings «chosen» for Napoleon's Museum, later returned.

Antolínez, José. *Seville (and possibly, Madrid), 1635; died in 1675 same city. Working in Francisco Rizi's workshop, he was noted for his quarrelsome, turbulent, proud and insufferable character. Although dexterous, his death was a consequence of a fencing assault at thirty seven. Outside of Spain his pictures are conserved in Munich, Saint Petersbourg, Hamburg and Amsterdam.*

Num. **591,** His masterpiece, *Death of Mary Magdalene* or *Ecstasy* or *Vision* deals whit her transition since Mary Magdalene was not actually raised to heaven in mortal flesh. The saint, with a very beautiful face and her hands, crossed upon her chest, is aided by the angels to heaven. On the ground lay several books, one of them opened. Antolínez is another painter whose palette gave forth rich colors. (Bought by Fernando VII for 2500 *pesetas*.)

The famous **Claudio Coello** *was born in Madrid in 1642 and died in the capital in 1693. Gifted with a great precocity he soon merited and received reknown. After painting for the Alcázar of Madrid he was named «King's painter» and later «Painter of the Chamber». His portraits of Carlos II, «The Bewitched», of his mother Doña Mariana of Austria, and of his second wife Doña Mariana of Neuburg, contributed greatly to his fame. However, his masterpiece is the ample* The Holy Form *(El Escorial), with more than fifty portraits. When Neapolitan Lucca Giordano arrived in Spain he was promptly lavished with the court's enthusiasm which later resulted in an undervaluation and contempt placing him in a deep melancholy that hastened his death.*

Num. **660,** *Virgin and the Child.* Surrounded by virtues and Saints. Coello was never startled by large compositions and he maintained a looseness of movement readily seen in this work with its fourteen symbolical and carnal figures. We reconize: St. Elizabeth of Hungary, St. Francis of Assissi and St. Antony of Padova.

Num. **661,** *The Virgin and Child Worshipped by Saint Louis, King of France.* The most beautiful figure is that of the king with his royal crown abandoned on the ground and holding the crown of thorns. Note the signature close to the right foot of St. John. (Carlos II acquired it from the Marquis of the Ensenada.)

Num. **664,** *Triumph of St. Augustin.* The bishop of Hipona appears upon a cloud dressed in pontifical garments; he triumphs over paganism and a dragon while two angels carry his staff. The scene is equally composed in the transversal from left to right as in its delineation and color. (It reached us from the Augustinian Convent in Alcalá de Henares.)

Herrera «the Young», F. *He was a painter and architect born in Seville in 1622 and who died in Madrid in 1685. He was the younger son of Francisco Herrera the Old, a good artist (but with an unbearable temper, and to avoid his temper the son fled to Italy). Upon his father's death the son came to Madrid where king Carlos II, the Bewitched, named him the «king's painter». Probably because he believed himself envied by the other painters, his signature is frequently bitten by a lizard or gnawed by rats. When he was named the palace architect he abandoned his painting. In Rome he learned the technique of frescoes which he employed in San Felipe el Real and in Nuestra Señora de Atocha.*

Num. **833,** *The Triumph of St. Hermenegildo.* Son of the Visigoth king Leovigild he was converted to Christianity, and happily accepted the martyrdom to which he was condemned. We see him transfigured in an extremely graceful pose clutching the crucifix and surrounded by angels musicians and singers, while others carry his crown of martyrdom and the instruments of his punishment. In the lower part we find King Leovigild, with an expression of terror, and the Arian bishop from whom the Saint refused to receive Holy Communion. It is a canvas with magnificent transparent qualities, and a certain roughness and freedom deliberately sought in the lower portion figures.

Carreño, Juan. *He was born in Miranda de Avilés (Asturias) in 1614 and died in the «City of the Prado» in 1685. Although he studied under Bartolomé Román he acquired his best traits while painting with Velázquez. Requested by Velázquez, he painted the Hall of Mirrors in the Palace of Buen Retiro. After the death of Felipe IV (1665), he was honored with the title of «king's painter». Although not a genius he was a conscientious, honest and correct artist. He took advantage of every occasion to gain inspiration including Rubens's* (Portrait of a Moscovite Ambassador) *and Van Dyck's* (Portrait of the Duke of Pastrana), *These masterly-applied inspirations were un-equalled among the followers of Velázquez. He married Doña María de Medina but had no children.*

Num. **642,** *Carlos II* (Pl. 27). Dressed in black with gorget, the decoration from the Order of «Toison d'Or» around his neck and a hat to the left. The background is the Hall of Mirrors of El Buen Retiro. Carlos II was the son of Felipe IV and Doña Mariana de Austria, born in 1661 and died in 1700. While Felipe IV's heir, Prince Baltasar Carlos, was still alive, his father chose Doña Mariana of Austria to be his wife. Then his descendant died prematurely and the elderly king married she who would have been his daughter-in-law and who incidentally was his niece. The abnormalities of both sides, caused a degenerated and sickly child. The child was very realistically painted by Carreño (so much so that those by Claudio Coello resemble Adonis in comparison).

Num. **644,** Now we see *Queen Doña Mariana of Austria*, who was the mother of the previous. She is dressed in a widow's headdress, as in the replicas of Bilbao, Castellá, Munich and Vienna. This is a portrait of a lamentable realism: the eyelids fall, the large and fat nose falls, the lower lip falls, the jaw falls, and the whole face is gravid, discolored somewhat like a corpse standing in a nun's habit. Those profund and black habits that Carreño learned from Velázquez and those magnificent white ones which he did not have to learn add inmeasurably to the effect. (This portrait and the previous were primarily in the Alcázar and later passed to the Buen Retiro.)

Num. **650,** *Duke of Pastrana* by name Don Gregorio de Silva Mendoza and Sandoval, Duke of Pastrana and Estremera, Prince of Melito and Eboli, Count of Saldaña, Knight of Santiago and Toison. This collector of titles is dressed in black, his valet adjusts his spurs and another awaits him with the horse. It is the best work by Carreño de Miranda and does not detract from Van Dyck's best portraits.

Alonso Cano *is an extraordinary figure in Spanish art: architect, sculptor, and painter. He was born in Granada in 1601, and became co-disciple of Velázquez in the workshop of Pacheco. Being gifted with exceptional qualities for art which he knew how to develop, he led a turbulent life with two marriages. A duel with a rival obliged him to flee from Madrid. As sketch master of Prince Baltasar Carlos he did not quite sympathize with his disciple, and upon returning to Granada·his second wife was discovered assassinated in her bed. He was accused of the crime, but he denied it after suffering innumerable torments. At the end of his life he wished to be a clergyman and obtained a place of prebendery in the Cathedral, but because of his unbearable character the capitulars drew him out of the choir. Finally he was ordered subdeacon. When he was about to die he asked for a crucifix but refused the one offered to him saying that it was an unworthy carving and requested two crossed sticks fastened with a cord. He died September 3, 1667. He left disciples who soon became famous.*

Num. **2806,** *The Miracle of the well.* The child who has just been saved by San Isidro Labrador is seated on the well's railing. Although the picture represents a miraculous scene, in which the least interesting is the figure of the Saint, the charm of this canvas is due to its genre-like painting: the boy who collects the water in his hand, the dog drinking in the puddle, the child back to the spectator who is looking at the jet, and the two women who comment about the happening. (It was painted for the Church Santa María, and entered the Museum in 1941.)

Villavicencio, Pedro Núñez de. *This Murillan disciple was born* *in Sevilla in 1635 and died in Madrid in 1700.* The Children's Game *was a particular favourite of Carlos II, who showered his friendship and favours upon the artist. The Andalusian Knight was of the Order of St. John of Malta (he visited the island) and received the commission of Bodonal.*

Num. **1235,** *The Children's Game,* a «genre» scene in which two children are playing while a third snatches the money and others look on. He painted a series of canvases of typical Sevillan street urchins (Munich), similar to those of Murillo. The painting is somewhat lacking in color but the scene is well composed.

Cerezo, Mateo, *who died at forty in Madrid was his father's disciple. At fifteen he went to Madrid in order to work with Carreño, later becoming an assistant to Herrera the Young during the decoration of the Church of Atocha's dome. In Valladolid his best work is entitled* The Supper of Emaus.

Num. **658,** *The Assumption.* While the angels lead Mary to heaven the apostles in the earthly scene, look inside the sepulchre to convince themselves that it is truly vacant.

Escalante, Juan Antonio. *Born in Cordoba, 1630, and died in Madrid, 1670. He was a pupil of Francisco Rizi. He copied many works by Tintoretto, the brilliant hues of which denounce the influence. Most of his paintings are bright. He painted for a great many churches, among them that of the Carmelitas Descalzas, in Madrid, and that of the convent of El Puig, near Valencia. His best canvas is the* Most Pure Conception, *in the Budapest museum, on the walls of which many Spanish works are hung.*

Num. **3046,** *The last communion of St. Rose of Viterbo.* A picture of large proportions, signed in its lower center part: Ivannes, Antonio Escalante Ft. St. Rose is covered with a large, dark coloured mantle, she kneels down and shows the paleness of death receiving her Last Communion from the hands of an old Franciscan. Angels with lit candles and an incensory are present at this soft scene. Clusters of roses are on the floor. In an opening in heaven and among the clouds, the Holy Trinity can be seen.

Room XXX.—EL GRECO

(See page 61).

Room XXX A.—SPANIARDS OF THE 17th CENTURY

Herrera «The Old», Francisco. *Born in Sevilla 1576, and died in Madrid, 1656. He Commenced painting under the guidance of Luis Fernández. A lover of great apocalyptic themes, of tormented visions, his painting is of rough orchestration, so fantastic that it could be Michelangelo's, even though more contrasted and incorrect. His character is reflected in his painting: he was acid and unbearable. His wife separated from him, his daughter took refuge in a convent, his son fled to Italy, the other, «the Fair» died in the prime of his life. Embittered by his solitude, he left for Madrid, where he painted for the Merced Convent and for El Paular. In Madrid, he died with neither friends nor family at his side.*

Numbers **2773** and **2774,** *Head of an Apostle.* They are two studies for a composition on the Ascension of the Virgin. At this moment it is the only piece that can be seen by this painter (seeing that the Museum possesses other works), and naturally, only of an idea far from his usual mode of painting.

Herrera «el Viejo». Num. **3058,** *Decapitated Saint.* A very realistic head with a mortal paleness.

Bartolomé Román. *He was born in Madrid in the year 1596. He was distinguished by his historical themes. He studied together with Velázquez and was the most distinguished disciple of Carducho: of a pusillanimous character, this painter lived without glory or fortune, although his works were quite appreciable. He was specially outstanding because of the richness of his colouring and the elegance with which he painted the clothes. He died in the year 1659.*

Num. **3077,** *St. Beda the Venerable.* He is shown to us in a cell reading a book attentively. There are other books and a miter on the table. The venerable Beda was a Benedictine monk and an English historian. He was born in the year 672 and died in 735. He spent his life in a monastery submitted to all kinds of privations. Among other works, he wrote a book called the «Ecclesiastical History of England» which is a true milestone of erudition.

Pantoja de la Cruz, Juan. *Born in Valladolid 1553. Died: Madrid 1608. Although a disciple of Sánchez Coello, who did not quite attain his master's psychological insight, his colouring excelled. The portrait of Felipe II in the Library of El Escorial, serves as a contrast.*

Num. **1034,** *A member of the military Order of Santiago.* Torso. Black suit with stiffened neck stock. The symbol of Santiago on his coat and mantle. Signed in the background, at the height of the right ear: «Juan Pantoja de la f. in the year 1691». The picture did not suffer in the fire of the year 1734.

Ribalta. Num. **1065,** *St. John and St. Matthew.*

Antonio Puga. *Contemporary and, according to some, disciple of Velázquez, whom he tried to imitate. He cultivated essentially material themes.*

Num. **3004,** *Portrait of my mother.* This is a charming portrait which expresses a deep intimacy: the smiling face, the crossed hands, the straw seat, the lock of hair, the cat, the engraving on the wall, as the Flemish painter Nicolaes Maes used to represent it... The force of expression, the fresh colouring and the know-how of his brush in such a way that nobody would imagine that the work was painted three centuries ago. (Gift of Mr. Frederick Mont, New York, January 1961.)

Ribalta. Num. **1062,** *St. Francis comforted by an Angel Musician.* The joyous concurrence of the sketch and color is wholly obtained in this work that well defines the Levantine master. St. Francis sick and alone in his cell, is surprised by a heavenly visitor and the apparition of an angel musician comforts him. A small symbolic lamb is upon the wooden couch. Both surprise and complacency are expressed in the saint's face and the richly molded hands are aqually expresive. The dark background permits one to see a monk's shadow, as candle in hand, he brings the meal. (This canvas was painted for the Capucin church of Valencia from whom Carlos IV bought it.)

Fray Juan Rizi. Num. **2510,** *St. Benedit blessing the Bread.* Three natural-size figures in the style of Zurbarán. A kneeling friar is presenting him with a piece of bread. On the right side is a gentleman with his hat in his hand.

Ramírez, Felipe. A painter cited by Ceán, his *Still-life* is catalogued as number **2802.** We see a thistle, lily, partridge and two clusters of grapes. No other work by this faithful observer of nature is known. (We owe this work to the Fernández-Durán's legacy.)

Maino. Num. **2595,** *A gentleman.*

Num. **2441 a,** *St. Buenaventura receives the sackcloth from St. Francis.* The scene represents a temple, the altar is on the right and, in the background on the left, there is a tribune. St. Buenaventura, dressed in a long black robe is kneeling in front of St. Francis. The sackcloth and the Franciscan monk's rope belt are on the floor. The Saint Founder seems to be sitting among the community: on the right, a very old brother introduces him to the postulant.

This canvas was painted at the same time like three of Herrera and four of Zurbarán for the church of the College of San Buenaventura in Sevilla. The order given to the painter was dated on December 30th 1627. (A gift made by Dr. Joaquín Carvallo from the

province of Extremadura, a doctor and collector, former owner of
the Castle of Villandry in Turenne, France.)

Anonymous Spaniard. Num. **1037,** *Portrait of the First Wife of
Felipe IV*, Isabel de Borbon (Pl. 25), daughter of Henry IV of France
(the Bearnés) and of Mary of Medici. She was born in Fontainebleau
in 1602 and in 1615 was married by proxy. She arrived in El Pardo
in 1620 and in 1644 she died in Madrid. It is definitely elegant and
vibrant due to the richness of the jewels and robes. According to
Allende-Salazar it perhaps was painted by Angelo Nardi, who lived
all his life in Spain. On the other hand, Gómez-Moreno believes it
to be an original by Zurbarán.

Arias, Antonio. *Born and died in Madrid, 1620-1684. Pupil of
Pedro de las Cuevas, he was one of the best painters in Madrid. In spite
of having been well favoured and of irreprochable habits, he died destitute in the Hospital. He left a daughter who showed a keen interest in
painting.*

Numbers **3079** and **3080,** *St. Thomas and St. James the Minor*.
Two handsome types of man, both solemn; both of them are dressed
with mantles with wide folds and a magnificent neatness who make
one think of the apostles of Durero.

Fray Juan Rizi. Num. **2510,** *St. Benedict blessing the Bread*.
Three natural-size figures in the style of Zurbarán. A kneeling friar
is presenting him a piece of bread. On the right side is a gentleman
with his hat in his hand.

Num. **2600,** *The Supper of St. Benedict*. A large size canvas with
two figures. St. Benedict is sitting at the table on which there is food,
a water jar, a glass and bread. Standing by him we see a famulus
with a candle. The artist sought the effect of the light on the faces
and hands. The position of the table adds to give depth to the scene.

Arellano, Juan de. *He was born in Santorcaz (Madrid), in 1614
and died in the capital in 1676. At thirty-six he entered the workshop
of Juan Solís, where he copied the flower pots by the Italian, Mario
Nuzzi, «Mario de Fiore», which enlivened his fondness for this popular
art of the 17th century. He was followed in this genre by his son, José
and his son-in-law, Bartolomé Pérez who excelled the former and at
times even his own master. Those of Juan still conserve the fresh tints
of the original painting; but in general they have darkened, maybe due
to the intense stamping of the canvas.*

Numbers **592** and **593,** *Two Flower pots*.

Tristán, Luis. *About 1584 he was born in Toledo and died there
in 1624. He was Greco's best follower. Tristán married Catalina de la
Higuera who Aragonés believes to the celebrated* Dama of the Ermine
painted by «El Greco». It is not too possible. In the Dama *one can see
a very select woman, and on the other hand, Tristán had hardly died*

when his widow married a vulgar shoe-maker. He was a good portrait painter, as witnessed in his portraits of Cardinal Sandoval y Rojas, and Lope de Vega, etc.

Num. **2836**, *Saint Monica.* Num. **2837**, *Tearful Saint.* Both are in profile, both in mourning, both tearful, the elder and the younger. These canvases, not of great dimensions, figure in the altar-piece of Yepes and were finished two years after Greco's death. They suffered deteriorations in 1936, and were later restored.

Hamen, Juan van der. *A member of the Spanish school, he was born in Madrid in 1596 and died item.*

His *Still-life* number **1164** was painted in 1622.

Anonymous madrilenian of 1627. Num. **2833**, *Brother Luke Texero in front of the corpse of V. P. Bernadinus of Obregon.*

Orrente. Num. **1020**, *The return to the sheepfold.* Very beautiful, it reminds one of similar themes of the Bassanos.

J. G. de Espinosa. Num. **701**, *St. John.* Resolved in diagonal, artificially illuminated and with a countenance which seems more mystic than ascetic.

Room XXXI.—(Left Passageway)

Several works by French painters of the 17th and 18th centuries have been collected in this room, as well as some pictures by the Spaniard Vicente López.

The portrait of *Elizabeth Farnesio* and *Felipe V* by Ranc, to whom we shall later refer, are hung here together with two battle scenes by Courtois and some long and narrow landscapes by Verner.

Robert, Hubert. *Paris 1733-1808. He was called «Painter of Ruins» due to the attention he gave them while in Rome. He expertly used his golden tones to best express the passing of time and to give them a strength and at the same time charm.*

Num. **2883**, *The Colosseum.* In this canvas the characteristics o Hubert Robert's art are well defined, because this portion of the ancient Rome is majestic to the extreme that it might be better minus the four women of the arch. (The Count of Cimera generously willed it in 1944.)

The following portraits by Vicente López Portaña are also included in this room; Doña María Cristina, Don Juan de Zengotita, Doña María Josefa Amalia, Fernando VII, Father Gasco of the religious. Order of the Mercy, Mrs. Carvallo, child, and the Infante Don Antonio.

Entering into the short passageway we find some pictures by Giaquinto, Tiepolo, Carnicero and Charles de la Traverse, and turning again this corridor we still find some Giaquintos together with works by Carnicero and Amiconi.

Giaquinto, C. *Was an Italian painter born in Mofetta in 1700 and who died in Napoles in 1765. His masters were Solimenes and Sebastiano Conca. Felipe V sent for him and he came to Madrid where he lived from 1753 to 1762. Thanks to his obliging and complacent art well-liked by the Court, he was honored and rewarded. He painted some frescoes in the Royal Palace but his best work is in the Prado to be found in room XXXIX, and those in the present room are almost all sketches or previous studies of more important works destined for roofs and ceilings.*

Perhaps the most successful is number **104,** *Justice and Peace* in which the artist illuminates his symbolic figures upon allegorical thrones of clouds. In general: Giaquinto was a superficial, pompous and facile painter.

Amiconi, Giacoppo. *Born in Naples about 1682 and died in Madrid in 1752. Some still believe him to have been from Venice. He remained in Spain for five years, became painter of the Chamber in 1747 and created religious pictures, portraits and «cartoons» for tapestries. Corrado Giaquinto succeeded him upon his death.*

Num. **2792,** *Portrait of a Lady,* is of half figure and cut. (Who it is has been ignored.)

Carnicero, Antonio, *was born in Salamanca in 1748 and in 1814 passed away in Madrid.*

Num. **641,** *The Ascent of a Montgolfier Balloon in Madrid.* In a large orchard that is possibly the Retiro, a multitude of *majos* and *majas* watch the balloon rise. This «photograph» of the epoch was acquired for the sum of 3000 *pesetas* in the Casa de Osuna auction.

Menéndez, Luis. *Although born in Naples in 1716, he spent almost all his life in Spain except for a few sojourns in Rome and in his birthplace. He died in 1780 in Madrid. He has been called, the «Spanish Chardin» due to his realistic still lives, so similar to those of the French painter. This realism denotes their only similarities. A slave to nature no other realm interests him and no other still-life painter can surpass him in his almost blind faithfulness. For Menéndez everything is as nature created it.*

His *Still-lives* to be found, in room XXXI are fruits, cheese, fish and vegetables of which it is commonly said that they «escape from the canvas giving the spectator a desire to clutch them». Nothing else interested him and without doubt he achieved his ideal as few others have.

Curtois, Jacques *«the Bourguignon» (from Burgundy), French painter and Jesuit, born in Saint Hipolite, in 1675. From a family*

La Reina Isabel de Borbón, mujer de Felipe IV.— The Queen Isabella de Bourbon.—La Reine Isabelle de Bourbon.—Die Königin Elisabeth von Bourbon.—La Regina Isabella di Borbone, sposa di Filippo IV

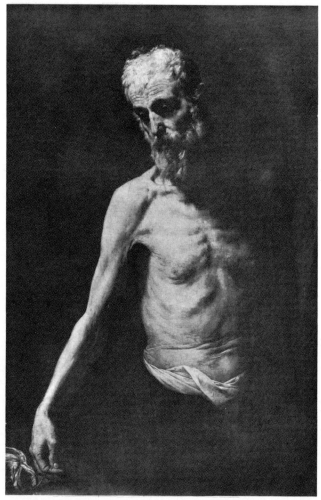

San Andrés.—Saint Andrew.—St. André.—Der Heilige Andreas.—S. Andrea

**Retrato de Carlos II.—Charles II's portrait.—Charles II.—Karl II.
Ritratto di Carlo II**

La Maja desnuda. — The «Maja» naked. — La «Maja» nue. — Die unbekleidete «Maja». — La «Maja Desnuda»

Doña Tadea Arias de Enríquez

Retrato del Infante D. Carlos María Isidro.—Portrait of the Infant D. Carlos María Isidro.—L'Infant D. Carlos María Isidro.—Bild des Infanten D. Carlos María Isidro.—Ritratto dell'Infante Carlo María Isidro

Louis XVI

El Parnaso.—The Parnassus.—Le Parnasse.—Der Parnass.—Il Parnaso

*of painters, he served his apprenticeship at his father's side. He led quite
an adventurous life. Enlisting in the Spanish infantry of Italy and
continued thus for three years. Free from his war-life he visited the
country, meeting and dealing with Guido Reni, Albano, Peter of Cortona
and other painters. He married the daughter of a painter and was very
unfortunate. After her death he entered the Company of Jesus, where
he remained until his death.*

Num. **2242,** *Battle between Christians and Moslems.*

Num. **2243,** *Battle for the Possession of a Fortress.* Two pictures
of war recall the belicose life of their author, who dealt equally with
weapons as pencil and paints. Of these two pictures, the second is
the better with great precision of observation and magnificent sketch.
(It was acquired by Felipe V, as the previous by Carlos IV.)

Panini, Giovanni. *Also an Italian, was born in Piacenza in 1691
and died seventy years later. Like Hubert Robert he was a painter
of ruins.*

His most characteristic work is classified as number **276,** *Ruins
with a Woman Speaking to a Group,* she is probably a Sibyl or pro-
phetess.

Maella, Mariano. *He began his studies with his father and later
continued them in Madrid at the Academy of San Fernando. He spent
five years in Rome and later returned to work in the Palace of Orient
under Meng's direction. Soon after he became a «royal painter» and
director of the Academy of San Fernando. What he lacked in qualiyt
he made up for in quantity. His best work being available in the Casa
del Labrador and in the Palace, in Aranjuez. Maella also illustrated
Quevedo's works. He was born in Valencia in 1739 and died eighty
years later in Madrid.*

Num. **2440, Carlota Joaquina.** *Spanish Princess and Queen of
Portugal.* Born in 1775 to Carlos IV, she later married the future
John IV of Portugal anb died in the first part of 1830. She comes before us dressed in pink and standing next to a table with a bird cage on
top while the canary poses himself on her right hand. The dull colors
make it inferior to Goya's works, and he was only one of many eclipsed by Goya.

Numbers **2497** to **2450,** In *The Seasons* we see Spring, Summer
and Autumn represented with the symbolical Flora, Ceres and Bacchus and Winter by two old men next to a fireplace. The compositions
are candid and well-delineated.

Esteve, Agustín, *was born in 1753 in Valencia, although he was
still living in April 1820 the exact date of his death is unknown. He won
a prize in the Academy of San Fernando, not long after painting royalty, for example Don Carlos María Isidro and his wife Doña María
Luisa de Borbón. He is considered to be a genuine disciple of Goya. In*

*fact some of his later portraits have been attributed to Goya, this of course,
being the greatest praise possible.*

Num. **2581,** Is entitled Portrait of *Doña Joaquina Téllez Girón.
Daughter of the Dukes of Osuna* and was drawn when she was not
yet fifteen showing her leaning on a globe. She was the daughter of
Doña María Josefa Alonso Pimentel, Countess-Duchess of Benavente,
whom Goya previously painted in the family portrait and Don Pedro
Téllez Girón, ninth Duke of Osuna. She married the Marquis of Santa
Cruz. The portrait is very lovely with its finesse of expression and
rich white transparencies. (It joined our collection in 1934.)

Room XXXII.—GOYA

Goya, Francisco de. *Born in Fuendetodos (Saragossa) in March
of 1746, he was the son of a goldsmith who took him to the workshop of
José Luzán the painter, in Saragossa. After remaining with him for
six years at twenty he moved to Madrid, to the shop of Francisco Bayeu,
of Aragón, whose sister Josefa he later married. The reason for his flight
from Madrid in the company of some bullfighters travelling to the south
has remained unknown. Soon after he went to Italy and just as quickly
returned to Spain, where he worked on the Arches of the Temple of Pilar
in Saragossa. Returning to the Court, Mengs encharged him with the
painting of cartoons for the royal tapestry factory of Madrid. Soon
aferwards his work, in competition with others for the church of St. Francisco el Grande, began his ascent to fame. He was well praised by the
king who aided him in joining the court's aristocratic circles. In 1776
he became the king's painter and then due to an illness he became completely deaf. In 1798 he painted the frescoes of the very famous Hermitage
of San Antonio de la Florida, and in 1800 The family of Carlos IV.
During the War of Independence he remained in Madrid secluded
in his cottage, «Quinta del Sordo», on the banks of the Manzanares,
from where he witnessed with his telescope the fusillades of the Moncloa.
Part of his* Caprices, The Disasters of the War, *and the «Black Paintings» were given life in this cottage. More and more fatigued by his
illnesses and the passing years, he went to Bordeaux to recover. He
managed to return to Madrid for a two months' stay of which Vicente
López took advantage to paint the master's portrait for the Prado. Once
again in Bordeaux he painted his last canvases and died on April 16,
1828 at eighty two. In 1899 his remains were returned to Spain to be
interred in Madrid's Hermitage of San Antonio de la Florida, not too far
from the present-day Plaza of the Moncloa.
Goya has been one of the most genial and productive painters of*

all times, painting everything although at his best in the realms of por-
traits, Kings, princesses, ministers of the crown, courtiers, nobles, generals,
comedians, majas, bullfighters, workmen...; and his brushes were at
home in each social state. To these subjects he added the offspring of
his solitude and melancholy; witches, monsters, goblins, nocturnal birds,
delirious dreams conceived in a deaf man's subconcience. At the same
time his brushes reproduced historical, religious, bullfights, popular
pilgrimages and «genre» scenes. Goya was extraordinarily gifted as
an artist and employed sumptuous reds, profound blacks, pearl greys,
unprecedented in Spanish painting. Although sometimes incorrect in
his designs this fault was counter-acted by a vivid vitality which shines
forth in his figures and compositions. He did not alter them because he
preferred the spontaneous rashness of his first impulse rather than the
polished retouching of the academist. It is interesting to note that although
in bad humor he preferred the popular cenacles with guitarrists, majos
and madrileñas of the lower classes instead of the un-inspiring court
frolics.

Goya has been the genuine Spanish artist, unbound by tradition
and details, realistic and impassioned, with all the defects and virtues
inherent in Spaniards, and with the concepts of art that only had been
equalled and occasionally surpassed a century and a half before, by Ve-
lázquez.

Numbers **741** and **742** (Pl. 28): *The Robed Maja* and the *Naked Maja.* Of the ladies of the period, the most beautiful and undoubtedly the most brilliant was María del Pilar Teresa Cayetana, Duchess of Alba. Much has been written and spoken about the supposed love affairs of the Duchess with Goya, but we doubt that they passed the bounderies of a sincere and affectionate friendship. He represented her in various sketches and portraits. Prematurely widower upon the death of the Duke, she retired to the palace of Rocío in Andalusia, where the artist lost little time in meeting her. During this stay he painted the two *majas*, the robed and the naked, which popular curiosity believes to be the portraits of Cayetana. Not the slightest facial similarity exists although the corporeality and the finess of proportions and line resemble the whole portraits which we know of the Duchess.

The Robed Maja is undoubtedly taken from the natural and could well serve her aristocratic friend, with the intentionally disfigured head, as a model. There are in this painting lights and qualities —the truth of an undeceptive reality— that only can be reproduced from the natural. On the other hand, *The Naked Maja* definitely is painted from memory or, to put it better, «deduced» from the previous, supposing that the carnation is false —too bloodless and porcelain-like, lacking vitality— and with arbitrary and unsteady lightings.

Of course the most beautiful and also the most provocative is the *Robed Maja*. Goya has left in the latter vibrant brush strokes, anticipating impressionism. From his easel has come a charming harmony of colors, from the little yellow jacket to the green silks of the divan, passing the warm rose of her sash to the changeable whites in her blouse and the counterpane and small pillows. (These canvases belongued to the Duchess of Alba and passed on her death to Godoy and later to «the private rooms» to be kept until they entered into the Academy of San Fernando and later to the Prado.)

Num. **726**, *The Family of Carlos IV*. This canvas painted in 1800 in Aranjuez shows Carlos IV with his wife, María Luisa of Parma, and between them the child Don Francisco de Paula. The queen's right arm rests upon María Isabel (who later married the heir to the Naples Crown). To the side we see a group of four: a young lady turning her head, the elderly Doña María Josefa, older sister of Carlos IV, the Asturian Prince, Don Fernando (later Fernando VII) and his younger brother Don Carlos María Isidro. Behind Carlos IV are four others who from right to left are: Princess Doña María Luisa (daughter of Carlos IV) with a baby in her arms, her husband Prince Don Luis de Parma, Doña Carlota Joaquina (the king's older daughter) and the Prince Don Antonio Pascual, the monarch's brother. In the background to the left we discover a self portrait of Goya behind the canvas. The young lady who hides her face toward the background, «the unknown lady», represents Fernando's future wife, at the time unknown because she was yet to be chosen. However it was María Antonia, daughter of Fernando I of the two Sicilies, who four years later married Fernando and thus became the «unknown lady».

In this canvas everything is brilliant and dazzling from the silks, jewels and sashes (the Order of María Luisa worn by the ladies, and of Carlos III by the men) to the fancy decorations. The painter glories in his technique of profound greyish transparencies obtained by successive velaturas of fluid color and of the genial and free brush strokes. Each brush stroke disseminating merits prominence in enriching fine handworks, embroidery and gems. The painter's presence in the background may be an attempt to imitate Velázquez. Other than this detail not a single similarity exists between this canvas and that of *The Meninas*.

Num. **719**, *Carlos IV on Horseback*. The son of Carlos III and María Amelia of Saxony, he was born in Portici (Italy) in 1748. Due to his weak character he was ruled by Godoy, favorite of the queen and he neither reigned nor governed. In March of 1808 he abdicated in honor of his son Fernando and later lived in poverty with his wife in Paris afterwards travelling to Italy where he died in 1819. We see him in his colonel's navy blue uniform of the Guards of Corps carrying the Toison and the sashes of Carlos III and Saint Jenaro. His reddish golden and kind face has been admirably portrayed.

Num. **720,** *Queen María Luisa* was the daughter of the Duke of Parma and of Louise Elizabeth of France. Born in Parma in 1751, she married her cousin Carlos IV, when less than fourteen, and through the years completely dominated the king's will. Years later she and her husband went to Rome where she died seventeen days before him. She also wears the uniform of Colonel of Guards of Corps. Goya painted her just as she was: ugly, conceited and lacking teeth (as one detects by the puckering of her lips). She is mounted upon *El Marcial* which her favourite, Godoy, gave her (the two portraits became part of the Prado collection in 1819.)

Num. **729,** *Princess Doña María Josefa*, the spinster sister of Carlos IV, who died in Madrid. This painting is a Goya pre study painted before his undertaking of *The Family of Carlos IV*. The background coloring is definitely the priming of the canvas.

Num. **730,** *Prince Don Francisco of Paula* who was the son of Carlos IV and María Luisa (and who appears in the family portrait between his parents). Later he married Luisa Carlota of Bourbon (Naples), giving birth to Don Francisco of Assissi and Paula, who married Isabel III.

Num. **731,** *Prince Don Carlos María Isidro* (Pl. 30.). He was the younger brother of Fernando VII, in the family portrait appearing behind him. This was the same prince who upon the kings's death raised the legitimist flag against the successor's rights of young Isabel II, thus provoking the first Carlist War. He died in Trieste in 1855.

Num. **732,** Is *Don Luis of Bourbon*, *Prince of Parma*. It is a preliminary sketch of the *Family Portrait* in which he is second to the right. His parents were Don Fernando, Duke of Parma, and the Archduchess María Amelia of Lorena. Piacenza was his birth place, and he married the daughter of our kings María Luisa Josefina (in the main painting who is at his side), after being crowned king of Etruria. In 1801 he died in Florence two years later.

Num. **733,** *Prince Don Antonio Pascual*. The brother of Carlos IV, he was born in Naples in 1755, married his niece María Amelia and later died in Madrid in 1817. This is also a preliminary sketch of the same larger portrait.

Num. **740,** *Doña Tadea Arias de Enríquez* (Pl. 29). A lovely full-length portrait, full of expression and coquetry. The dress with its rich transparencies shows this to be the master's best period, and understandably so when we realize that he received 10 000 *reales* for it. Her grandsons donated it in 1896.

Num. **722,** *Josefa Bayeu*, *Goya's wife*. Josefa was the sister of Francisco and Ramón Bayeu painters from Aragón. If this portrait actually represents his wife, as it is believed, we cannot deny her a dignified and gracious face. His wife presented him with twenty children but only Xavier outlived his father. At any rate the portrait was acquired from Don Román de la Huerta for 300 *escudos*.

Num. **734,** *Isidoro Máiquez*, painted more than once, was an admired Spanish actor friend of the artist.

Num. **2448,** *The Marquess of Villafranca*. She is sitting and painting her husband's portrait. She was not only a painter but moreover an Academician of Bellas Artes. Her mother was the Countess of Montijo and her name was María Tomasa Palafox, as we read on the palette held in her left hand. She married one Borja Alvarez de Toledo, Marquis of Villafranca and Duke of Medina Sidonia. (Willed by the Count of Niebla, in 1926.)

Num. **2449,** *Duke of Alba*, José Alvarez de Toledo y Gonzaga, the oldest son of the marquises of Villafranca, and husband of Duchess Cayetana whom he married in 1775. He is standing leaning on a piano and we see musical composition by Haydn, so well loved by the Duke of Alba that during a rivalry with the Dukes of Osuna, he engaged the composer and his works for a complete year.

Num. **2450,** *Don Manuel Silvela*. Goya's friend was called «Frenchified» because of his post as mayor of the «Casa y Corte» under Bonaparte's reign. He emigrated to Bordeaux when Fernando VII returned. (Catalogued as num. 2450 it was acquired by the Ministry of Public Instruction from the heirs in 1931.)

Num. **721,** *The Painter Francisco Bayeu*. Brother of painters, Ramón and Fr. Manuel, and of Goya's wife Josefa, he appears in half-lenght seated with a brush in his right hand in a grey smoking jacket. Due to Bayeu's death Goya had to employ the former's self-portrait in order to finish the work. It is a masterly work because of the simplicity of technique employed without an apparent thickness in the carnation, and the beautiful grey tint of the smoking jacket. (It was acquired for 400 *escudos* from Bayeu's descendants.)

Num. **2546** and **2548,** *Commerce and Industry*, are two circular canvases that Goya never finished. Apart from their plastic values, they serve as a study of Goya's technique. They were painted for the Library of Godoy's palace which later was the Naval Ministry who left it in charge of the museum in 1932.

Room XXXIII.—CALLET

Callet, Antoine François. *French painter, born and died in París (1741-1823). He painted the ceiling in the Gallery of Apollo in the Louvre, and entered into the Academy of Fine Arts, in 1870.*

Num. **2238**, *Louis XVI* (Pl. 31). He wears an ermine mantle, and collars and insignia appropriate to the scene of consecration. Only the French painters have known how to paint such opulent and resounding portraits: Son of the «Dauphin», grandson of Louis XV, he was born in 1754, crowned king in 1775 and guillotined during the French Revolution in 1793. Of the three that Callet painted, this one was given to the Count of Aranda, Ambassador in Paris, by the King himself ten years before his execution. (Acquired by Isabel II in the Duke of Hijar's will, and sent to the Museum in 1864.)

Room XXXIV.—FRENCH PAINTERS

When Lucca Giordano came to Spain in the 17th century, called for by Carlos II, the last of the House of Austria, the last and most brilliant star of the constellation, Claudio Coello, was unjustly neglected. The Bourbons gained the Spanish throne; and not finding painters to satisfy their needs, they called for their own. Thus a series of French artists of the royal families entered into Spain.

These last monarchs likewise acquired works of their countrymen, thanks to which our Museum is so rich in important works of the French schools.

Ranc, Jean. *French painter born in Montpellier in 1674 and who died in Madrid in 1735. Son of an almost unknown painter, Antoine, he studied under Rigaud, whose niece he married. Rigaud protected him greatly, entering him in the French Academy of Fine Arts and procuring that Felipe V name him «Painter of the Chamber». With this commission he arrived in Spain, making himself well-liked by the Monarch, who found his art reminiscent of that of Rigaud. By reason of Felipe V's trip to Portugal the student was taken along among his retinue, in order that he might paint the royal Portuguese family. His art does not have the solidity of his master's but still with fewer artistic facilities he knew how to paint a large number of royal portraits that speak well of him in an XVIII French Gallery.*

Num. **2333**, *Fernando VI* (child). Son of Felipe V and María Luisa of Savoy, he was born in 1713; became king of Spain in 1746 and died in 1759. He wears the Band of the Saint-Esprit. (Came from La Granja in 1848.)

Num. **2334**, *Carlos III* (child). This son of Felipe V and Isabel Farnesio, was born in 1716, was king of Spain in 1759 and died in

1788. He appears in his drawing room classifying some flowers. (It entered the Museum the same year that the previous portrait.)

Num. **2265,** *The Prince-Cardinal Don Luis Antonio of Bourbon.* He is in the picture, *The Family of Felipe V by* Van Loo. Here he appears as a child with a little black and white dog and wearing the emblem of Saint-Esprit Son of Felipe V and of Isabel Farnesio, he was born in Madrid in 1727. At eight he was named Archbishop of Toledo, at nine, Cardinal; and at twenty-seven he renounced all these titles saying that as of yet he had not been ordained a priest. He received the title of Count of Chinchón and contracted a morganatic marriage with Doña María Teresa Villabriga. He died in Arenas de San Pedro in 1785.

Num. **2266,** *María Teresa Antonia of Bourbon, Dauphine of France.* Oval as the previous. She also figures in *The Family of Felipe V* by Van Loo. Here she is dressed in blue with a pink mantle. Sister of the previous, she was born in Madrid in 1726, married at fifteen in Versailles the Dauphin Louis of France, son of Louis XV, and died in the same city upon reaching twenty years of age. This work was previously and incorrectly attributed to Michel Ange Houasse. (Was inventoried in the Retiro.)

Num. **2326** and **2329,** *Felipe V.* In the first, he appears on horseback with partial armature, followed by a page who carries his helmet. In the second, more than a bust-size. Son of the Great Dauphin (who in turn was the son of Louis XIV), he was born in Versailles in 1683. The first king of Spain of the House of Bourbon, he was crowned in 1700 and died in Madrid forty six years later.

Num. **2330,** *Queen Isabel Farnesio.* Wife of the previous, daughter of Eduardo, Duke of Parma, she was born in 1692, married Felipe V in 1714 and outlived her husband by twenty years. Very much interested in art, especially in Murillo and other Spanish artists of her period, she counted an extremely important collection which figures in our Museum.

Num. **2332,** *Luisa Isabel of Orleans, Queen of Spain.* Daughter of Felipe of Orleans, Regent of France, she was in fact Queen of Spain, since she married Prince Louis, later Louis I, whom she called «The king silhouette».

Num. **2336,** *María Ana Victoria of Bourbon.* Eldest daughter of Felipe V and Isabel Farnesio, she is the same portrayed by Largillière in num. 2277.

Van Loo, Louis Michel. *French painter born in Toulon in 1707 and died in Paris, 1771. After studying with his father, Jean Baptiste, he left for Rome in order to perfect his studies. Returning to Paris, he came to Spain in 1737 in order to substitute for Ranc, who had died two years before. He remained fifteen years in the Court as the leading painter,* *squandering his money lavishly; he ended up ill paid, and at times unpaid. In 1752 he returned to France never again to visit Spain.*

Num. **2283,** *The Family of Felipe V.* A canvas of colossal proportions in which appear from left to right, María Ana Victoria, Bárbara de Braganza, Prince Fernando, Felipe V, Infante-Cardinal Don Luis, Isabel Farnesio, Don Felipe, Duke of Parma, Luisa Isabel of France, María Teresa, María Antonia, Fernanda, María Amelia of Saxony and Carlos, King of Naples. On the floor María Luisa, daughter of the Duke of Parma and María Isabel, daughter of Carlos. It is supposed that they are listening to a concert (the only invisible tie uniting them in their pose for the portrait). This decorative, numerous and dazzling court substituted for a sick, poor and melancholly young man and a widowed queen who silently tugged at her nun-like headdress of mourning. Carreño and Van Loo: each one reflected a different epoch and art. They would not have understood each other. That which in the former is intimacy in the latter is occupation. At any rate, the French painter did this large superficial painting with much decoration and satisfied the tastes of a Court that asked for no greater show skill. (It was in the Retiro.)

Num. **2282,** *Prince Don Felipe of Bourbon, Duke of Parma.* Son of Felipe V, he married Luisa Isabel, daughter of Louis XV, King of France. He wears the sashes of the Saint-Esprit and of Saint Michel. (Entered in the Museum in 1847, proceeding from the Palace.)

Num. **2281,** *Luisa Isabel of Bourbon,* wife of the previous. Signed in Madrid, 1745.

Houasse, Michel Ange. *French painter, born in Paris in 1680 and died in Arpajon in 1730. Disciple of his father, René Antoine, called for by Felipe V, came to Spain where he remained for 13 years and through his father he was able to study with Le Brun.*

Num. **2387,** *Louis I.* Here is a beautiful portrait of this king who hardly counts in the historiography of the Spanish monarchs. Son of Felipe V and of María Luisa Gabriela of Savoy, he was born in 1707 reigning only seven months. In the portrait he appears at the age of ten. He is entirely covered by a silverish tone, with an almost vanishing head, the vestiges, laces and feathers are praises to his brushwork. It is one of the works that, due to its elegance, is closer to the English painters than to the tradition of the courtiers of Louis XIV. The attribution is owed to Don Elías Tormo, but the same René Antoine, disciple of Le Brun, the collaborator of Simon Vouet and Jouvenet, would have been astonished by this portrait of his son.

Num. **2269,** *View of the Monastery of El Escorial.* As a painting it is of little value, but it is interesting because this landscape gives us an idea of the surroundings of El Escorial at the beginning of the 18th century. The figure of the monk (Order of Saint Jerome) reading in the foreground to the left could not possibly be more unfortunate. (From Felipe V, in La Granja.)

Largillière, Nicholas. *French painter, born and died in Paris (1656-1746). Son of a hat making father he was sent to London in order to perfect his work; he returned to become a painter. After six years as apprentice in Paris he returned to London, earning the protection of Carlos II, who encharged him with his portrait and the decoration of Windsor Palace. Several disagreeances took place due to his religion, Catholic, which caused him to return to his native land, where Le Brun favoured him. Soon a path opened for him and he began to stand out in his feminine portraits which he endowed with an un-paralleled elegance, far superior to that of his contemporaries. His stay in London can be witnessed through his works. When Jacob II ascended to the English throne he was called for in order to portray the new king and his wife. These were to be his best works, and upon finishing them he retired. Once again in Paris as Director of the Academy, he died leaving a fortune. It has been stated that he painted more than 1500 portraits.*

Num. **2277,** *María Ana Victoria of Bourbon*. She was the eldest daugther of Felipe V and Isabel Farnesio, born in 1718. She was meant to be Louis XV's wife, since the marriage was concerted when the princess was three years old, but it was cancelled and in 1729 she married Don José Manuel of Braganza, Prince of Brazil and later king of Portugal with the name of Jose I. The same year his sister Doña Bárbara of Braganza married the Prince Don Fernando, later Fernando VI of Spain. It is a beautiful portrait of rich qualities as well in the mother-of-pearl dress as in the mantle with an ermine lining. Signed in 1724. (Proceeding from La Granja it entered the Museum in 1848.)

Room XXXV.—RIGAUD AND OTHER FRENCH PAINTERS

Mignard, Pierre. *A French painter born in Troyes in 1612 and died in Paris in 1693. After having been Simón Vouet's disciple he went to Rome and remained there more than twenty years. Apart from the decoration of some palaces, he did the portraits of the Popes Urban VIII and Innocent X. His fame having reached París, Mazarin commissioned him to do a portrait of Louis XIV, which he finished in three hours. After this success he was called to Spain to portray the Infanta María Teresa —Felipe IV's daughter— who was to marry the King of France. The mission completed, he tried to gain the protection*

*of Louis XIV, in fact he managed to replace Le Brun in the palace
approximately in 1690. He received an immediate naming as Rector
of the Academy of Fine Arts. After working during seventy three years
he died rich and covered with honors.*

Num. **2288,** *Philippe of Orleans, Regent of France.* Portrayed as
a child, dressed in half Roman armature. Son of Philippe of Orleans,
grandson of Louis XIII and father-in-law of Louis I of Spain, he
was portrayed in 1687.

Num. **2291,** *Maria Teresa of Austria.* She is the daughter of our
Felipe IV, wife of Louis XIV. She takes her son, the «Great Dauphin»,
by the hand. The drying up of both figures and the richness of the
dresses and embroideries is surprising. But one notes that both mother
and son are disguised, the Queen carrying a mask in her right hand.

Num. **2369,** *Philippe of France, Duke of Orleans.* Second son of
Louis XIII and brother of Louis XIV.

Num. **2400,** *Henriette of England.* Daughter of Charles I of England —executed by order of Cromwell— and of Henriette Maria of
France, wife of the Duke of Orleans. (From the Retiro.)

Poussin, Nicholas. *French painter, born in Les Andelys (Nor-
mandy), in 1594, he died in Rome in 1665. As a youth he fled to Paris
and later to Rome, where finally in 1624 he managed to enter into the
workshop of Domenichino, who caused him to grow fond of the beauties of
the classic antiquity. He lived poorly until Cardinal Barberini's protection, enabled him to marry a wealthy young lady, Anne Dughet, and from
then on de had access to the palaces where fortune at last smiled upon
him. Louis XIII called him to Paris in 1640 encharging him with important works and naming him «his painter». This caused him to be
hated by his rivals who had remained in Rome. He left for the Eternal
City never to return.*

*Poussin wanted to be the restorer of the classic beauty, and in part
he was. He became enraptured before the ancient marbles, the friezes and
the temples; he also praised the outdoor life with its young shepherds,
and wise old men seated beside the ancient ruins. He resuscitated the
mythological themes, quite forgotten after the great Venetians, etc.; but
in general, more than an «innovator» he was the «resumer» of a past
art. A magnificent sketcher, his colors did not quite achieve the same
perfection; his tones are somewhat repetitious and monotonous. However,
his name is unquestionable in French art.*

Num. **2320,** *The Hunt of Meleager.* The theme is already known
by us, if it is that of the title and not *The Triumph of Aeneas*, as other
suppose. Two horses advance in solemn march, two others rise on
their hind feet, a dog watches the curvet, some figures stand, others
walk, others contemplate... It lacks unity of composition. (It proceeds
from the Retiro.)

Watteau, Antoine. *A French painter, born in Valenciennes, in 1684 and died in Nogent-sur-Marne in 1721, he was the son of an artist slate-cutter.*

He did not wish to follow in his father's footsteps and fled to Paris where he lived in the strictest penury. Since he was not satisfied with several occupations proportioned to him, he preferred rather to spend his hours in the garden of Luxembourg and in the Bois de Boulogne, studying the foliage and the effects of the light. When he became known he was well esteemed but negligent and disinterested, almost with a hatred for money, he continued to live poorly, When finally his efforts were crowned with success, instead of enjoying it he escaped to London, where the climate combined with his deprivations caused tuberculosis which soon carried him to his grave. He returned to Paris, left for Nogent in search of a better climate and died at thirty seven in the arms of his friend Gersaint.

Watteau does not have predecessors in French art; such superiors would have to be in Flanders, and certainly in Rubens; in a luminous Rubens seen through a minifying-glass. His pictures, generally of small size, are charming and even when the scenes obviously desire to be amusing, they all breathe, nevertheless, a certain melancholly, as is the case in the Harlequin, *the* Gilles, The Indifferent One.

Num. **2353,** *Capitulations of Country Wedding and Dances.* Thus the canvases of Watteau are usually gilded reflections between foliages of blue and dark green, and with little figures, as in this case, that have along with the grace of the Flemish, the elegant robustness of the tops of Versailles. In these activities of the wedding, beneath the artificial light, the marriage takes place (Note the notary, pen in hand), while the guests dance to the airs of the violin. It is a scene highly poetic, aristocratic and popular at the same time, without clumsiness debilitating the beauty of the moment.

Num. **2354,** *Party in Park.* Once again a shady place, with a play upon lighting effects and suave darkness in which children and couples in love amuse themselves; with statues and fountains beneath the leafy trees. Courtly parties, more likely imagined than witnessed by the painter, but full of poetry and even of mystery. Watteau was one of the most elegant artists of his century, and possessing a most excellent taste. It is not the same as in the case of Claude Lorraine, who miniaturized as a last resort. Watteau's figures could be giants without decline of their exactitude nor of the pattern of their sketch. Observe any one of the five groups of persons who constitute the animation of this park and you will see that any one of them could be amplified successfully. Apart from the «minuettos of Watteau» and cognizant of the pure plastic values of his painting in the Prado (unfortunate ill-conserved), this painter of Valenciennes ought to be reputed as one of the great figures of the French 18th century, and of those who have most contributed to give French painting the tone distinction (not always merited) famous in Europe.

Rigaud Hyacinthe. *Was born in Perpignan in 1650, son of Spanish parents, and named Jacinto Rigau, or Rigó, and Sors; but he frenchified his name and signed his surname as «Hyacinthe Rigaud». He went to Paris at twenty-two carrying with him very little money; but definitely possessing the fire, impetuosity and the passion of conquest inherent in a meridional. To the personal spirit of enterprise which characterized him, he united the soul of an artist of first quality. If he had not been such he would not have triumphed so greatly, nor would his life have been a collar of successes without parallel. It is sufficient to know that at one time in his life five kings sought his work simultaneously.*

Rigaud has been one of the most brilliant personages in art. He had an extraordinary ability for empty grandeur, the olympic afectation and the sonorous eloquence of color. He was undoubtedly an artist. But his impulsive faculties were lucky in arriving during the times of a Court radiant und swollen, plethoric in vanity, ability and self-confidence. Rigaud fits into the picture very well. But his brushstrokes recall that greatness far better than history.

Num. **2343,** *Louis XIV* full length, standing with armature and band of the Saint-Spirit. It is a beautiful portrait that defines the style of the artist. Everything in it is solid and tight, rich in sketch and qualities. The head appears outlined. The landscape with a battle-field for background was painted by Parrocel. (Property of Felipe V, in La Granja.)

Num. **2391,** *Louis XIV,* in a round canvas, is the copy commissioned by the King to be sent to Spain. (It proceeds from the Palace of La Granja.)

Num. **2597,** *Louis XIV, old man.* It is a bust, copy of a portrait probably painted by heart. (Willed by the Duke of Arcos in 1935.)

Num. **2294,** *A Prince,* bust steel armature, red suit and white mantle. In other times it was attributed to ther painter Nattier, but the attribution has been disproved.

Num. **2390,** *Louis of France* «The Great Dauphin». Son of Louis XIV and of the Princess Maria Teresa, daughter of our Felipe IV; they had contracted marriage in San Sebastián in 1660. The same Louis of France was the father of Felipe V, who, because of heritage received the «Treasure of the Dauphin» that is exhibited in Room LXXIII of this Museum. It is a copy in which the portrayed wears the Band of the Saint-Spirit.

Num. **2337,** *Felipe V.* Son of the Great Dauphin and grandson of Louis XIV, born in Versailles in 1683. He was proclaimed king

of Spain in November 24, 1700. Since this portrait was signed in
Paris in 1701, it would seem that before leaving for Spain he wanted
to be portrayed in the Spanish manner with black dress and gorget.
He wears the Toison and the emblem of Saint-Spirit. (From the
collection of his wife, Isabel Farnesio, proceeds from La Granja and
entered the Museum in 1848.)

Room XXXVI.—FRENCH PAINTERS

Poussin. Num. **2312**, *Bacchanals*. Num. **2318**, *Bacchic Scene*.
Here Poussin boasts with nudes, gods, satyrs, and although the waste
of figures is manifest, it has no comparison with similar themes by
Tiziano or Rubens. On the other hand, the painting has blackened
and results in confusion. However, some *Landscapes* with their classical buildings and distant blues are charming.

Num. **2313**, *The Parnassus*. (Pl. 32). It is, along with *Shepherds of
Arcadia*, one of the culminating works of the painter. Homer, crowned
by Calliope, kneels before the god Apollo. A few cupids in the foreground offer the elixir of life to those crowned with laurel. The
Graces and the Muses present a beautiful entirety beneath the trees
where other little cupids weave crowns. In the center of the composition Castalia, completely disrobed, is floating upon the fountain
(Bought by Felipe V, proceeding from Aranjuez.)

Num. **2307**, *Landscape*. We see an Arcadian scene with a youth
and an elderly man together beside a classical temple, very typical
of the author. Num. **2315**, *Battle of Gladiators*. The painter returns
to historical reconstructions with many naked figures. The canvas
is ill-preserved, and the monotony of color is obvious. Num. **2322**,
Landscape Polyphemus and Galatea. If these mythological scenes
present a certain Baroque sumptuousness they appear cold and tas-
teless. Num. **2319**, *Landscape with a Sleeping Diana* by a disciple of
Poussin.

Claude Lorrain. *Born Claude Gelée in Champaigne (Lorraine),
in 1600, he died in Rome eigty-two years later. His first position was
that of a pastry cook. He left for Rome as servant to a painter, at whose
side he began his studies of art. Returning to his fatherland, he once
again departed for the Eternal City, where he perfected himself, more
so in color than in sketch, and thus managed to attract the attention of
Pope Urban VIII, who encharged him with several works. His fame
increased but was embittered by a cripple, whom he protected and who
denounced the painter maintaining that the pictures which the master
signed and charged for, were in reality his work (the cripple's) and thus*

*demanded a large sum. Lorrain, in order to avoid the annoyances of
the courts, handed over the demanded amount. In spite of this, however,
he remained wealthy and upon dying, left both a large financial and
artistic heritage.*

Numbers **2254, 2255, 2257** and **2259,** *Landscapes.* Claude
Lorrain always failed in figures, but dominates well landscapes. Such
landscapes usually had for *leit motive* river and canal banks with architectural palaces at their margins. He liked to put twilights upon the
distant confines of the waters, in order to decrease the shades from
the foreground to background and stumping the outlines so as to
submerge them in the final atmosphere. Thus he obtained very beautiful effects; but upon viewing just a few of his works one notes his
«manner», the impossibility of acquiring notable landscapes out of
the same means.

He recognized his sketches as inexpert and never dared to deal
with the human figure other than miniaturized, and flattened by
the immensity of its location.

But even so his human figures cannot resist a detailed analysis,
as one observes in num. **2254,** *Embarkment in Ostia of Saint Paola
Romana;* in num. **2255,** *Landscape with Toby and the Archangel Raphael* num. **2257,** *The Ford,* and num. **2259,** *The Penitent Magdalene.*
All those are landscapes in which the figures are the least important.

Vouet, Simon, *was a French painter born in Paris in 1590 and
died in the same town in 1649. He painted in London and later in Constantinople where he portrayed Hamet I. He remained several years in
Italy and worked in Venice, Genoa and Rome assimilating in such a
manner the Italian style that some of his canvases have caused some
confusion. He painted in St. Peter's and left a beautiful portrait of Pope
Urban VIII. Upon his return to Paris María Medici protected him
and he was commissioned to paint the portrait of her son Louis XIII,
becoming the latter's professor and a good friend of Richelieu. Brilliant
disciples succeded him as Le Brun, Mignard, Le Sueur, etc.*

Num. **539,** *The Virgin and the Child, with St. Elizabeth, St. John
and St. Cecilia* is a canvas admirably composed, which was believed
to be of the Bolognese school, until H. Voos accredited it to the genuine works of Simon Vouet. It was thought that it should have been
painted in Rome.

Philippe of Champaigne, *a French painter, was born in Brusels,
1602, and died in Paris in 1674.*

Num. **2240,** *Portrait of Louis XIII,* by Philippe de Champaigne.
He was the son of Enrique IV el Bearnés and of María de Médicis,
born in 1601 in Fontainebleau; he married Ana de Austria in Bordeaux
in 1615, daughter of Felipe III of Spain.

Num. **2365,** *(No title),* of the French School. A painting with a strange theme, in which Christ with the cross on his shoulders, is followed by a half naked young girl, also loaded with another cross, both of them moving with difficulty over ground which is scattared with crosses.

No number): *Wordly pleasures.* An allegorical painting, very fresh with color. Two youths abusing the Time, who appears thrown away with the scythe and the sand clock.

Num. **2317,** *Saint Cecilia,* by **Poussin.**

Room XXXVII.—ITALIAN PAINTING OF THE 17th

Castiglione, Benedetto, *painter and engraver. He was born in Genoa in 1616, and died in Mantua, 1670. Painter of the Chamber of Carlo I, Duke of Mantua. He was a great landscapist and aquafortist, and he left more than seventy engraved metal plates. His greatest work is the Crucifixion of the Palazzo Bianco in Genoa.*

Of his six works figuring in the Museum, only num. **86,** *Jacob's Journey* and num. **88,** *Diogenes* (which is signed) are considered authentic. The more characteristic work of Castiglione is the former. In summarizing we might say that his compositions were less outstanding. (Both proceed from Aranjuez.)

Furini, Francesco. *Born in Florence about 1600 he died there in 1646. After finishing his apprenticeship with Roselli he left for Rome where his nude figures soon caused him to become famous.*

A good friend of Giovanni de Saint Giovanni, he left Florence in order to finish some works that the latter had left unterminated. He returned to Rome where he led a dissipated and licentious life before he finally repented. He became a Priest and lived in the parish of Santo Sano in Mugello; no longer painting nudes, he dedicated himself entirely to religious themes.

Num. **144,** *Loth and His Daughters.* They are shown attempting to enebriate their father. It is one of the best works of this painter, although one notes that the background appears to be re-painted. But the two nude figures are marvellous, richly illuminated in the subtle flesh tones and delicately wrought forms. It is said that this work was painted for the Emperor, Ferdinando II. It was also among those sent to the Academy, entering the Museum in 1827.

Caravaggio, Michelangelo Amerighi. *Born in Caravaggio (Bergamo) between 1560-65, died in Porte Ercole in 1609.*

Num. **65,** *David, winner of Goliath.* With strong light and shade contrasts, as it is peculiar of this great painter. David's head lies in the shadow and his body is strongly illuminated. Following Berenson and H. Voos this picture does not belong to Caravaggio but to a disciple.

Guercino, *by name Francesco Barbieri. He was born in Cento in 1591 and died in Bologna in 1665. From a family of artists his master is unknown, although he is not too distant from the influence of Caravaggio and also of the Caracci, at least during his stay in Bologna. He stayed in Venice where he worked with Gioccoppo Palma and later was called to Rome by Pope Gregory XV, where he decorated the «loggia» of the Benediction. He received the title of Knight from the hands of the Duke of Mantua. One of his most original works is* The Dawn, *from the Casino of the Villa of Ludovisi (Rome), with an architectural perspective courageous as not other.*

Num. **201,** *Susana and the Old Men.* Susana has emerged from her bath and is drying herself; to the left the two libidinous judges, Arquian and Sedequia, waylay her. It is a very beautiful picture, one of the best by this artist, of brilliant coloring and marvellous execution, especially in the forms of Susana and the tremendous expression of the two old men. One notes the influence of Caravaggio in the contrasts of light and darks. (It was in El Escorial.)

Maratta, Carlo. *An Italian painter, born in Camurano in 1625 and who died in Rome in 1713. Still young he was taken to Rome where he entered in Sacchi's workshop. He painted many Virgins, so many in fact that his rivals called him insultingly «Carluccio delle Madonne». considering him unable of greater works. But he surprised them all with his work, suggested by Sacchi, entitled* The Destruction of the Idols by Constantine. *Thanks to it he obtained the protection of Popes Alexander VII and Clement XI, the latter even named him Knight of the Order of Christ. He possessed numerous works of art.*

Num. **327,** *The Painter Andrea Sacchi.* This is the bust-sized portrait of his master showing him when he was sixty years old. In Room XCII the portrait he did for Pope Clement XI is hung. (It was in the Granja, belonging to the Collection of Felipe V, acquired in the public auction of Maratta.)

Gagliardi, Filippo. *An architect and painter, he worked in Rome about 1640 and died in 1659.*

Num. **145,** *Interior of Saint Peter's in Rome.* An ample canvas with the interior of Saint Peter's of the Vatican shown from one of the naves and exposing the canopy of Bernini. The perspective is excellent, and obviously by an architect-painter. It gives a precise idea of the interior of the Basilic at the middle of the 17th century. It is signed on the base of a pillar to the right. (Proceeds from the Retiro.)

Sacchi, Andrea. *An Italian painter born in Nettuno about 1599 and died in Rome in 1661.*

Num. **326,** *Painter Francesco Albani.*

Guido Reni. *Born in Calvezzano (Bologna) in 1575, he died in 1642. Son of a musician father he flourished in Bologna when this city was one of adventurers, of games and of crime. During the legation of Cardinal Vidoni fifty five homicides were commited in one night. The episode of the extremely beautiful Beatrice Cenci —portrayed by Reni— put to death in 1599, reveals the contemporary environment. Guido, who was notably good-looking, elegant and genteel was the victim to gambling which persecuted him to the end of his days. He studied under the mastership of Calvaers, a Flemish-Italian, and later entered the Academy of the Carracci. He went to Rome and through the commission of Cardinal Borghese painted the* Martyrdom of Saint Peter. *He was accused of plagiarising Caravaggio and the case was submitted to the decision of Annibale Carracci. The later accused him of being a traitor to the art of Bologna unjustly (at least in reference to plagiarism which he did not commit). Il Caravaggio was rude and Guido, in contrast did a work suave, soft, sweet and triumphant in feminine figures. He died engulfed in debts, but without wishing to separate himself from a collection of one hundred original sketches of Rafael, acquired in his adventures, and which fell into the hands of his servant Marchino, who was a true and loyal friend. Signorini, the heir of the master, sold out all the heritages of Guido and payed the creditors until the last cent.*

Num. **210,** *The Virgin of the Chair.* Of course one cannot compare her with the Virgin of Rafaello: but this one also has a sweet feminine charm that is overcoming. One notes in this canvas the influence of the ecclesiastical art of the Carracci. This was one of the pictures which Joseph Bonaparte carried to France. (It entered the Prado collection in 1837.)

Room XXXVIII.—VARIOUS ITALIAN PAINTERS (17th CENTURY)

Guido Reni. Num. **211,** *Saint Sebastian.* Almost a full-length portrait, he is shown fastened to a tree with an arrow piercing his chest. All his representations of this saint resemble each other. Palazzo Rosso in Genoa; Museo Capitolino in Rome, etc.) and can be reduced to a young man with a woman's head with Hercules-like forms in great dissonance.

Num. **216,** *Saint Mary Magdalene,* and num. **208,** *Lucrece killing herself,* both by **Guido Reni.** The two paintings were Isabel Farnesio's and were in La Granja.

Num. **91,** *Circus elephants,* a large painting by **J. Castiglione.** An anticipator of modern circus scenes.

Crespi, Daniel *(1590-1630). He was disciple of Giovanni Battista, and very much influenced by Michelangelo.*

Num. **128,** *Piety* (Pl. 33), and num. **129,** *The Scourging.*

Spada, Lionello. *Born in Bolonia, 1576 and died in Rome, 1622.*

Num. **353,** *Saint Cecilia.* A very delightful picture. Saint Cecilia plays the organ; at the back, an angel and on the table, a lute. At one time, this work was attributed to Domenichino.

Albani, Francesco, *an Italian painter, born and died in Bologna (1578-1660). Disciple of Calvaert, a Flemish painter established in Bologna about 1570, and friend of Guido Reni, he left with the latter for Rome, where he decorated some patrician mansions. When his friend died, he changed his themes, dedicating himself this time to mythological ones. Later his workshop became a mercantile center; he signed and charged for the pictures done by assistants and students, and therefore it is very difficult to discriminate among the abundance of his work which are actually his. He is one of the clearly manneristic painters.*

Num. **1,** *Dressing-table of Venus.* Num. **2,** *The Judgement of Paris.* In both themes one notes, through Calvaert, the distant influence of Rubens. Both canvases belong to the second epoch of the painter. (They were sent to the Academy, and were saved from the fire. They entered the Museum in 1827.)

Il Domenichino. *His true name was Domenico Zampieri, and he was born in Bologna in 1581 and died in Naples in 1641. He received the names of «Domenichino» due to his small stature. The son of a poor minstrel, he entered the Academy of the Progressives, of the Carraccis but also dominated by Caravaggio, he found himself between these two opposing tendencies, who were even personal rivals. Persecuted by Corencio he fled to Naples leaving his wife and children abandoned in Rome with many unfinished works. Corencio put the fugitive's family in prison, and they spent many horrible hours. Seeing that since he was a timid man he did not dare face the situation. Protected as a result of the supplications, he was allowed to finis his work. He returned to Naples and according to some he was poisoned to death. He is one of the obvious exponents of the 17th century baroque.*

Num. **131,** *The Sacrifice of Abraham.* The Angel detains Abraham's arm; Isaac is upon the faggot of fire-wood.

Malombra, Pietro. *Born in Venice, 1536, and died in the same place, 1618.*

Num. **245,** *The saloon of the Venice School.* It probably refers to the reception of the Spanish Ambassador, Don Alfonso de la Cueva. He is seated at the right of Duke Leonardo Donato. Felipe V had this picture in La Granja in 1746.

Room XXXIX.—TIEPOLO, VICENTE LOPEZ AND PARET

This room shelters **Juan Bautista Tiepolo's** paintings and the best works of **Vicente López,** who is also the painter who decorated the wide allegory covering the ceiling. It was painted in 1818 for the root of the little Palace «Casino de la Reina» given to Isabel of Braganza, Fernando VII's second wife, by the city of Madrid. In this Room we can also find two canvases of **Paret.**

Battoni, P. *This Italian painter was born in Lucca in 1708 and died in Rome in 1787. He abandoned his father's jewelry workshop and went to Rome becoming a disciple of Conca. Many ecclesiastical dignities protected him. Due to his friendship with Mengs and the influence of Rafaello, Tiziano and Correggio, his works lacked originality. However, he was the most appreciated painter of his time. His* Magdalene *of Dresden is very well. known, and shows his sweet and mellow style.*

Num. **49,** *A Gentleman in Rome* is a dandy in a very studied attitude, with a plan of Rome. In the background, and on each side of the figure, we see St. Angelo Castle and St. Peter's. In this portrait we observe Meng's influence. (In 1814 the picture hanged in Don Carlos room in the Royal Palace.)

Gian-Battista Tiepolo, *was born in Venice in 1696, when the Venetian school had already said the last word; nevertheless it would breath until Tiepolo's last blow. His immediate masters were Lazzarini and the Piazetta, but was mainly inspired by Paolo Veronese. He had a warm imagination and was happy when he had to paint huge allegories. In Italy he decorated many palaces until Carlos III sent for him and was commissioned to work in the Royal Palace. Anthony Mengs was already one year in Madrid, called by the same Monarch, when Tiepolo arrived in 1762.*

Both represented two different conceptions of art. The imagination of the Italian was decorative and Rococo giving the precise liberty to his brush strokes for the creation of sumptuous and pleasant forms; the Bohemian was inclined to the polished classicism, somewhat like an ancient beauty's plaster mask. Soon after Madrid was divided in two groups the «Tiepolists» and the «Mengsists». With the Italian, Tiepolo, were the sentimentalists while the intellectualists were with Mengs, but honoring the truth, there was neither conqueror nor conquered. However Mengs received the best praises. We know of the first The Triumph of the Monarchy; *and of Mengs* Trajano's Apotheosis. *Tiepolo married*

*the sister of the Venetian painter Guardi, and they had nine children
whose two elder Domenico and Lorenzo, were his assistants. He died in
Madrid in 1770.*

Num. **363,** *The Conception.* In the upper zone is the dove representing the Holy Ghost, underneath and standing upon the world
is the Virgin smashing the serpent with her feet and surrounded by
angels and cherubs. The grave face seems to contemplate the space.
The figure is less than modest: it is arrogant. (The Spanish version
displays more humility.) However, it is a magnificent pictorial piece.
Tiepolo has been able enough to dominate color with accord of a
very sweet serenity. His palette although being dull and apparently,
limited is very rich in subtle tones. It seems a vaporized painting but
at the same time its coloring is difficult to obtain. It was painted
for an altar-piece of the Church of St. Pascual in Aranjuez. (In 1828
figured in the Museum's catalogue.

Num. **364,** *An Angel bearing the Eucharist.* The angel carries the
reliquary with the Holy Wafer in his hands followed by little cherubs.
The background is a temple. Tiepolo who knew Venetians very well,
and whose style he did not want to repeat, wanted to resolve the
outdoor's and light's problem in different ways to those followed by
Giorgione and Veronese. However he was aware of his insufficient
means and searched to accentuate his personality in technical details:
the pleats of the fabrics, the subtleness of the colors, the lighted half
tone, the conjunction of a golden symphony (Giorgione) with a silvered one (Veronese). These were his problems successfully resolved in
his canvas, which is only a part belonging to the altar- piece of the aforesaid church in Aranjuez. Soon after its placement it was violently
outdrawn to be substituted by a work of Mengs.

Num. **364,** a): *San Pascual Baylon,* is the previous picture's lower
part. (Errazu's legacy.)

Num. **365,** *The Olympus,* is a sketch for a ceiling representing Jupiter, Juno, Diana, Mercury, Venus, Minerva and Saturn.

Num. **365,** b): *St. Francis of Assissi.* Due to its proportions this
picture harmonizes with the *Conception* whose coloring we have
already studied. The Catalogue of 1949 says about this canvas: «It
was painted for the Epistle collateral side of the altar-piece in the
Church of San Pascual of Aranjuez, before August 29, 1769.» (Let
us remember that Tiepolo died six months later, few years after it
was outdrawn.) In 1914 it was discovered, broken and crumpled
by D. J. Garnelo, the Museum's Subdirector; F. Amutio restored it
and the portion between the lower part of the angel's right wing
and the inferior side is definitely new.

Num. **633,** *An Angel with a White Lilies Crown,* was painted for
the same altar-piece as the two previous. (It belonged to Eugenio

Lucas, and in 1933 was acquired by Dr. Frey, the Parisian collector, by means of the Count of Cartagena's legacy.)

Num. **2464,** *Abraham and the Three Angels.* This canvas presents a composition somewhat theatrical, and seems more a vision of the sleeping patriarch than a real happening. The coloring is beautiful, always in the subtle tones which characterizes the painter. (Given in 1924 by Mr. and Mrs. Sainz.

Paret, Luis. *Was born in Madrid in 1746, and died in item in 1799. He became pupil of the Academy of San Fernando and disciple of González Velázquez. Through the French painter Charles de la Traverse, who came to Spain, he knew Watteau; and Paret without imitating the colors of the latter, was interested in these themes to the extreme that someone has called our painter* the Spanish Watteau. *The parties are gallant with gardens and stores of silks, always according to the Spanish taste, because Paret, never renounced his* «madrileñismo». *Nevertheless, his insatiable curiosity induced him to paint the most various subjects, especially popular ones, pilgrimages, bullfights, etc. He travelled a great deal. Carlos III held him in great esteem, because he was satisfied with the court's themes painted by Paret under his commission. Thus he painted among others,* Fernando VII's Oath as Prince of Asturias, The Royal Couples, *etc. Mengs was also his protector.*

Num. **2422,** *Carlos III, Eating before His Court* is a picture of reduced size for the large scene represented and in which there is also a great free space. The room is magnificently adorned; in a corner at the table, we see Carlos III alone, a kneeling page offers him a plate, some courtiers are talking beside the walls, and among them and near the table are the king's mastiffs. The canvas reflects historical intimacy, with the contrast of light and shade, and the «performance» is beautifully treated. In imitation of the *Greco* he humoristically signed it in Greek characters: «Luis Paret, his father's and mother's son, did it.» (Proceeding from the Palace of Gatchina, in Russia, was acquired in 1933 with the Count of Cartagena's legacy.)

Num. **2875,** *The Masquerade Ball* which takes place in the Prince's Theatre, in Madrid. Even more reduced than the previous it represents numerous masked scenes full of life and color. One cannot ask more charm of composition, grace and light. (This picture was unknown until 1944, and was acquired with the same legacy as the previous.)

Procaccini, Andrea. *This Italian painter, born in Rome in 1671, came into Spain, requested by Felipe V in 1720 who entitled him «court's painter». He died in La Granja in 1734.*

Num. **2882,** *The Cardinal Borja* was named D. Carlos de Borja Centellas Ponce de León. the ninth Duke of Gandía born in 1663, and promoted Cardinal in 1720.

Vicente López, *was born in Valencia in 1772 and died in Madrid in 1850. In his province he was a disciple of P. Villanueva and of the Academy of San Carlos and in Madrid follower of Maella. When he arrived in Madrid he was already famous and Fernando VII soon sought him for «royal painter». Later López was the teacher of María Isabel de Braganza and Josefa Amalia of Saxony. He painted portraits of the royal family, and of the most important figures, including Goya in 1827. He truly merited his directorship of the Academy of San Fernando. Kind and humble Vicente López, was well esteemed during Goya's life and even more so upon the latter's death. Mengs had a notable influence upon him. He was not a genius but an expert sketcher and very scrupulous painter who meticulously reproduced the natural.*

Instead of continuing with the rest of his overly polished and sickeningly sweet portraits let us turn now to num. **870,** *Queen Doña María Cristina de Borbón,* showing Fernando VII's fourth wife. It is a portrait of the Court and for the Court, in which we see even minute details. The fantasies and feathers of the hat, the pendent jewel, the silks and laces of the dress, have all been obtained by brush point, without being obvious. As most of his portraits it is a finished face of a simpleton expressing little else because he never reached the interior of his subjects. He was-satisfied with the superficial, and those whom he painted required little else. María Cristina was the daughter of Francisco I of the two Sicilies and of María Isabel de Borbón (daughter of Carlos IV and therefore, niece of Fernando VII, whom she married in 1829). She was born in 1806 and died in Le Havre in 1878. (This portrait was brought from the Palace in 1847.)

Num. **865,** *The Queen Doña María Cristina of Bourbon, Fernando VII's Wife.* It is another portrait of this queen in which the painter has worked with the patience of a friar in the embroidery, laces, jewels and plumes, and one must recognize its faithfulness. Everything is in its place. All this minuteness was demanded to the portrayer being his main quality. A lady dressed for the portrait for the first time, would no more wear the dress. Vicente López was held in great esteem by the royalty, precisely because his bestowing character and his ability for the details proportioned him frequent success. The plastered face of the queen appears more like a «biscuit». It should have been painted on occasion of her wedding at the end of 1829, when the princess was about twenty four.

Num. **864,** *The Painter Francisco Goya* (Pl. 34). We can say that in this portrait Vicente López has surpassed his own measure. It is the most beautiful portrait he ever painted and one of the best Spanish portraits of this Museum. Upon a short trip of Goya to Spain, at the. middle of 1826, Fernando VII commissioned López to do the portrait The painter of the «Majas» accepted reluctantly, because he did not appreciate the future artist, and only did it to content the king. López began his work and not without worry. In a few sittings he succeeded in sketching the head completly. When Goya saw it he liked the sketch and recommended the painter to leave it unfinished and in reward he offered to show López a new and skilfull manoeuvre in the bullfighting. But the fact is that the portrayed did not consent the portrayer to polish any more the head, and returned to Bordeaux, leaving the picture unfinished. López nevertheless terminated it without the model, and left this work of so rich modelling and irreproachable carnation. It is said that one can guess his deafness through his gloomy gesture, but anyway undoubtedly the portrait is as beautiful in the handling as in its interior life. Goya did not see it finished. The signature reads: «López to his friend Goya.»

Num. **2901,** *Don Antonio Ugarte and his Wife Doña María Antonia Larrazabal.* He was from Navarra, Fernando VII's minister and ambassador in Torino. (Doña Margarita Calvache y Aréchaga doned it in 1946, in her mother's memory.)

Room XL.—EARLY FLEMISH

> *Coming back to the ingoing rotunda (Room I), take the door to the right and then turn to the right in order to arrive in room XL.*

This room and those immediately following are devoted to early Flemish works, with which our museum is very richly endowed. Many of these works formed part of the royal collections since the period of the Catholic Kings. Due to the relationship through marriage of their sons with members of the House of Austria and to the fact that a sister of the Emperor and a daughter of Felipe II were rulers of the Low Countries, many tablets from the Flemish school were acquired.

Hubert and **Jan van Eyck** (Schools of). Num. **1511,** *The Fount of Grace or Triumph of the Church Over the Synagogue.* Some believe this tablet to be a copy of a lost original; but in any case it would have to be a copy by one of Van Eyck's best followers. The general color is subtle, as it still lacks the *velaturas* of oil that would intensify it to the point of giving it an enamel-like quality. The work is frankly Van Eyckian and the scene is depicted in three areas, in the superior Gothic architecture predominates treated with miniature-like beauty. Three figures appear in it; the Virgin, in the form that the Ghent

Brothers created and has served as a model until Jan Massys's last years; Christ, Who in Ghent's Polyptich is believed to be «God the Father» and Saint John, the Young Evangelist writing the Apocalypse. At the feet of Our Lord we see the *Mystic Lamb*. Below is the Fount ot Grece upon which the Holy Communion wafers are floating.

In the central part angels are playing their instruments upon a green lawn adorned by little flowers while angels singing in the tribunes repeat the verse «fons ortorum» (Hymn of Hymns). Finally in the lower part the Church of Crist is opposed by the Synagogue which is repelled —some with their eyes covered— the Christian version of the Eucharist indicated by virtue of the Pope's forefinger. The Pope is seen kneeling before the Christian gentlemen. Previously this tablet belonged to the Monastery of Parral (Segovia).

Master of Flemalle ·or **Robert Campin.** *There has been so much investigation and criticism that both names are quite unidentifiable.*

Num. **1513,** *St. John the Baptist with Master Henry of Werl,* little door of a triptych that goes with the following. Observe the valuable detail in the folds and gatherings of St. John's red mantel as in the massive habit of the persons praying, and the realism of the hemispherical mirror that reflects a part of the room with other miniature-sized figures.

Num. **1514,** *Saint Barbara.* This reminds us of previous pictures supposedly by Van der Weyden. Everything in this work is delicate and lively. The open door permits one to see a tower, the Saint's emblem. The little flower vase, the pious statue with its candle, the iron work, the hails in the beams of the ceiling —nothing is lacking in the sweet intimacy of this piece, in which the Saint is attentively reading an old prayer book while her fingers are poised in the air ready to turn the page. (Both tablets were acquired by Carlos IV and brought from Aranjuez in 1827.)

Num. **1887,** *The Betrothal of the Virgin.* This tablet has been attributed to Van der Weyden. Inside the temple are the pretenders for Mary's hand. The marriage ceremony of St. Joseph is in the Gothic hall. (Entered in El Escorial in 1584, and in this museum in 1839).

Num. **1915,** *The Annunciation.* An Angel observes Mary from the threshold while she reads oblivious of God's forthcoming message. The scene is a Gothic interior.

Thierry Bouts. *He was born in Haarlem (Holland) about 1420 and died in 1475.*

Num. **1461,** *The Annunciation; The Visitation. The Adoration of the Angels and the Magi.* A triptych with four scenes. These are beautiful works of composition and color. The triptych was previously attributed to Petrus Christus, but now it is generally believed to be an early work of T. Bouts.

J. Gossaert or **Mabuse.** *Born in Maubege about 1478 it is believed that he died in Middlebourg between 1533-1536.*

Num. **1510,** *Christ with the Virgin Mary and John the Baptist.* The figures are painted upon paper which is fastened to a tablet. This picture has also been attributed in many different ways, which is logical when one realizes that the early Flemish did not sign their works. They dealt with the same art models and also repeated identical themes and copied from each other. These three figures are amplified copies of the smaller ones that figure in the superior zone of the *The Mystic Lamb Polyptych* in the church of St. Bavon in Ghent, which is the work of the Van Eycks, Hubert and Jan. (It was brought from El Escorial.)

The Master of Divine Blood. *Thus he was called because of the Chapel of Divine Blood, in Brussels. He is believed to be a follower of the Q. Metsys's school.*

Num. **1559,** *Ecce Homo.* (Triptych acquired in Valencia for Fernando VII in 1829.)

The Master of Hoogstraten. *An anonymous disciple of Q. Metsys.*

Num. **1617,** *Saint Francis,* is a free copy of an original by the Van Eyck brothers.

Alimbrot, L. A. *Painter from Brussels, who was in Valencia about 1439, and died in 1460.*

Num. **2538,** *Scenes from Christ's Life.* A triptych conserving the original frame. C. H. R. Post suggests that it is a work of Alimbrot.

Ysenbrandt, A. de. *Very little is known of this artist other than he was a disciple of G. David. He established himself in Brussels in 1510 and died in 1551. Although he painted for Spaniards in Flanders and for Spain, his main works hang in the museum of The Saviour in Brussels.*

Num. **2544,** *The Virgin and the Child with St. John and three Angels.* A little tablet in which Friedlander sees Gossaert's influence. (Was willed by Don Luis de Castro y Solis in 1925.)

Disciple of J. Van Eyck. Num. **2696,** *The Virgin with the Child* (willed by Don Pablo Bosch in 1915).

Metsys, Q. *He was born in Louvain about 1466. In 1491 he established himself in Antwerp. It is believed that he travelled to Italy. His jewel,* St. Anne's Descent, *is in the Classical Museum of Brussels. A. Dürer visited his workshop in Antwerp, and Metsys entertained him in the company of Patinir. He died in 1530 leaving two sons, Cornelis and John who were also painters.*

Num. **2801,** *Christ Present to the People.* This is a composition of stark realism and one should contrast Christ's resigned posture with the characteristic and bestial faces which surround him. The same faces are very similar to those that J. Bosch painted in Bois-le-Duc.

(A legacy of Don Mariano de Lanuza it entered in the Museum in 1940.)

Room XLI.—VAN DER WEYDEN, MEMLING

This room need not envy the previous one, because here we see beautiful early Flemish works belonging among others to R. Van der Weyden follower of R. Campin and J. Memling, a disciple of Van der Weyden.

Van der Weyden, R. *Born in Tournai, although of Brabant, about 1400. He married at twenty-four, lived by his art and after a life of ease died in Brussels in 1464 leaving four sons, one of whom was a painter. His best works can be found outside of his country, some of which, as the Triptych of St. John (Berlin), belonged to the Cartuja in miraflores (Burgos).*

Num. **2825,** *The Descent from the Cross* (Pl. 35). It was bought by Queen Mary of Hungary for her brother, Emperor Carlos V, and she in return was promised some church organs and an exac copy of all work by M. Coxcie. An original amplification of the higher border of the panel permits one to discover the cross on which Our Lord has been nailed; Joseph of Arimatea sustains him by the armpits and Nichodemus holds him by the legs in order te place him in Mary's lap, who, sunken to the ground, is helped by St. John and Mary Salome. A hooded holy-lady, what a marvellous expression she has as she mourns Christ's Death! In the opposite part a pious gentleman carries a balsam flask and Mary Magdalene writhes with sadness in a slightly exaggerated manner. The inexpressive Gothic characteristics have disappeared from this work; each person is almost real with his own individual expression. One's eyes go directly to the white figure of Christ, which occupies the center of the composition.

Numbers **1888, 1889** and **1891,** *The Redemption* a large triptych with exterior figures. The left part: the Angel expels Adam and Eve from Paradise, two characteristic early Flemish nudes (reminding one of the Polyptych of St. Bavon in Ghent); in the center with a Gothic temple in the background, Christ is crucified between the Virgin and St. John. The central panel is one of marvellous and magnificent decorative value, with scenes of the Passion in the arch and of the Sacraments in the tribunes of the side towers. On the right hand side a representation of the Last Judgement. Christ all powerful Judge with the Virgin and Saint John and in the lower part the Resurrection of the Dead and a separation of the just and the wicked. (It belonged to the convent of the Angels in Madrid.)

Num. **2540,** *La Pieta.* An admirable tablet because of the colors and Mary's expression. (It belonged to the Duke of Mandas and was acquired by the Museum in 1925.)

Num. **1558,** *The Adoration of the Magi.* A copy by Memling.

Num. **1886,** *The Crucifixion,* painted by a disciple of Van der Weyden it carries the apocryphal monogram of A. Dürer, 1513. (From the Alcázar it passed to El Escorial; being added in 1830.)

Num. **2663,** *The Crucifixion.* Friedländer considers this work to be by the Master of St. Catherine. (Willed by Don Pablo Bosch.)

Memling, J. *The biography of this early Flemish is full of anecdotes although the only fact that is certain, is that he was born in Memling about 1433 and died in Brussels in 1494. His most beautiful collection of Tablets is to be found in Bruges where he painted with Van der Weyden. Memling fled from any pathetic scene in order to represent only the charm and softness of the sweetest religious scenes.*

Num. **1557,** *Adoration of the Wise Men;* in the central panel. In the background of this tablet one discovers the city of Bethlehem; the Virgin sustains in her lap the Child Jesus while the kings look on. The kings being in reality, Carlos el Temerario («the Daring») and Philip the Good. The third king, the negro, is a curious creation of this painter that has been copied until the present. He is the young king who enters with gold and while unhooding himself he greets those present with a bizarre gesture. At his side we find the contrast of the humble and pensive Saint Joseph who seems very remote from the scene. Another similar tablet, although smaller, is to be found in the Hospital of the Saviour in Brussels. On the left hand part *The Nativity* (Pl. 36) in the moment that the Virgin and angels adore the Child. On the right side *The Purification.* (This triptych belonged to Carlos V and adorned the oratory of Ateca Castle. It entered the Museum in 1847.)

Num. **2543,** *The Virgin and the Child between Two Angels.* A well-restored tablet which was donated to the Museum in 1894 by the Marquis of Cabriñana.

David, G. (Disciple). Num. **2542,** *The Crucifixion.* Mary Magdalene between the Virgin and St. John, at the foot of Our Lord.

Flandes, J. de. *Thus we refer to a master whose name is unknown although he could be identified with J. Sallaert painter from Ghent (who joined the service of the Catholic Queen and died in Palencia about 1519). He belongs to the Spanish-Flemish school.*

Num. **2541,** *The Visitation of the Virgin to St. Elizabeth.* This work marks the decadence of the painter. It reminds us of a similar work in the Museum of Cádiz. (Acquired in 1928 by the Church of St. Lázaro in Palencia.)

Cock, J. de. *A painter from Antwerp in the first half of the 16th century. Flemish school.*

Num. **2700,** *St. Anne, the Virgin and the Child, willed by Pablo Bosch.*

Room XLII.—FLEMISH PAINTERS

The Flemish works continue, some of which are after those masters already cited in the preceding room. They have already begun their trips to Italy the «Queen of Gracefulness», that will terminate the proverbial rigidity of the early Flemish school. Now the human coloring will be more varied and natural. Pleats and folds will enjoy a larger flexibility, and a spontaneous movement of the figure will lend a superior realism to the compositions.

Gossaert, J. or **Mabuse.** Num. **1536,** *The Virgin of Louvain,* a tablet that does not seem to be by the same hand as the following. Some consider it by Van Orley.

Be sure to observe the Renaissance architecture in the background. (It was the propriety of Felipe II, willed by the city of Louvain and came to El Escorial in 1839.)

Num. **1930,** *The Virgin with the Child.* Now the painter has been in Italy and in this picture everything is succulent, fresh and modern reflecting the ease of life itself. Had he not left Flanders we would not detect the liberty represented in the Virgin's form. Mary's face is not that of the conventional early Flemish, nor do we see in the opulence of the forms of the Child anything similar to those reduced forms characteristic of their masters and predecessors. We are before figures now more Italian than Flemish, as much in expression as in attire and folds, etc... And the same background is Renaissance rather than Gothic. Flanders is loosing her own characters and this change is perhaps destructive to her painting. But instead, the Latin Canon, which the primitive considered as novelty, continues uninterrupted. (It belonged to El Escorial where it was located as early as 1572.)

Orley, B. Van, *born to the painter Valentine in Brussels about 1490; in 1540 travelled to Italy where he met Raphael who became an inseparable friend. He was also a great admirer of Michelangelo. When Albrecht Dürer was in Flanders he accompanied him to the Brussels and Antwerp workshops of their masters, and offered him such a grand banquet that the German painter mentions it in his travel comments. In Flanders he became the Court's main portrait painter. Among his*

*works are portraits of Emperor Carlos V, of his wife Isabel of Portugal,
of his sister Mary of Hungary, and of his aunt Margaret of Austria
and many others. In 1542 he died a very famous man.*

Num. **2692,** *The Holy Family.* Van der Weyden had already been
dead over a century when this painter began to flourish in Brussels. Van Orley inherited «the scepter» of Brussels painting, developed
from Flemish formation to the more pure Italian form. It is well
realized in this painting, which is a model of mobility and composition. The eyes of the Child follow the flight of the angel who comes to
crown his Holy Mother. St. Joseph's head is Italian, Raphael-like,
without exception. The angel who carries the basket of flowers has
a lengthy Italian tradition: only in the serious and pensive expression
of the Virgin can one discover the thread that unites his work to the
typical Flemish paintings.

Num. **1932,** *The Virgin and the Child.* (From Aranjuez in 1827.)

David, G. *A Dutchman born in Oudetwater in the 1460. From
there he went to Bruges being attracted by Memling's art. He married
Cornelia Cnoop and they worked many years in illustrating breviaries,
In 1515 he established himself in Antwerp where he painted untill 1523-
25. when he died. His best followers' were Adrian Ysenbrandt and A.
Benson. Soon after his death his name became unknown and his tablets
were attributed to Memling until 1902 when the first catalogue of his
works was printed.*

Num. **2643,** *The Rest during the Flight into Egypt.* A very conventional scene. The «flight» is represented by small figures that go
through the forest of pines. However, the figure of St. Joseph is lacking. (Willed by Don Pablo Bosch.)

Num. **1512,** *The Child and Two Angels crowning the Virgin.* According to Friedländer it was painted in Bruges about 1520 as a
derivation of the Virgin of the Monkey by A. Dürer. This is a bust
of the Virgin with a gold background.

Num. **1537,** *The Virgin with the Child.* This does not seem to be
by G. David.

Anonymous Flemish. Num. **1361,** *Triptych of the Adoration of
the Wise Men.* In the center, The Adoration; to the left Herod receiving presents from the emissaries of the Wise Men. Note the group
costumes. To the right the Queen of Saba before Solomon representing the Epiphany. (From El Escorial in 1839.)

Coecke van Aelst, P. *Born in Alst in 1502 and died in Brussels in 1550.*

Num. **1609,** *St. James the Elder and the Praverful eleven.* It is the
left part of a triptych. Num. **1610,** *St. John the Evangelist with two
ladies and two prayerful girls.* It is probably the right part of the previous triptych. (The two tablets entered in 1870.)

Num. **2223,** *The Adoration of the Wise Men.* A triptych with a king in each one of the tablets.

Master of Frankfurt. *He lived between 1460 and 1515 or 1520 and worked in Antwerp from 1491, greatly influenced by the coloring of J. Van Cleve.*

Num. **1941,** *St. Catherine*, in a sumptuous attire of the time, with background of a landscape and a miniature-sized group of the decapitation. (This comes from the Convent of Sta. Cruz of Segovia.) Winkler believes this to be work of Van Orley.

Num. **1942,** *Saint Bárbara.* This tablet and the previous one are the small sides of a triptych. Behind we see the towers that characterize the Saint.

Ysenbrandt, A. Num. **1943,** *The Mass of St. Gregory.* It is the version of the miracle which, happened when the body of Christ in the moment of the consecration appeared to the Pope St. Gregory. The miracle is only visible to the Saint. (Entered in 1822 proceeding from the Palace of Madrid.)

The Master of the Holy Blood. Num. **2694,** *The Virgin and the Child with Musician Angels.* The tablet has been restored. (Willed by Bosch.)

Room XLIII.—BRUEGHEL, PATINIR AND BOSCH

This room is dedicated to three famous Flemish masters: **P. Brueghel, J. Patinir** and **J. Bosch.** With these three one can say that the great classical Flemish school terminates after lasting less than a century. They fight in order to maintain the forms and spirit of their fatherland in contrast to the Italian influence.

Brueghel, P., *also called* the Old. *According to some authors he was born in Brogel, Limburg, in 1525. In Brussels he was the disciple of P. Coecke van Alst whose daughter he married. He travelled twice to Italy though he was influenced very little by her artists. Because he only painted for ten years his authentic catalogue paintings number no more than thirty. The larger part of those which one finds in museums are copies of his descendents. His friends from Brussels called him «the joker» because of his joyful kermesses and popular parties. He began imitating J. Bosch although in his main works he was independent. Brueghel died in Brussels in 1569 leaving two sons painters J. Brueghel de Velours and C. Brueghel d'Enfer.*

Num. **1393,** *Triumpf of Death*, a tablet which is not in the usual theme of this painter. He tells us that death reigns and triumphs above all the pleasures of life. Here love delivered to its raptures, there the passion that excites the game, over there plagues and fires, as death awaits everyone with his coffins, and leading all in the boat of Caronte. The distant landscape is covered with phantoms, macabre and fiery scenes. Brueghel, as *El Bosco*, wishes to be a moralist in this painting. (Proceeding from San Ildefonso, entered in 1827.)

J. Patinir. *Born in Dinant in 1480 soon made his entrance into the society of the Antwerp masters: First he married F. Buyts and as a widower later J. Nois at whose wedding A. Dürer was present. His production was limited and he died in 1524 leaving a painter son.*

Num. **1616,** *Crossing the Stygian Lake.* Caronte leading the souls in the boat to hell is surrounded by a beautiful landscape of marvellous and intense blues. Patinir is the foremost Flemish lansdcapes painter. His beautiful tones full of transparencies, and his ample perspectives are the fundamental themes of his works in which the presence of humans is but a mere pretext. To the left one sees Elysian Fiels with angels and also to the left Tartaros guarded by Cerberus.

Num. **1615,** *The Temptations of St. Anthony.* As in the previous, the landscape is of prime importance, the figures not being painted by Patinir, but rather by Massys. If the distant blues remind us of *Bosco*, the temptation scene follows a different conception. A flattered woman appears by virtue of a procuress witch. There are three beautiful damsels, one of which caresses the hermit while another offers him a carnal apple and a third one seems to be seducing him by means of flatteries. The repugnant monsters representative of vices and sins do not figure in the central part of the composition (look beside the Saint's hut), and only a monkey remains conspiring to cause the material downfall of the hermit.

Num. **1614,** *St. Jerome and a Landscape* is a beautiful landscape with a coast and river and steep rocks. Below a monastery, in a hut, St. Jerome removes a thorn from the lion. Note the miniature scenes in the background. The tablet is signed by Patinir and according to Baldas it is one of his latest works. (Sent by Felipe II to El Escorial it came to the museum in 1839.)

Num. **1611,** *Rest in the Flight into Egypt.* A beautiful landscape that extends to the sea with village settlements, country scenes, and in the upper zone the episode of the downfall of the innocent saints. Mary rests with the Child and St. Joseph carries a small pitcher of milk. (The tablet came from El Escorial.)

Patinir, E., son of Joachim. Num. **1612,** *Rest in the Flight to Egypt.*

Disciple of Patinir. Num. **1613,** *Rest in the Flight to Egypt.*

Bosch, J. *His true name was Hieronymus van Aeken of the Acken*

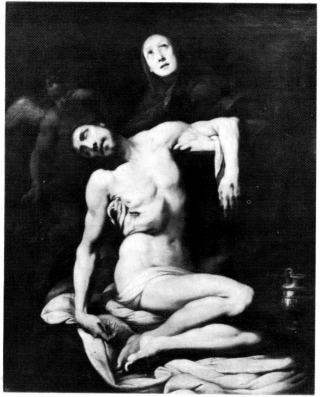

Piedad.—Pietá.—La Piété.—Die Pietät.—La Pietá.

Retrato del pintor Goya.—A portrait of Goya.—Portrait du peintre Goya. Bildnis Goyas.—Ritratto del pittore Goya

**El Descendimiento de la Cruz (detalle).—The Descending of the Cross.
La Descente de Croix.—Die Kreuzabnahme.—La Deposizione dalla Croce.**

La Natividad.—The Nativity.—La Nativité.—Die Geburt Jesu.—La Nascita di Gesù

El Jardín de las Delicias (detalle).—The Garden of the Delights.—Le Jardin des Délices.—Der Garten der Vergnügen.—Il Giardino delle Delizie

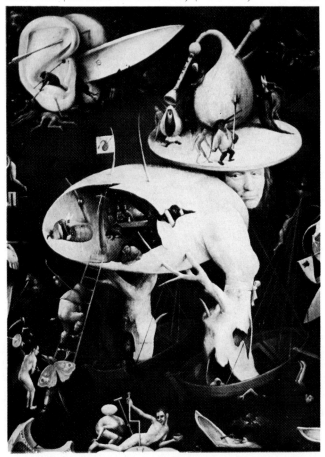

**El Jardín de las Delicias (detalle).—The Garden of Delights (fragment).
Le Jardins des Délices (fragment).—Der Garten der vergnügen.—Il
Giardino delle delizie.**

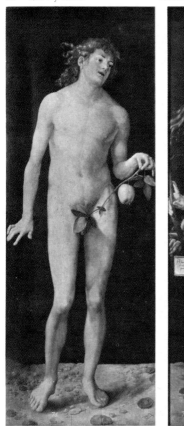 

Adán y Eva.—Adam and Eve.—Adam et Eve.—Adam und Eva.—Adamo et Eva

**La Virgen y el Niño.—Virgin and Child.—La Vierge et l'Enfant.—Die
Jungfrau und das Kind.—La Madonna con il Bambino Gesù**

of Acken. Born in Hertogenbosch (Bois-le-Duc), he employed the name of his birthplace for his last name. Bosch was born about 1450, he was outstanding in the Netherlandish school and died in 1516. (Some authors believe him to be Spanish but he never set foot in Spain.) The Catlolic Queen possessed some of his tablets. One of his Last Judgements was painted for Felipe the Handsome and at the death of Felipe de Guevara, (who is known by the Spaniards as El Bosco.)

Num. **2822,** *The Table of the Mortal Sins.* This is one of his early works. Around Christ in a circular fashion are represented allegories of the seven capital sins, each one of which receives its suitable punishment. In four circles the last phases of life appear: death, judgement, hell and glory. (Felipe II owned this work and it now belongs to El Escorial.)

Num. **2056,** *The Extraction of the Stone of Madness.* A very characteristic and curious painting in which we see a doctor covered by a funnel and a cooking pot to his waist, and an assistant discussing the victim. We also see an undaunted woman sustaining and balancing upon her head the Book of Wisdom. The inscription reads in Gothic characters: «Maester, suijt die Keye ras. Myne nema is lubbert das». This is spoken by the patient to the surgeon: «Master, remove this stone quickly. My name is *Lubbert Das*» (which means timid or lacking in virility).

Num. **2048,** *The Adoration of the Wise Men.* A very balanced and fine triptych with a beatiful landscape in the middle part and a huge city in the background. In this work the author breaks completely with the Flemish tradition, and from all Italian traits in order to show his absolute creative independence. In the side parts the doners are seen with the saints and those who are praying. (Sent by the Duke of Alba from Flanders to Felipe II and was added in 1839.)

Num. **2049,** *Temptations of St. Anthony.* El Bosco has dealt with this theme many times. The Saint has gone to search for water, but his retiring manner implies that the monsters lurk nearby. Seeing that he does not yield to temptation they set fire to the hermit's hut. (Note that there is no woman in the picture.) In the tablet of Lisboa a nude and semihidden woman in the hollow of a tree. In the Gutmann Collection of Haarlem a nude woman bathes in a lagoon. In the Palace of the «Signoria» (Venice) a nude woman is sitting behind a canvas. (From El Escorial.)

Num. **2052,** *The Hay Cart.* A triptych interpreting the Holy Scripture. It represents sensuality and lubricity behind which run so many mortals that resemble beasts. The Pope, the Emperor and the King are incapable of restraining the impulse of their passions. In spite of the imploring angel who raises his eyes to Christ some try to scale the cart on whose top love triumphs. Some fight for a portion of stolen grain while still others are crushed by the heavy wheels. In the left part the scenes of Paradise and in the right Hell. (The central panel is signed.)

Num. **2695**, *The Archer*. It is the head of one of the soldiers of the tablet. *The Crowning with Thorns*.

Num. **2050** and **2051**, The first tablet is a copy of *The Temptations*, of Lisbon; the second copy is also signed.

Bramer, E. *He was born in Delft in 1596 and died there in 1674.*

Num. **2069**, *Hecuba's Sorrow*, showing her on her knees before her son Polydorus. To the right a young maiden finds Polyxena's body. (Acquired by Carlos IV.)

Room XLIV.—GERMANS

This room treasures one of **J. Bosch's** great jewels and the rest is dedicated to German paintings, especially by **A. Dürer, Holbein, L. Cranach** and **Baldung Green** are also represented, but our German collection is small. The empire of Carlos V of Germany did not last long and due to the Reform was even less calm. There were not then art interchanges, which ordinarily take part through lasting and cordial relations.

J. Bosch. Num. **2823**, *The Garden of Delights* (Pls. 37 and 38). Triptych during the painter's last years, in which he shows an overflowed imagination, delirant, with the most genial and extravagant creations that painting of any epoch registers. Any machine of modern creation, any conceptions as hallucinant and absurd as they could seem, have already their precedent in this triptych multitudinaire, with a richness of miniaturized nudes completely without preterite. Father Sigüenza wrote in the 16th century: «The difference in my opinion between the painting of this man to those of others, is that they tried to paint the man as he looks outwardly; only he dared to paint him as he is inwardly». J. V. L. (traslation by Cardenal Iracheta) makes a complete description of the central panel. In the impossibility of reproducing it wholly we describe one of its parts: «Two lovers appear captive in a fragile and transparent glass globe, which rests on another solid globe adorned by a tropical plant whose end is a peacok's tail. This second globe has a glass cylinder as a unique aperture, and in the left side one sees the face of a man and in the right a big mouse. Nearby this extravagant scene, a man plunged into water separates his legs widely, and going between them is a red globe topped

by a heron, and pierced by a branch with a bird on top. A little far-
ther a man and a woman float on a queer construction, and present a
large bunch of currants to the man in the water. In the shadow of the
re tent an analogous scene is offered, formed by two large boards with
branches. One of them carries a bird with a big cherry in its beak
while a large group of men, their mouths widely-opened, look on.
There are men and women hidden in a solid tower, others under a
glass cup, and others simply amusing themselves near a garden by
eating and pulling up fruit. Under these a couple with their backs covered by a sort of red egg shell, madly dancing with large cherries in
their hands. In spite of this we have not yet arrived at the end of the
confounding surprises offered to us in this gallery of enigmatic scenes.
One fellow carries an enormous mollusc on his back. This creature
busies himself by guarding two human beings and three pearls, symbols of the vanity of earthly richness Another man bows to a large
marble globe which also imprisons two men. Their heads and legs
extended by both breaches and opposite and bowing to the same globe
are three other men. One has a big red strawberry on his back showing
a wide cut adorned by a flower of evil. Several groups press themselves
around other enormous strawberries and bunches of red, violet and
blue currants. Finally, a woman, that the painter has located in a very
visible place, shows the posterior part of her body adorned by flowers
symbolizing the vanity of man's pleasures.»

A different interpretation has been given to each of these delightful imaginations; but the secret of most of them remains with
the author. The little door on the left presents the creation of our
first fathers and to the right the city of Dite with the condemned.
This tablet defies description. Dante himself could not have imagined
such pains and torments. (It was bought by Felipe II at an auction
held by the Duke of Alba's natural son, and now belongs to El Escorial.)

A. Dürer, *was born in Nuremberg in 1471 and died in item fifty
seven years later. He travelled a great deal, and lived amidst the Reformation and its problems without being convinced by the new doctrines.
He was one of the most well-known painters of his epoch. Son of a silversmith, he entered in the workshop of a Volgemuth silversmith. Among
his many works his best are in the Royal Gallery of Vienna and in the
Classic Pinacothec of Munich. He drew and engraved two Passions,
the Great one and the Green, and repeatedly painted himself in sketches
and oils. Through his trips to Flanders he met and accompanied the best
painters; in Italy he became a good friend of Raphael, with whom he
exchanged some drawings. His impermeability to influences may be
guessed and resolved in the way he treats the greatness of the Renaissance in* The Apostles *(Munich).*

Num. **2179**, *Self-portrait*. The first self-portrait was made when he was thirteen in a drawing conserved in the Albertina (Vienna). At twenty he painted the one of the Louvre Museum, carrying in his hand a wild spear-plume, symbol of his forth-coming marriage.

Between this self-portrait and the frontal of Munich is the one of the Prado, when he was twenty-six years old. One can say that he is wholly «full of coquetry». Now he has been in Italy and knows the smart and fancy Venetian habits, which begin by the nice cap followed by the shirt with the golden lace, the waist with black border, the robe with a silk string crossing the breast and finally the white gloves. He has curled his hair carefully and put himself before the mirror, trying to avoid if possible the line of his horse-like nose. In short the exterior appearance is modern but the self-portrait is much nearer to medieval Gothicism than to the realistic liberty of the Renaissance. His pencil has been working patiently hair after hair, fold after fold, crease after crease, with the minuteness of a Lowlander. (The Municipality of Nuremberg gave this tablet and the following as presents to Thomas Howard. Felipe IV bought it in the auction by Charles I of England.)

Num. **2180**, *Unknown*. Mayer believes it to be the portrait of Hans Imhoff, Dürer's banker, but other authors have disagreed proposing different names. Whomever the portrait represents, it is a tablet of superior greatness and of the artist's last phases. It is almost impossible to reach a higher end in human portraits. The character of the man depicted is shown by means of the eye-brows that meet, the lurking eyes, the tightened lips and the active chin. Rich is the complexion with good modelling, thanks to the light and darkness in which he excells, and to the fact that he is not hidden by the large hat and furs that cover his breast. The fatty hands, far from being the long and bony forms of the Flemish and early Germans, have the surprising realism of the carefully studied natural.

Num. **2177**, *Adam*. Num. **2178**, *Eve* (Pl. 39). Two original tablets, a replica in the Uffizzi (Florence). Dürer always cared about the human proportions in the man and in the woman. He studied the Venetian canon and then painted these two prodigious nudes cut on a background with a movable and tight drawing. Adam, beginning from the head is of Apollo-like beauty; he has in his left hand the apple of temptation that Eve has just given to him; the right hand opens with a light nervous twitching while one of his legs is disposed to advance. One notes the face with anxious eyes, the mouth half-opened and the nose lightly dilated, in which palpitate the emotion of desire. Eve's head and her falling shoulders mark the German form but all the rest is Latin. Note the soft curve of the hips, the abdomen (un-deformed by the corset), and the thin and long legs. The author has depicted a face as seductive as it can be, though the arms break a little the ideality of the unity. One of the hands receives the apple from the serpent; the other one maintains the little branch which covers the flank, pending from it an inscription saying that the picture was painted after the Christmas of 1507. They are two realistic nudes of very rich formation with soft tones of bronze in the man and of milky rose in the woman. (Both tablets were given to Felipe IV by Christine of Sweden, and remained a century in a «private room» until Fernando VII's death.)

J. Holbein, the Young. *Born in Ausburg, in 1497; after having dedicated himself to beautiful workmanship, he became consecrated to his suited vocation portrait-painting. Gained to the Reformation, he painted its principal leaders: Luther, Melanchton, Catherine of Bora, and many times Erasmus of Rotterdam. Afterwards he abandoned his wife and sons and moved to London, where he began a new family. Because he was a friend of Henry VIII, he became the royal painter and a favorite of the court personages. He died in London at forty-six. His principal work,* The Ambassadors, *hangs in the National Gallery (London).*

His work in our museum num. **2182,** *Portrait of an old man,* is one of the painter's masterpieces and before being correctly attributed it was said to be by Joos van Cleve. He who knows the collection of portraits by Holbein, of the Bâle Museum, realizes immediately that it is in the same line. It consists of a face of a great interior life, sceptic or disdainful, well-characterized by the sinuous and enormous nose betwen the small semi-opened eyes. His perfect modelling does not surprise us when we see his un-paralleled light and shade qualities.

J. Baldung Green. *He was born in Gmund (Swabia) in 1480 and died in Strassburg in 1545. Dürer visited him in his Strassburg workshop and ranked high in his esteem. His influence was indeed great on this italianized painter who never visited Italy. He was called «Green» because of the greenish tones that he generally lent to his compositions. He particularly dealt with nudes:* The Young Girl and Death *(Bâle).* Adam and Eve *(Frankfort), numerous sketches and engravings on wood and copper (Albertina, Vienna), and those paintings in the Prado, as well as those in Strassburg prove this inclination.*

Num. **2219,** *Harmony or the Three Graces.* It represents the three Graces with Cupids at their feet. The harmony is not to be found in the two musical instruments in the painting, but rather in the happy placement and arrangement of the three (more Italian than German) beauties who contemplate their beauty in the mirrors. (It belonged to Felipe II.)

Num. **2220,** *Death and the Ages.* A composition of disagreable contrast.

L. Granach, the Old. *The Cranaches represent three generations of painters. The most famous, the Old, born in Cranach (Franconia) in 1472 died in Weimar in 1553 after a life of travel. He painted the Reformers whose doctrine he accepted and practised. Lucas was the official portrait painter of Martin Luther. He was best in sketches and engravings on wood but at times this perfection resulted in dryness of style.*

Numbers **2175** and **2176,** *Hunting party in honor of Carlos V in the Torgau Castle.* These are two aspects of the same scene. The Emperor, the Elector of Saxony, a knight of Toison, ladies... rough scenes, with deer hunts on a lake, and a castlecrowned forest. The interest of this tablet lies in the persons painted.

A. Ysenbrant. Num. **2818,** *Christ the Sufferer.* Is a tablet with the Redemptor seated and His hands bound to the cross. Other scenes are of the Passion, and Jerusalem is in the background. (Entered in the museum in 1941.)

Room XLV.—(Central staircase)

On the ceiling the canvas by Corrado Giaquinto *Death of Absalom* and on the wall two works by **Titian** and two by **Ribera.**

This room is the central staircase where two **Riberas** appear: Num. **1113,** *Ticio,* who is seen tied to the rock of Tartarus, and, scarcely visible, one of the two vultures pulling out his entrails. Palomino relates that this painting was in Amsterdam, at the home of Jacoba Ussel, whom, in the susceptible, critical moment of first sight, gave birth to a monstruosity as a consequence.

Num. **1114,** *Ixion,* tied to the wheel which crushes him continually, by the sentence of Jupiter, in punishment for having tried to seduce Juno. To the left, in the lower part, a devil is discovered who is tormenting him.

There are also two **Titians** Num. **426,** *Sisifo,* condemned to carry a rock to the top of a hill, then to roll it down the opposite slope. The painting is in rather bad condition due to a fire.

Num. **427,** *Ticio:* the same theme of **Ribera,** before. A vulture also devours his entrails in punishment for having violated Letona.

Room XLVI.—(Corridor)

A. van Dyck. Num. **2526,** *The Count of Arundel and Thomas his grandson.* The Count of Arundel, named Thomas Howard, an

English diplomat is portrayed armoured; his grandson dressed in salmon coloured satin. In other times it was believed that they were the portraits of Guzman el Bueno and his son. It does not appear to be an original of **Van Dyck.** The hands, especially those of the Count, are completely faulty.

Num. **2565,** *The Infanta Elisabeth Clara Eugenia.* Now old and with a widow's head-dress. It is the copy of a lost original. A legacy of Duque de Tarifa.

Num. **2569,** *The Infanta Elisabeth Clara Eugenia.* Another portrait similar to the former, but with only half the body. A legacy in 1930 from don Xavier Laffite.

Num. **1499,** *Charles II of England.* Son of Carlos I, seven years old, he is on foot, armoured, with a pistol in the right and a plumed helmet in the left. It is a copy of **Van Dyck,** or perhaps a replica. The original is found in Windsor Castle.

Room XLVII.—(Hall)

(This room is bare of paintings)

Room XLVIII.—(Corridor)

Bayeu, Ramón. *He was born in Saragossa on 1746 and died forty-seven years later in Aranjuez, and was Francisco's younger brother and Goya's brother-in-law. Upon seeing the six genre canvases that hang in this room one understands why Francisco's efforts to place his brother before his brother-in-law were useles, and Ramón remained relegated to the mediocrity which he merited. His colors were not bad but he was never gifted by God to be an outstanding artist. Let us study the faces: the are insipid, inexpressive and obviously painted to be «pretty», resulting in a resemblance to mannequins. The fact that they were cartoons for tapestries does not pardon them, although it does explain the strong contrasts of colors and the sharp tendency to silhouette. Having studied the faces, one is even more convinced that they are deficient, especially in comparison with those that Goya finished in 1791.*

Num. **2521,** *The «majo» with the guitar.*

Num. **2453,** *Country treat.*

Goya. Num. **2555,** *Æsop.* Copy of the canvas by Velázquez. Number **2554,** *Menippus.* Ibidem.

Num. **2857,** *Shooting party,* a «cartoon» for tapestry.

Bayeu, Francisco. *A disciple of Luzán and later in Madrid of*

*González Velázquez and of Mengs. Bayeu was held in great esteem
by them. He was bron in Saragossa in 1734; later he became royal
painter and director of the Academy of St. Fernando. At first he influenced Goya but it was not long before they became rivals, and of
course the Genius of Fuendetodos came out on top. Bayeu nevertheless,
was a great portrait painter and later when he recognized the superior
talents of his eminent brother-in-law he was his zealous defender. Had
Goya not outshown him, Bayeu would have been the best painter of his
period. He died in Madrid in 1795.*

   Num. **2590**, *La merienda. (The picnic.)*

Room XLIX.—SPANISH PAINTERS FROM THE 16th CENTURY

   This room is one of the most important in the field of
Spanish painting in the 16th century. It brings together
some very beautiful italianized examples by Yáñez de la
Almedina, Juan de Juanes, Pedro Machuca, Sánchez Coello, etc.

   Pantoja de la Cruz, Juan. *Born in Valladolid 1553. Died: Madrid 1608. Although a disciple of Sánchez Coello, who did not quite
attain his master's psychological insight, his coloring excelled. The portrait of Felipe II in the Library of El Escorial, serves as a contrast.*

   Num. **1040** A): *St. Augustin.* A severe and noble head.

   Num. **1040** B): *St. Nicholas of Tolentino.* The Augustinian habit
appears star-embroidered. To the left we see the revived partridge
on a plate. The comet refers to one of his miracles. (This canvas and
the previous one were painted for Doña María de Aragón's School,
that existed where later palace of the Senate was erected.)

   Sánchez Coello. There hangs here a beautiful canvas. Number
1144, *The Mystic Marriage of St. Catherine.* Very graceful figures
dressed in lively colours garments with metallic-glittering carnations.
At the feet of St. Catherine is evident the instrument of her martyrdom: the prickle-wheel and the sword. The artist mistook St. Catherine of Alexandria (the portrayed) for St. Catherine of Siena, who
was the one concerned with the mystic marriage with the Child Jesus.
Other painters in this Gallery have incurred in the same mistake.

   Morales, Luis de, *named «the Divine», was born in Badajoz
around 1500 and died in item in 1586. He started his education under
the protection of the bishop of his birthplace, D. Jerónimo Suárez, and
although he never left Spain, he was evidently influenced by the early*

Flemish and also by the Italians. He worked in Valladolid, Toledo and El Escorial, but it seems that he did not please Felipe II very much. He married Doña Leonor de Chaves and had two sons, one who died prematurely and Cristóbal, who was a painter. It is said that he became wealthy and led a gaudy life, but that he died poor and with many debts. Morales has a very particular personality and a mystical sense which pairs him with Greco more than with any other painter. His holy figures are also deprived of substance, scarcely realistic and spiritualized and they proceed rather from his interior fire. The abundance and inequality of his works lead us to think about the possibility of assistance from his son Cristóbal.

Num. **2656**, *The Virgin and the Child* (Pl. 46) a much repeated theme where the Child is seeking the breast of His Mother.

Correa, Juan. *There are no data concerning his birth and death. We only know that he used to paint in the 16th century while living in Toledo, where he worked for the Cathedral in the years between 1539 and 1552. He painted the tablets of the altar-piece of the Monastery of Guisando, as well as those of the Convent of St. Bernard in San Martín de Valde-iglesias.*

Num. **690**, *The Nativity*. A large painting, much harder «painted» than the former. It has reminders of Rafael or, at least, of Julio Romano. Angels, musicians and singers in groups of three. Fresh landscape and river and bridge at the back.

Luis de Morales. Num. **2512**, *The Annunciation*. The figures are too stiff and dry, especially the announcing angel.

Num. **943**, *The Presentation of the Infant Jesus*. We see Mary and Joseph with the group of virgins and their offering; old Simeon holds the Child in his hands.

Juan de Juanes. *Son of the painter Vicente Macip, he was born in Fuente la Higuera (Valencia) in 1523 and died in Bocairente in 1579. He has been called the «Spanish Rafaello», although he seems never to have been in Italy. Juan was an artist with deeply religious beliefs who prepared himself by prayer and fasting before beginning his works. He painted for the churches near Valencia and his art was well-liked for its softnes and beauty, and colorful style of a sweet fluency.*

Numbers **838**, **839** and **842**, about the *Episodes of the life of St. Stephen*. In the first tablet we see the Saint discussing with the Doctors in the Synagogue; in the second he is accused of being blasphemous, which causes the Doctors to cover their ears and in the third he is placed in the sepulchre. It is supposed that the figure appearing in the background to the left could be the portrait of the painter. In the present tablet he tends to dramatize the scenes, as much in the posture as in the expression of the faces. His soft and crome-like technique is the same that we have seen in previous works, especially in another altar-piece of St. Stephen in Valencia. In 1801 Carlos IV acquired them.

Macip, Juan Vicente, *was Juan de Juanes' father and master, born about 1475. In 1513 he lived in the Roteros' Street, Valencia. He willed in his old age in 1545 and died before 1550. At the end of the 15th century he probably visited Venice.*

Num. **843,** The Martyrdom of St. Agnes. Num. **851,** The Visitation, and num. **852,** The Crowning of the Virgin reminds us of Juan de Juanes technique. The three were acquired by Fernando VIII for 12 000 *reales.*

Juan de Juanes. Num. **846,** The Last Supper. In this one can detect the Lombard influence immediately (far more than that of Raffaello). Christ has one han on His chest and He raises the Holy Wafer in the other. In front the Holy Chalice of the Valencian cathedral is pictured. The apostles contemplate Christ in mystified amazement. In the halos appear the names of the twelve apostles and to the side that of the traitor Judas Iscariot, who is seated with his back to the viewer. Juan de Juanes has had an engraving or reproduction of *The Last Supper* by Leonardo da Vinci before him. (This panel was bought by our king Carlos IV. Then Joseph Bonaparte brought it to France, and later it was returned in 1818.)

Correa. Num. **689,** The Visitation.

Picardo, León. *He was born in Picardy but established himself in Burgos in the first half of the 16th century. He was painter for the Condestable of Castille.*

Num. **2172,** The Purification. The figures are disproportionate and their faces lack shadows and modelling.

Rincón, Fernando. *Had it not been for the authentic document that have reached us, many different opinions have been expressed about this painter. Some have denied his very existence in spite of Palomino's assertions. Others believe him to have been a disciple of Andrea del Castagno and of Domenico Ghirlandaio. and consider him a Knight of the Order of Saint James as per acknowledgment of the Catholic Kings (as his biographer states). It is known that he used to paint at Guadalajara, where he probably was born, about the end of the 15th century and that he still lived in 1517. Jusepe Martínez says about him «Some say he was a Portuguese, others that he was a Castilian; at any rate he was a great painter and his heads are very appreciated.»*

Num. **2549,** The Miracle of the Saint Physicians Cosmas and Damian. Background and clothes are overcharged with golden colours. The subject represents the substitution of the leg of a white patient for that of a negro. On the right side is the man who has ejected the snake he swallowed while asleep.

Picardo, León. Num. **2171,** The Annunciation. Subject treated in a very archaic way, without perspective and accentuated in excess. Curious enough is the pigeon included in the composition.

Master of the eleven thousand virgins. Num. **1290,** *The Coronation of the Virgin.* Golden background. Jesus Christ sitting on His throne is crowning the Virgin. Some winsome musician and singer angels make a merry composition.

Master of La Sisla. Num. **1256,** *The Adoration of the Magi.* There is no black King. The three Kings represent the three ages of man: an old man, a full-grown one and a boy. The subject is treated in a very religious way.

Num. **1255,** *The Visitation.* Num. **1254,** *The Annunciation.* Num. **1258,** *The Circuncision.* Num. **1257,** *The Presentation of the Child in the temple.* Num. **1259,** *The Death of the Virgin.* Though the scenes are ingenuous, the faces appear full of expressiveness. The Virgin, an old Lady, is holding the candle given Her by a mournful St. John.

Master of Perea. Num. **2678,** *The Visitation.* It is a large tablet with golden ornaments. The forms are still, dry and without expression. Very interesting is the popular detail of the girl spinning the spindle at the entrance to the house. So is, too, the figure of St. Joseph, on the left side, greeting with his hat in his hand.

Anonymous. Num. **1335,** *The Virgin of the Knight of Montesa,* thus titled in honor of the diminished doner kneeling on the right of the composition. St. Benedict and St. Bernard are standing on both sides of the Virgin and the Child, and the background is a temple. It is an extremely interesting picture because of the ivory-like technique employed in the flesh coloring and in the vibrance of some of the fabrics. A curious note is liberty of the Child's movement as he slips from his mother's lap in order to reach one of the staffs, while the fingers of his right hand are about to give a blessing. (This picture entered in the Museum after being purchased by popular subscription in 1920.) It is believed that the painter is **Rodrigo de Osona** who, during the last part of the 15th century, painted in the Levantine region.

Yáñez de la Almedina, Ferdinando. *He is considered a native of La Mancha, perhaps born in Almedina (Ciudad Real) and his name is associated with his namesake, Fernando Llanos, who also painted in the Cathedral of Valencia from 1505 to 1506. Later he painted Cuenca. It is believed that «Ferrando spagnuolo» refers to him and that he helped Leonardo da Vinci in the preparation of the sketch for the Battaglia d'Anghiari. But anyway, it is certain that he was in Italy. According to María Luisa Caturla, he not only was inspired by da Vinci but also by Giorgione. One easily discovers the undeniable derivations of Leonardo in St. Catherine, in the Prado and the Adoration of the Shepherds (in the Valencian Cathedral). So it is impossible to deny a relationship between Leonardo and the Spaniard in mention.*

Num. **2805**, *St. Anne, Our Lady, St. Elizabeth, St. John and Jesus Child*. The curving of the mouths and the shading of the flesh remind the style of Leonardo but there is no beauty in the faces.

Num. **1339**, *St. Damian*. Note the Italian influence.

Num. **2902**, *St. Catherine*. This painting of the Saint is an extremelly beautiful and un-precedented work of the most excellent that Spain created in the 16th century. She is standing sword in hand (the sword-point touches the wheel with which she was killed), and her crown is placed upon the shelf. The figure has a soft scattering of lights and darks in the face, hands and vestments that create a very pleasing effect. For the first time coloring is wrought with sufficient ease, as similar to the Venerians as to the Lombards, Whith the exception of Morales we can now bid farewell to the Flemish school in order to follow, where there are influences, the Italian modulations. (It belonged to the Marquis of Argudin, acquired in Paris, and entered in the Museum in 1946.)

Machuca, Pedro. *He was born in Toledo about the end of the 15th century and died in Granada in 1550. His work on the Palace of Carlos V was later to be continued by his son, Luis. The versatile Pedro was a painter, sculptor and architect.*

Num. **3017**, *The Descent from the Cross*. This work marks the «exitus» of the painter.

Correa. Num. **2828**, *The Annunciation*. A large painting; a rather disproportionated beautiful angel, a phylactery in his hand and the index finger pointing to the Eternal Father in a shoal of Cherubins. At the entrance of the chamber of the Virgin appears the Holy Ghost. The angel has the noble movement of one who hurries to communicate good news. The countenances are without shadows. The hands of the Virgin are a delight of modelling. The coloring is of soft, fine tints. The flower vase below the room on the foreground is pretty and delightful.

Machuca, Pedro. Num. **2579**, *The Virgin and the Souls in Purgatory*. The Virgin with the Child is surrounded by angels. The breasts of the Virgin give milk to quench the flames of the Purgatory, full of sobbing souls and in the lower corner one sees the gateway to heaven. There is also an extraordinary Italian influence upon this panel.

Juan de Juanes. Num. **855**, *Portrait of D. Luis de Castellá. Lord of Bicorp*. This is an exact portrait which deviates from the feminine gentleness of the preceding panel. It is very well done, especially in the union of the green and gold of the sleeves with the back of the suit. And on the chest of D. Luis we see the gleaming emblem of the military Order of Santiago. He was the protector of novelist Jorge de Montemayor (who dedicated his «Seven books of Diana» to him). (This portrait was owned by Carlos IV.)

Correa. Num. **2832,** *Apparition of the Virgin to St. Bernard.*

Sánchez Coello, Alonso. *Benifaró (Valencia) was the scene of his birth in 1531 and he died in Madrid in 1588. This famous portrait-painter of the epoch of Carlos V and his son, Felipe II, painted religious works in El Escorial, although he excelled in portrait work. By the emperor's wish he went to Portugal with A. Moro (Dutch) in order to paint the portraits of the royal family. Then after the un-foreseen separation of Holland he was named to be the painter of Felipe II who held him in great esteem and who frequently was known to watch the painter at work. Coello worked on portraits of the royal Spanish family and for some foreigners who came to Spain. He died rich and famous, and his works hang in many European museums and private collections. (Note Anton Moro's influence.)*

Num. **1137,** *Portrait of the Princess Isabel Clara Eugenia.* She was born in Valsain in August of 1566, daughter of Felipe II and of his third wife Isabel of Valois, and died in December of 1633. The Princess married the Archduke Albert and was the ruler of the Lower Countries. We see before us a charming portrait with cold tones, but very wisely harmonized. The minuteness of detail with which the laces, cloths and jewels are treated lessens in importance before the realism of the child-like face. It is said that it is a portrait of a sick woman under whose skin circulated more lymph than blood. The slightly reddish eyes are full of tender melancholy; the palid face and hands are bloodless and seem to be capable of dissappearing momentarily. What an unusual contrast between the childish face and the girded and firm body of a mature woman! In spite of the sickly appearance of the princess she lived to be sixty seven years old, and our Museum displays portraits of her through different epochs of her life.

Num. **1030,** *Portrait of Queen Elizabeth of Valois.* This portrait was painted by Pantoja from an original by Sánchez Coello that disappeared in the 1604 fire. It represents the third wife of Felipe II, the daughter of Henry II of France and Catherine Medici. She married the Spanish King in Guadalajara in October of 1568, and some romantics invented non-existent love stories regarding the queen and her step-son, Prince Carlos. It is a beautiful portrait definitely not inferior to the original. The garments as well as the jewels are richly represented.

Num. **2861,** *St. Sebastian between St. Bernard and St Francis.* The subject is divided into two scenes: a heavenly one where the Trinity is seen together with the Virgin and the Cherubs; the earthly scene shows St. Sebastian naked and tied to a tree with many arrows stuck in his body. St. Bernard and St. Francis are on both sides, the former receiving a prize for his defence of the virginity of Our

Lady and the latter is receiving the stigmae. The archers disappear
in the background.

Num. **1036**, *Portrait of Felipe II*. Born the son of Emperor Carlos V and his wife Isabel of Portugal in Valladolid, May of 1527 he
died in El Escorial in September 1598. Pale, with a deathly pallor,
very few times have his face and expressionless glance been so well
represented. In his black attire the face of the solitary gentleman
of El Escorial seems to be even more emaciated. The observing spirit
of the artist has penetrated the very intimate psychology of his
Austrian figures. Among the predecessors of Velázquez, Sánchez
Coello is the most sharp, severe and clearsighted Spanish portrayer.

Num. **1136**, *Portrait of the Prince D. Carlos*. He was the son of
Felipe II and of his first wife María of Portugal. Born in Valladolid
in July 1545, the Prince died in Madrid in July of 1568. The unfortunate son of the judicious king is seen in this portrait almost a child,
he about whom romantic theatre has imagined so much. However,
he is well-characterized with a grave look of restrained irritation
directed to the spectator. In spite of his orange-colored waist coat,
his ermine wrappings, and his green stockings the picture, like all
of those by Sánchez Coello, has a cold intonation. It is said that this
portrait was originally full length.

Room L.—SPANISH ALTAR-PIECES

In this room many notable altar-pieces by early Spanish
artists of the 15th century are united. Some are unsigned,
others are known only by «Masters» by a figure represented,
by the scene of the work, by the theme, etc. Others, when
the origin or theme is ignored or un-recognized they are
referred to as «Anonymous». The city officials commissioned
such portraits to be done by masters already well-estab-
lished and whom they knew well. They would sign the con-
tract, do the work, which they did not sign, and if the document disappeared within the third generation it became
almost impossible to attribute the work correctly. And for
this reason there are so many «Anonymous» works.

Anonymous Spaniard. Num. **1321**, *Altar-piece of the Archbishop Don Sancho de Rojas*. It belongs to the style that Lafuente Ferrari
calls «international», because the Italian influence stands out upon
the background typical of Gothic art. The altar-piece consists of

a central tablet and three wings, with a variety of themes based on the *New Testament, The Nativity, The Adoration of the Magi, The Elagellation, The Fifth Dolor, The Crucifixion, The Ascension*, et cetera. The identification has been made thanks to the coat-of-arms of Señor de Rojas, five blue stars in a silver background, that mark the pinacles of the third plane, and therefore of the Prelate Don Sancho de Rojas, who accompanied the King, Don Fernando, in the capture of Antequera. In the central part of the altar-piece the Archbishop appears kneeling before the Virgin who places his mitre, the Child Jesus crowns the King. (This work was acquired by the Parish of San Román de la Hornija. Valladolid, in 1929.)

Pedro García de Benavarre. *It is supposed that he was born in Benavarre, Huesca, and pertained to the cycle Aragón-Catalonia. He flourished during the middle of the 15th century.*

Num. **1324,** *Saint Sebastian and Saint Policarp Destroying Idols.* The first refers to Mark and Marcelinus.

Num. **1325,** *Martyrdom of the Saint Sebastian and Policarp.* Both Saints appear martyrized. The painter is very inferior to Bernardo Martorell who preceded him.

Master of Arguis. *Thus called due to the altar-piece of Arguis, province of Huesca. This master painted about 1410.*

Num. **1332,** *The Legend of St. Michel.* It illustrates the medieval legend of Gárgano, who is seen wounded in a dramatic pose by the same arrow that he had shot against the runaway bull, the battle of the archangel against the rebelious angels and the victory against the Antichrist, whose foot-prints remained upon the rock when he intented to re-mount, but was lowered to the ground by St. Michael between the loud laughs of those nearby and to the surprise of the little devils on the side. There are six others seated on the predella or bench.

Master of Sigüenza. Num. **1336,** *St. John the Baptist and Saint Catherine.* This altar-piece is formed by five tablets, to which it is believed three more from the Cathedral of Sigüenza could be added, with which this work would remain complete. In the central tablet are St. John the Baptist and Saint Catherine, who are responsible for the title; to the left, Salome, Herod and the scene of the beheading. The tablets proceed from the Chapel of the Arces in the same cathedral. It has been suggested that the other be the master Juan Arnaldin. (It was acquired by the Patronages of the Artistic Treasure and the Prado in 1930.)

Nicolás Francés. *It is not known if his surname is topographic or inherited from his father, and it is only known of him that he painted in León before 1434 and that he still lived in May of 1468.*

Num. **2545,** *Altar-piece of the Life of the Virgin and of Saint Fran-*

cis. It is a splendid gothic work with very Italian figures. One would say that the author knew the frescoes of Giotto. In the central part and the right side are scenes from the life of the Virgin; to the left, from the life of Saint Francis of Assissi. The part representing St. Francis surprised by the thieves is of a very impressive plasticity. In the predella, bust of various saints. (Proceeds from La Bañeza, León, and was acquired by the Patronage of the Artistic Patrimony in 1932.)

Anonymous Spaniard. Numbers **2668** and **2669**, *Removal of the Body of St. James*. It deals with two tablets of equal size with scenes from the martyrdom of the Apostle in Palestine and the removal of the body in Iria Flavia. It is supposed to be by an anonymous disciple of Miguel Ximénez (see Room XXIV). They proceed from the province of Lérida. (Bosch Legacy.)

Huguet, Jaime. *He painted in Barcelona between 1448 and 1487. Son of the painter Pedro Huguet, the most important figure of the contemporary painting from Catalonia.*

Num. **2683**, *A Prophet*. A small tablet, probably of a sub-predelle, that cannot begin to give us an idea of the great artistic personality of this early Catalan (Bosch Legacy).

Master of the Archbishop Mur. It was painted in the 15th century. Num. **1334**, *Saint Vicent, Deacon, Martyr*. A beautiful tablet well ornamented and of excellent golden reliefs. The Saint is standing above a Moor. The doner is kneeling, at the side.

Other less important tablets, among them. Num. **2675** by a disciple of Luis Borrasá.

Room LI.—(Rotunda)

This room is decorated with eight canvases of **Snayers** of battle themes. In an expansion is a type of chapel with mural pictures of the 12th century, proceeding from the Hermitage of the Cruz de Maderuelo, Province of Segovia.

Room LII.—CARRACCI

There were three **Carracci** brother, Agostino, Annibale and Giovanni Antonio. The three were well gifted, especially Annibale. They were born between 1550 and 1560. When adults they resented the painters who busied themselves solely

Los fusilamientos del 3 de Mayo de 1808. — Fusillade of the 3rd May 1808. — La Fusillade de 3 Mai 1808.
Die Erschiessung am 3 May 1808. — Le fucilazioni del 3 Maggio 1808

**María Tudor, esposa de Felipe II.—Mary Tudor, Queen of England.
Marie Tudor Reine d'Angleterre.—Die Königin Maria von England.
Maria Tudor, sposa di Filippo II**

Dama y niña.—Lady and Child.—Dame et son enfant.—Dame und Kind.
Dama con una bambina

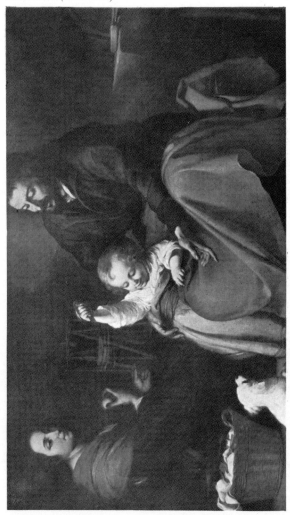

Sagrada Familia del pajarito.—The Holy Family with a litle bird.—La Sainte Famille au petit oiseau.—Die heilige Familie mit dem Vögelchen.—La Sacra Famiglia dell'Uccellino

La Adoración de los pastores (fragmento).—The Adoration of the Shepherds (fragment).—L'Adoration des bergers.—Die Anbetung der Hirten. L'Adorazione dei Pastori

Jesús Niño en la puerta del Templo.—The Child Jesus at the Door of the Temple.—L'Enfant Jésus à la porte du Temple.—Christuskind am Tempel Tor.—Gesù Bambino alla porta del Tempio

El Tránsito de la Virgen.—The Death of Our Lady.—La Dormition de la Vierge.—Der Tod der Heiligen Jungfrau.—L'Assunzione della Madonna

La Dama de Elche

in imitating art of the great masters, and through the initiative of their uncle, also a painter, they founded the «Academia degli Incaninati», a group of independents, in order to represent an eclectic art. That is to say an art not devoted to a set personality or school, but rather to the choice of the best available.

Carraci, Annibale. *He was born in Bologna in 1560 and left with his brother, Agostino for Parma in order to study the local painters, and especially Correggio. Later they went to Venice where they studied the art of Tiziano, Tintoretto and Veronese. Upon returning to Bologna they founded the Academy and decorated various palaces. Annibale stood out and was called to Rome in order to decorate the Farnesio Palace but he took his brother along. They quarreled, Annibale was not well treated and returned disgusted to Bologna. He went to Naples and died in 1609, being buried beside the tomb of Raphael.*

The six works which figure in this Room are frescoes passed to canvas, three oval-shaped, and three trapezoidal, painted in the Chapel of San Diego de Alcalá, in the church of Santiago de los Españoles in Rome. They were passed to canvas in the times of Fernando VII. Others from the same chapel remain in Barcelona.

Mohedano, Antonio. *A Spanish painter, born in Lucena (Córdoba) about 1569 and died there in 1625.*

Num. **2911**, *Saint John the Evangelist.* It is a fresco upon a drumskin of a wall in a niche (Donated by Señores de García, of Lucena.)

Room LIII.—SKETCHES BY GOYA

What a marvellous collection! There are displayed in this extensive room some innumerable dozens of sketches by Goya, executed with varied techniques, that later served for his «Caprices». All of them spontaneously done on the first impulse, without pretensions of public exhibition —other had this destination, his jealously guarded plates. They deal with «previous documentation», and thus ought to be considered as such —sketches— the larger part unintentional and even containing moralizing tendencies.

We do not pretended to describe them, because in addition to the fact that interesting publications have already been devoted to them, this **Guide** is of pictures. In other respects we advise the curious visitor to stop for a while in this genial room, whose works although small are very important. They complete the physiognomy of the Goya who embraced all the existing *genres* (and even invented a few he felt necessary in order to furnish nourishment and departure to his extreme enxieties). And they are important as much in the expression of the observer's attitude, as in the representation of an epoch. Goya has been one of the most eminent and fecund artists that humanity has given.

Room LIV.—GOYA

Num. **2447,** *Doña María Antonia Gonzaga, Marquess of Villafranca.* She was the daughter of Don Francisco Gonzaga, prince of the «Sacro Romano Imperio», and Doña Julia de Caracciolo. In 1754 she married the tenth Marquis of Villafranca, patron of the arts, and academician of San Fernando. She wears a blue striped grey dress and white shawl. (This was donated, along with **2448** and **2449** by Count of Niebla in 1926.)

Num. **739,** *The Dukes of Osuna and Their Children.* In this strange misty and vague work we see Don Pedro Téllez-Girón and his wife Doña María Josefa Alonso Pimentel. Countess-Duchess of Benavente. It definitely resembles the English school more than the Spanish and only those, well accustomed to Goya's style will recognize this to be by the master from Saragossa. Originally costing 12 000 *reales* it was later willed by descendents to the Museum.

Num. **2446,** *Cornelius Van der Gotten,* was the director of the Royal Tapestry Factory, for which Goya painted numerous «cartoons». It was signed in 1782 and became the property of the Junta Iconográfica in 1881 for 500 pesetas.

Num. **2862,** *Queen María Luisa in a Hoop-skirt,* shows the queen's vain, unbearable, and unvarying conceit. She is dressed in the 18th century fashion, which makes, her appear even more absurd and ridiculous but that nevertheless manage to «reveal» two well formed arms. Goya's unpleasant tasks were many. (It came from the Buen Retiro to the Museum in 1847.)

Goya. Num. **738,** *Cardinal Don Luis María of Bourbon and of Villabriga.* Son of the Prince-Cardinal. D. Luis Antonio of Bourbon (see Num. **2265** of Room XXXIV, who renounced his ecclesiastical titles to marry Doña María Teresa Villabriga), he was the grandson therefore of Felipe V. He was born in Cadalso de los Vidrios

(Madrid), in 1777, was Count of Chinchón Cardinal and Archbishop of Toledo and died in Madrid, in 1823. He wears the attire of a cardinal and displays a breast-plate, the crosses of Carlos III and of the Saint-Spirit and a medal. In his right hand he has a prayer book. (Sent to the Museum in 1906 by the Ministry of State.)

Num. **737,** *Charles III*, by Goya. He leans on the fowling piece with a dog resting at his feet. It is a picture of tremendous realism, without the least concession to the original. Carlos III was the son of Felipe V and Isabel Farnesio; he was born in Madrid in 1716 and died in Madrid in 1788. There are three copies of this portrait: the Duques de Fernán Núñez possesses one; another is in the Museo Municipal de Madrid, and the third is this of the Prado.

Num. **740** *a*): *Carlos IV* and num. **740** *e*): *María Luisa*, are two almost full length portraits of the kings painted about 1789.

Num. **745,** *Christ Crucified*. Many times it has been said that Goya did not feel religious painting and that his only exception is the painting for the Colegio de Escolapios of San Antón, *The Last Communion of St. Joseph of Calasanz.* Actually he was a good Christian. He even began his letters (to Martín Zapater) with a small cross and constantly invoked God's aid and that of the Virgin of «El Pilar». But nevertheless he did not feel a religious intimacy in his works dealing with sacred subjects. His *Crucified Christ* is a proof because the artist has contented himself only in painting a sculptured almost tactile mellow Apollo-like body. We can hardly say that his Christ is mortified by suffering and whip lashes. Our Lord is magnificently placed upon the cross; however, due to the lack of pain and anguish is not likely to inspire prayers. He presented this to the Academy in order to be admitted and it is not difficult to note his «academic» style. Perhaps in imitation of Velazquez's Christ he put a foot-ledge and four nails according to the French idea. The French say that three was a fourth nail brought from the Crusades by St. Louis and apart from the three from Loretto Spanish tradition, as well as the Italian and German, is of three nails, the third for both feet. It proceeds from the beautiful St. Francisco el Grande.

Num. **746,** *The Holy Family*, is one of his early works painted under the influence of Mengs and acquired for 8000 *pesetas* from the heirs of Don Manuel Chaves in 1877.

Room LV.—GOYA'S «CARTOONS»

In times of Carlos III the Royal Factory of Tapestries of Santa Barbara was more or less forgotten and wishing

His Majesty to restore and enliven it, he commissioned the task to the Bohemian painter Antonio Rafael Mengs. In 1776 **Goya** lived in Madrid protected by the so-called «Partido Aragonés» («Aragonese Party»), presided over by Aranda. This same year Goya received a letter from Mengs inviting him to paint patterns for tapestries destined to the palace of El Pardo. In that period Castillo, Napoli and Ramon Bayeu already painted such desings. At the beginning 8000 *reales* by year were alloted to him. The first «cartoon» delivered was *Picnic on the Banks of the Manzanares* for which he was paid 7000 *reales*.

These pictures were not actually «cartoons» but oil paintings, generally to be translated by the workers of the factory in excellent tapestries with polychromed threads; although Goya during the execution tried to be free from the straitness of a reduced palette and an excessive outline which harshly accised the constrasts. And so it happened that sometimes the workers complained of it to the director Cornelius van der Gotten, telling how impossible it was to be subdued to a chromatic tyranny to which they were not accustomed. However Goya did not resign and the workers had to submit leaving their obstinate routine and enriching the works with very esteemed boasting polychromes. Let us compare the aforesaid «cartoon» with the last two delivered by the artist in 1791, *The Nincompoop* and *Blind Man's Buff*, and a radical difference will be appreciated.

Goya. The description of each «cartoon» figures in the official Catalogue of the Museum as follows.

Num. **771,** *The Maja and the Hooded Man*. In a forest —the «Casa de Campo»?— is a *maja* with a courtier; to the left is a hooded man sitting; two others are in the background; more distant a *maja* is sitting and a *majo* standing.

Num. **772,** *The Bibber*. He is sitting and raises the «bota». To the left is a lad and in the foreground is a loaf and two onions. To the right there are three *majos*.

Num. **773,** *The Parasol*. Young lady sitting with a little dog in he lap: behind her is a *majo* hiding her from sun with a green umbrella.

Num. **778,** *The Blind Guitar Player*. The blind man sings playing the guitar; a varied group listens to him; to the right in the background is a water-carrier and a melon stand.

Num. **779,** *The Fair of Madrid*. A couple before a fripper's stand showing copper kettles; a bureau, a portrait, worn clothes. There are other groups before other stalls. In the background appears the dome of San Francisco el Grande.

Num. **784,** *The Ball-game with Racket*. Seven players and various spectators. Hills in the background with people.

Num. **787,** *The «Novillada»*. The young bull and four bullfighters; the one dressed in red looks like Goya himself. Behind the wall some spectators assist at the bullfight.

Num. **792,** *The Rendez-vous*. A sitting woman awaits someone, in the background are several figures, twilight.

Num. **795,** *The Vintage*. The young man sitting gives a bunch of grapes to a young lady; a child tries to take it; in the rear is another woman standing with a basket of grapes.

Num. **800,** *The Maids with Pitchers*. Three water-carriers with pitchers; to the left a boy; the fountain with a large basin. Country background with a building and hills.

Num. **805,** *The Hunter with his Dogs*. The hunter back to the spectator with the gun and two dogs; forest and hills in the background.

Num. **753,** *Dogs and Hunting Tools*. Two dogs, two guns, a pot with powder, etc.

As we see, the themes are popular scenes as those of the «cartoons» of Teniers. Nothing about mythology, neither triumphant battles, nor pompous parades. Goya is at his ease interpreting the scenes taken from the suburbs of Madrid and its surroundings. A beggar, a bibber, children playing, a stand of a market, a bullfight... With this he has enough to fill meters of a canvas with a bright and succulent painting, which is more than a design or a hint. They are finished works which can adorn the walls of the palaces salons with dignity.

Room LV A.—GOYA

Num. **724,** *Fernando VII in an Encampment*. Born in El Escorial in 1784 to Carlos IV and María Luisa of Parma, he died in Madrid in 1833. Fernando was sent for by Napoleon and stayed in France during the War of Independence becoming king of Spain, since his father's abdication in 1808. When the war ended he returned to Spain, and upon learning that Goya had painted the bust of Joseph Bonaparte in a symbolic scene he told him that he merited the gallows (this not lowering him the least bit in the court's esteem). He gave back all Goya's assignments and honors insisting that his back salaries be paid. Around his waist he wears a general's sash, Toison, and the band of Carlos III. The background is full of soldiers, their tents and bonfires. (It belonged to the School of Civil Engineering.)

Num. **748,** *May 2, 1808 in Madrid. The Fight with the Mamelukes.* The people of Madrid rose in rebellion against the bloodthirsty orders of the French General Murat, and took all sorts of weapons, each man ready to defend his country's independence. This incident took place in the Puerta del Sol —where the soldiers brought by Napoleon from Egypt were planning to overcome Madrid. But the task was not so easy as these *«pueblanos»* continued to successfully defend their Madrid with steel and irregular arms. Among the «mamelukes» there is a member of the Imperial Guard. It was painted six years after having taken place so we don't know if Goya actually witnessed the scene or not, nevertheless the scene is realistic without being melo-dramatic nor affected. The 1949 museum catalogue reads: «They left the museum (this canvas and the next) on November 21, 1936. Later, after several months they were transported from Valencia to Catalonia but on the way the truck carrying them had had an accident and upon breaking the box the two canvases were ripped. After being re-lined in Catalonia they were returned to the Prado and until this day the missing fragments have not been replaced in num. **748**».

Num. **749,** *May 3rd in Madrid* (Pl. 40). *The Firing-Squad in La Moncloa,* Isidro, Goya's servant who stayed with him in his Quinta in the banks of the Manzanares refers to the episode of Trueba in the following manner:

«From that same window my master watched the fusillades with a telescope in his right hand a small-mouthed blunderbuss with a handfull of bullets in the left hand. If the French arrive here, my my master and I are other Daoizes and Velardes. About twelve noon master said: Isidro, bring your blunderbuss and come with me. I obeyed him and where do you think we went? Well, we went to the Príncipe Pío Mountain, where the unburied bodies laid. I remember everything as if it had happened yesterday. It was a moonlight night, but the sky was full of menacing black clouds, one second it was clear the next dark. My hair stood on end when I saw my master with the blunderbuss in one hand and his notebook in the other gui-ding me towards the dead bodies. As if he was worried he asked me: Are you trembling, Othello? I, instead of answering him «I'm trem-bling like a fennel» I almost began to cry, believing my poor master had lost his senses, because he called me «Othello» instead of Isidro. Later we sat down on the river-bank, near the dead bodies and my master opened his notebook, placed it upon his knees and awaited the moonlight which was temporarily hidden by a large cloud. Some-thing hovered over the river-bank grumbling and panting. Me, well, I trembled like quicksilver; but my master tranquilly continued as if it were daytime preparing his pencil and sketch. Finally the moon shone as if it were daylight. In the middle of the puddles of blood we saw a group of cadavers some open-mouthed others head down, some as if they were kissing the ground, others with their hands bound...»

This reference has the un-deniable depth of being by an eye-witness. Isidro evidently, was there on the night of the fusillades and regarding Goya it is sufficient to see his canvas of the episode to realize that he saw the whole scene of the shootings and the spectacle of the cadavers crumpled upon the blood-soaked ground. It is a canvas that produces a complex impression: horror and protest blend as it actually horrifiers by its realism. Each hero is «one», he is separate, individual and unrepeatable. While this one covers his eyes so as not to see the shootings, that one his ears to avoid hearing the shots. One grasps his head so as not to lose his sanity, while another with arms outstretched like Christ reproaches the assassinators. And it is the latter, completely illuminated by lantern light that blends all the other facial expresions. -Only he is the spirit of the battle, the shabby hero of the war. In front of him we see the undistinguishable mass lined up as a human machine firing and slaying. And in the background a desolate mountain and the distant silhouette of Madrid adds to the rare naturalness and drama. A great solitude and hushed silence surround and blanket the tragedy.

The painter has not wished to impress the spectator as he passionately and angrily commanded his brush-strokes to «brutal» stains. What did the spectator matter to Goya? The episode itself is so pregnant with drama that any movement whatsoever intended to intensify the hues would be negative rather than useless. Yes, Goya saw the fusillades and sketched with a heap of cadavers before him, so this is a historical painting but not in the usual «historical» nor «literary» sense. (It was not listed in the Museum catalogue until 1872.)

Num. **723**, *Self-portrait*. Although small-sized, in this extremely attractive creation we see Goya in a sef portrait nonchalantly in his opened shirt. We see his bared neck and the play of richly modelled lights and darks upon his chest. His face with its marvellous expression betrays the artist's character (acquired by Don Román de la Huerta for 400 escudos).

Num. **725**, *General D. José Palafox on Horseback* shows Saragossa's heroic defender during the War of Independence, who gained the title of Duke of Saragossa, looking like he is about to give some orders from his camp; and in the background fire and smoke. Painted in 1814 it was willed by the General's son and put on exhibition in the Prado in 1884.

Num. **747,** *The Exorcised,* shows a dark church scene and a possessed man on the ground with a priest's stole around his neck while a priest and a woman hold him down and a third reads the incantation sprinkling the victim with the hyssop. Probably the painter witnessed a similar scene. In 1866 it was purchased from Don Román de la Huerta for 300 *escudos.*

Num. **740,** *The Beheading.* A scene of «genre» painted upon a tin plate and representing a naked woman kneeling before a man with a knife in his hand who is trying to behead her. Goya liked to paint this kind of atrocity of a particular contemporary incident in which he could boast an unpreoccupied realism. It was willed by Don Cristóbal Ferriz in 1912 and there is a replica.

Num. **2898,** *Don Juan Bautista de Muguiro.* Moratin, who emigrated with Muguiro to Bordeaux wrote that Goya was firm and valiant at eighty-one years and said that «with a rapier in his hand he feared no one». Nevertheless his pulse faltered him and he had to paint with double spectacles. This portrait of the gentlemen from Navarre was one of Goya's last and in the dedication we read: «Don Juan de Muguiro by his friend Goya, at eighty-one in Bordeaux, May, 1827.» Observe the work and you will detect that the brush work is firm and magnificent in color. (Willed by Muguiro's descendents in 1946.)

Num. **2899,** *The Dairy-maid from Bordeaux* is probably the master's final work. Even near his death his works continued to be marvels of design and color. It is said that in proportion to the proximity of his death his soul became more youthful. The blouse and shawl have the vivid qualities of their fabrics due to his famous strokes that the eyes love to pursue. The milk-maid's inclined head and her doubled posture indicate that she was definitely riding on a small donkey. Goya was at least forty years ahead of his time; about 1860 they painted in the same way even today! (Willed by the previous.)

Num. **735,** *Fernando VII in Royal Cape,* shows him in a red ermine-lined cape, with the decorations of the previous and an accepter in his right hand. The Imperial Channel of Saragossa boasts a similar work.

Room LVI.—GOYA

New «cartoons». In this room *Blind Man's Buff* figures, a marvel full of gaiety and movement, and a golden tone in the sky and landscape, which converts the cartoon into a lovely painting of genre. Goya joins in it the popular with the aristocratic: they are lonely personages amusing themselves as it might be done by the lads and maids of Fuendetodos in a thrashing floor of their village. With this work he left his will to the Royal Factory: it was the prophetical foresight of a mind which easily would conciliate with his: that of the Duchess of Alba —whom he still did not know— a prominent figure of the nobility who at the same time loved the most plain Madrilenian amusements.

Num. **788,** *The Guards.* In a field at the banks of a river are two internal revenue guards; in the rear we see two villagers.

Num. **789,** *The Boy of the Tree.* A boy semi-hanging from a branch; behind another with a basket.

Num. **790,** *The Lad of the Bird* is sitting, back to the spectator with a linnet in his hands.

Num. **794,** *The Thrashing-floor.* A group of countrymen; while some rest, one makes even the heap with a rake and two boys heap the gavels with winnowing-forks. In the background appears a castle.

Num. **796,** *The Mason Wounded.* Two workers carry a third one wounded; scaffolds in the background.

Num. **797,** *The Beggars at the Fountain.* A woman between a child and a dwarf; in the fountain is a pitcher. In the background a modest house.

Num. **798,** *The Snowfall.* Five men, followed by a dog and a mule carrying a dead pig, go through the snowed mountains.

Num. **804,** *Blind Man's Buff.* In a lawn at the banks of a river —Manzanares?— four ladies and five young men are playing blind man's buff. A mountainous background.

Num. **768,** *Picnic on the Banks of the Manzanares.* Five young men are sitting, they drink, toast and smoke, on the ground: dishes, bottles, meals, etc. On foot a maid who sells oranges; a little more distant, two groups; to the right a dog picks a bone.

Num. **769,** *The Ball at San Antonio de la Florida.* Two couples dance with guitar and bandurria music and clasp hands sound; three other couples are sitting; to one side runs a river and in the background appears the dome of San Francisco el Grande.

Num. **770,** *The Quarrel in «Venta Nueva».* To the right appears «Venta Nueva» (New Inn) and the table on which the game caused the quarrel; two groups of fighters and others who try to make peace. Country background with a distant village.

Num. **776,** *Children blowing a Bladder.* Two boys, and a couple in the rear. Country background.

Num. **777,** *Boys pulling up Fruit.* A boy on the shoulders of anotner one and grasping a tree makes apples fall down; to the right two boys are looking on.

Num. **781,** *The Soldier and the Lady.* The lady looks to the left at a couple appearing at a wall; to the right behind the lady and her attendant, a gentleman, another couple is sitting.

Num. **782,** *The Azeroles Maid Seller.* The maid, three hooded men behind her, one of them greets her. A crowded group of people.

Room LVI A.—GOYA, «Black Paintings»

This is a world-famous room belonging completely to Goya and sheltering his famous «Black Paintings» with which he decorated his Quinta. A French nobleman, Baron Emil d'Erlanger, bought the cottage in 1873, and had the murals transferred to canvas (a work done successfully by the painter D. Salvador Martínez Cubells). D'Erlander took them to Paris for the World Fair of 1878 and it has been said that they hardly drew attention, which is understandable if we consider those who attend such spectacles. We are sure that the representatives of «Impresionism» and those who stubbornly defended it were not of the same opinion. We can deduce their admiration from the resulting prominence of this artist who painted forty years ahead of his times.

Goya bought his Quinta during the ephemeral reign of Joseph Bonaparte but unfortunately his wife died soon after leaving him in the care of a second cousin named Leocadia who had married Isidro Weiss (he abandoned her and her small daughter Rosarito). In this cottage solitude and deafness began to place their claims upon the artist. He soon commenced to decorate the rooms with strange and absurd paintings that perhaps harmonize with his nightmares and hallucinations. Goya had witnessed a war and had contemplated horrible scenes; he rested in solitude, ignoring commissions and accepted patterns... The bitter sweetness of his solitude began to devour him giving vent completely to his dreams. Able to paint what he wanted, he gave an unlimited freedom to the nightmares of his sleepless nights, and he was enveloped in a monster's world of solitude and sadness where one's judgement fails to judge, where nothing is worth the trouble and everything is one and the same.

They were not meant to be ironic paintings to scare his visitors nor amusing sketches to entertain his friends. They are an escape from the concrete everyday world in which he lived for so many years. It is a purification of the ferocity that had been accumulated throughout so many intrigues, struggles and inanities. He unburdens himself and becomes quiet. (They are not *Caprices* aggrandized by his brush. A *Caprice* is a pedagogic moralisation; it is a fiery thrust aimed at the social larvae). The «Black Paintings» with their monster, goblings and witches, are the excretions of a soul tormented in one of those «diminuendos» of a life in which nothing is interesting nor desirable, when life fails to teach us anything new, because everything has been seen and attained. By painting in a careless manner, with his thumb, with sponges, with blows and scrapings of a spatula and utilizing only black, ochre, red and white he has created a magical world that attracts while disquieting.

Num. **754,** *A «Manola»*. It looks like a black stain upon a rock. (Previously it was in the dining room of his Quinta.)

Num. **755,** *Pilgrimage to the Fountain of San Isidro*. A group of mentally deranged are in the right foreground, a shapeless confusion near the mountain, and a landscape under a pelting shower. (It was in one of the halls.)

Num. **756,** *The Witches' Sabbath* shows two witches flying over a camp of soldiers, a bad omen. (Equally situated as the previous.)

Num. **757,** *Destiny*, is a woman with scissors in hand representing Death cutting the thread of existence. She wavers between the child being born and the old man who still wants to investigate the wonders of the world through his lens.

Num. **759,** *Two Friars*. One is clattering and the other cannot hear. (This and the previous were on the main floor.)

Num. **760,** *The «Romería» of San Isidro*, depicts a group of possessed who have escaped from an insane asylum, and come back from the «romería». (It was in the dining room.)

Num. **761,** *The Witches' Sabbath*. This fascinating painting reminds us of the fabulous sabbatical nights of Salazar and Zugarramurdi. Congregated by the buck in a friar's habit, the witches have come with their jars and ointments to listen to the advice of the «abracadabring» inspirer. What does this *manola* seated on a chair in *man-*

tilla and mufti represent? (Another picture which enhanced Goya's meals.)

Num. **762,** *Two Old Men Eating Soup,* is a representation of old age without dignity. (Previously on the main floor.)

Num. **763,** *Saturn Devouring his Son,* is a plastic and repugnant expression of the mythological god who devours one of his children and has savoured all axcept the head and an arm; his hands envelop the dead body.

Num. **764,** *Judith and Holófernes* is a sarcastic version of the Biblical episode. (Also in the world Goya managed to dine in peace.)

Num. **765,** *Two Women and a man.* In the three faces there is nothing else than evil. (On the main floor.)

Num. **766,** *The reading.* The only thing that occurs to one to ask is what the man is reading at the right, listened to with such avidity by the others. (On the main floor.)

Num. **767,** *A Dog Buried in the Sand.* On a barren and imposing scene the dog's head appears. Did he remain blocaded by a hurricane of sand? What possible significance could this painting of such dimensions and only one motive have? (It was on the main floor.)

Num. **758,** *Quarrel by Cudgelling,* shows one of those ferocious spectacles among the lowest classes. Probably witnessed by the artist, two rivals, provided with large clubs bury themselves up to the knees so they cannot withdraw from the fight. One of the two, or both, has to necessarily yield. The scene and landscape are barren.

Room LVII.—GOYA

We are in the last Room with «cartoons». Here is *The Nincompoop,* another of the famous works of the tapestry Factory. In the preceding rooms we have seen some themes about children. Here we meet them again. Goya felt a paternal fondness towards children. From his twenty sons with his wife Josefa Bayeu only one outlived, the who almost «killed him of joy» when Goya saw him again in Bordeaux. His excessive love to his grandson Marianito and the young Rosarito Weiss, shows his fondness of children in every epoch of his artistic life. And these «cartoons» are also an evident proof.

Num. **743,** *The Majo and the Guitar.* He is sitting and sings to the guitar music. Three figures in the rear.

Num. **774,** *The Kite*. A group of young people in the country let a kite go; some viewers; in the foreground is a smoker, etc.

Num. **780,** *The Crockery Seller*. A stand of çrockery of Alcora; a young girl with a cup in her hand; a coach with two lackeys and a lady inside who is contemplated by two young men with their backs to the spectator; in the background to the left are other figures.

Num. **783,** *Boys Playing Soldiers*. Two boys carrying a gun; another beats a drum; to the left another boy.

Num. **786,** *The Laundresses*. One is sleeping leaning upon the legs of another girl. This one and a friend pretend to frighten the first one by means of a lamb. In the rear are two other laundresses.

Num. **791,** *The Woodmen*. Three men, two with hatchets are destroying a fallen tree.

Num. **793,** *The Flower Sellers*. A young girl giving her hand to a child; another to the right kneeling with flowers, behind them a man who wishes to surprise the first one with a little rabbit. Country background with village and hills.

Num. **799,** *The Wedding*. Musicians and boys precede the suite; the betrothed —a young bride and old and grotesque bridegroom— are followed by the priest, the godfather, etc.; in the background an arch.

Num. **800** a): *Los Gitanillos*. Four boys are playing and another one in the rear. Country background.

Num. **801,** *The Stilts*. Two young men on stilts, accompanied by two flageolet-players, boys, men and women; to the right at the window is a young lady.

Num. **802,** *The Nincompoop*. Five young men toss a doll in a blanket. Trees in the background.

All the «cartoons» of these three rooms after their employment as patterns in the Royal Factory, were rolled and stored in a department of the Royal Palace in Madrid; after several years they were unrolled, cleaned and brought to the Museum to these rooms *ad hoc*, to display all their beauty.

Room LVII A.—GOYA

Num. **727,** *Portrait of Carlos IV*. Once again we see Carlos IV, this time in a vest, blue dress coat, and red trousers, Toison and the two sashes of Carlos III and saint «Jenaro».

Num. **728,** *Portrait of the Queen María Luisa*. In a black dress of *maja* with mantilla, pink bow and fan, we see her at forty eight. The graceful dress of the lower class Madrilenian women was far from suitable, however she was well aware of her attractive arms and took every possible opportunity to display them. (This portrait and the previous one came from Godoy's collection.)

Num. **2785,** *The Colossus,* or *the Panic.* It is said that it can also represent the war. The people flee frightened and only a donkey, who happily is un-informed about it, remains motionless before the general panic. The picture is related with the famous engraving, also by Goya entitled *The Colossus.*

Num. **750,** *The Pradera of San Isidro,* shows an angular river bank in the foreground on which banks appear the first figures in clear hues, and then the prairy background on May the 15th, the feast day of Madrid's Patron Saint. The prairy is crowded with a miniaturized throng on horseback, running in circles, and amusing themselves in a thousand ways. On the other side of the Manzanares river Madrid is visible, and we note the Royal Palace and San Francisco el Grande. (Obtained in the Casa de Osuna auction in 1896 por 15 000 *pesetas.*)

Numbers **751** and **752,** *A Dead Duck* and *A Dead Fowl* (were acquired from Sr. García Palencia in 1900 for 6000 *pesetas*).

Num. **744,** *A «Garrochista» on Horseback,* was already in the museum in 1828.

Num. **2895,** *The Flageolet-player,* is a tapestry «cartoon».

Room LVIII.—SCULPTURE AND PAINTING

This Rotunda which corresponds to that of Velázquez in the upper floor is consecrated to Sculpture. All the paintings hanging on the walls represent mythological themes and are generally copies by first-class Flemish painters.

Regarding the sculptural collection Bernardino de Pantorba tells us: «The sculptural pieces of the Prado Museum come in almost totally from the royal collections. They were acquired by our monarchs or presented to them. We can establish with the ensemble two very definite nucleus; the Greek-Roman and that of Renaissance and modern works (16th to 19th centuries). Here the representation of medieval sculpture is lacking.

«The origin of some pieces has not been entirely cleared up. Others, the main part, proceed from the collections of Felipe V and his wife Isabel Farnesio, who was a lady of an exquisite choice and was fortunate in buying in Rome (at a high price) a good deal of sculptures which had belonged to the Queen Christine of Sweden. We have also the group formed by what belonged to Carlos V and Felipe II and with the works sent by Pope Paul III to the Emperor and the presents of Cardinal Montepulciano. The worthy series of Roman busts presented by the diplomat Don José Nicolás de Azara to Carlos IV is also noticeable. These busts, acquired in Italy, sum up about thirty. Finally we must add the few examples which remain of the purchases made by Velázquez in Italy by order of his king.

«Among the classic marbles there are several of Pheidia's school which are excelling, as the beautiful head of an Athenian horse and the masculine torso (this one of the Zaya's legacy) which enrich Room LXXI. The most noticeable of the Hellenistic period are *The Venus of the Shell* and the *Hipnos*, and to the Praxitelian course correspond the *Group of St. Alphonsus* (two naked ephebes, which may represent Castor and Pollux) and *The Faun of the Kid*. The *Venus of the Dauphin* and *Aphrodite*, from the Zaya's legacy.

«From the Rennaisance group figure the illustrious names of the Italians Leone and Pompeo Leoni who left in Spain so wonderful bronzes: in our Museum the *Carlos V* of the Rotunda and *Felipe II* in Room XXI.»

Room LIX.—FLEMISH PAINTERS OF THE 16th CENTURY

In the Rooms on the main floor is seen the generation following the primitives of the XV century. Like **Juan Massys** (son of Quintin Metsis) and others, they had already been in Italy and had brought a concept less full of mannerisms about the human figure, though at the cost of sacrificing the modisms of the great eyckian epoch and immediately afterwards, that of Van der Weyden, for example. After that already seen in Room XL and the following, we shall point what is important in this one.

J. C. Van Oostamen. Num. **2697**, *Saint Jerome.*
Anonymous Flemish. Num. **1916**, *Triptych of the Mystic Marriage of St. Catherine of Siena*, and Donors on the little doors.
Master of the legend of St. Catherine. Num. **2706**, *Marriage of the Virgin* (small tablet).
Ambrose Benson. Num. **1933**, *St. Anne, the Virgin and the Child.* Splendidly coloured and beautiful cloth-foldings; a beautiful landscape in the background with delicate blue tones.
Pieter Coecke Van Aelst. Num. **2703**, *Triptych of the Annunciation, the Adoration of the Magi, and the Nativity.* The painter has included a black King following the tradition of Memling.

Master of 1518. Num. **2217,** *Triptych of the Adoration of the Magi.* The artist has included a brown King.

Master of the half figures. Num. **2552,** *Triptych of the Annunciation, the Nativity and the Presentation in the Temple.* Not so good as the former works.

Master of the «Virgo inter Virgines». Num. **2539,** *The Pieta.*

Christopher Amberger. Numbers **2183** and **2184,** *Portrait of the Goldsmith of Augsburg Jörg Zörer and his wife.* Two magnificent works by the great portrayer of the Emperor Charles I of Spain and V of Germany.

There are still in this Room six tablets by Ambrose Benson concerning episodes of the life of Jesus Christ, the Virgin, Saint Thomas of Aquino, and St. Dominic of Guzman.

Jan Prevost. Num. **1296,** *Zachary* is shown astounded at the birth of his son, with the palms of his hands turned up.

Room LX.—ANTONIO MORO AND VAN SCOREL

If there were Dutch painters who cultivated a humble and popular art against the decorative and baroque pomp of the Flemish, Holland can also present a record of first-class painters of portraits, as Rembrandt, Franz Hals, Van de Welde, Van der Helst, Vermeer de Haarlem, etc. Previous to all of them is Anton Van Dashorst, who in Spain is called **Antonio Moro** and in a certain way separates himself from the Dutch tradition in order to give to his portraits the elegance and solemnity of the great Italian portrayers.

Antonio Moro. *Born in Utrecht in 1519 and died in Antwerp in 1576. He was Jan van Scorel's disciple. He owes his entrance in Felipe II's Court to Cardinal Granvela who estimated him as the unusual gift of the artist deserved. During a trip of our King to Flanders he made the acquaintance of Moro through the cardinal. Antonio portrayed the monarch and painted also the portrait of the Duke of Alba. Felipe II, satisfied with the work, offered the artist the post of Painter of the King in the Spanish Court. Moro accepted it but asked the King's permission to visit Rome. He was allowed to and then he continued to perfect his art. Felipe II sent for him and commissioned him to stop in Lisbon to portray his betrothed, the Princess Doña María, Juan III's daughter. He also painted the portrait of her mother, the Queen Doña Catalina, Emperor Carlos V's sister. There was no marriage and Moro entered Spain* *in 1550. He painted again Felipe II's portrait and some personages of his family, When the marriage of the King with Mary Tudor, Queen of England, was formalized, Felipe II sent Moro to London, and he travelled with his wife Mergen. The artist sent the picture and in 1559 returned to Spain. In this period he painted the portrait of Isabel de Valois, new wife of Felipe II. Later he also portrayed his fourth wife Anne of Austria.*

For some reason which has not yet been sufficiently explained, Antonio Moro almost subreptitiously left the Court and Spain, going to Utrecht and establishing himself. Felipe demanded his presence in Spain and even required the Gran Duke to send him back. But the latter argued that Moro was painting a new portrait of him, and when it was finished he claimed that he had other works engaged. In short, Dutch painter never returned, but he left in Spain several disciples, the first of them being Sánchez Coello, who substituted for Moro as the King's painter.

Num. **2108,** *The Queen Mary of England, Second Wife of Felipe II* (Pl. 41). Daughter of Henry VIII and Catalina de Aragón, she was born in Greenwich in 1516, was crowned queen in 1553 and married Felipe II the following year dying four years later. This is the portrait which determinated the trip of the painter to London. The queen carries the jewel of the Austrias, the diamond «Estanque» and the pearl «Peregrina», and in her right hand the red rose of the Tudors. In spite of the painter's wish to embellish the Queen, who was eleven years older than her betrothed and who was his aunt, Felipe II was not too fascinated by the Queen's charms, although he accepted her with agreement because of State reasons. The portrait is a jewel of our Museum, and to find a match in this order of painting one should raise to the best portraits of Holbein.

Num. **2107,** *Pejeron.* Buffoon of the Count of Benavente and the Grand Duke of Alba. He holds a pack of French in his deformed hand and looks to the spectator with malignant eyes. In the rest it is a wonderful head, which deserves a better personage. He was probably a very esteemed and distinguished buffoon, because the Emperor himself speaks of him in a letter which he wrote from Brussels. (It figured in the Retiro.)

Num. **2109,** *Doña Catalina de Austria, wife of Juan III of Portugal.* The daughter of Juana la Loca (the Mad) and Felipe el Hermoso (the Handsome) was born in 1507 after the death of her father. In 1525 she married the King of Portugal. The portrait was purchased in 1552 and several copies were made. (Inventory of the Alcázar.)

Num. **2110,** *The Empress Doña María de Austria, Wife of Maximilian II.* She was the daughter of the Emperor Carlos I of Spain and V of Germany, born in 1528 one year after Felipe II. At twenty she married Maximilian.

Num. **2111,** *The Emperor Maximilian II,* son of Ferdinand I. (King of Romans, was born in 1527, at thirty seven Emperor and he died in Ratisbon in 1576. He boasts the Toison. (In the inventory of the Alcázar.)

Num. **2112,** *Doña Juana de Austria, Mother of King Don Sebastián of Portugal.* She was also a daughter of our Emperor Carlos V. Born in 1535; she married Don Juan, Prince of Brazil when she was seventeen. The unfortunate King, Don Sebastián of Portugal who died in Alcazarquivir, was her son. From her shawl hangs the little figure of an armed soldier. (In the inventory of the Alcázar.)

Num. **2113,** *The Lady with the Jewel.* The studious ask themselves who can this lady be who caresses the pearl of her jewel with two fingers. When Carlos III acquired the picture it was believed to be the portrait of Empress Isabel; later it was supposed that she represented Doña María of Portugal, betrothed to Felipe II. Allende-Salazar and Sánchez Cantón think that she may be the Infanta Doña Isabel, the IVth Duke of Branganza's daughter, who married the Infante Don Duarte. She was portrayed during the stay of Moro in the Court of Portugal around 1552. (Noted in the Retiro.)

Num. **2114,** *Metgen, the Wife of the Painter,* When Antonio Moro went to London, commissioned by Felipe II to paint the portrait of María Tudor, he took with him his wife, Metgen. This one and the Queen present the same pose, with the only difference that the Queen has in her right hand the red rose of the Tudor and Methen holds a little white dog.

The technique of both of the two portraits is the same. (In the inventory of the Alcázar.)

Num. **2115,** *The Duchess of Feria* (?). It figures in the «Catalogue» with this question mark indicating the supposition that she is Doña Juana Dormer, Sir Williams's daughter who was a good friend of María Tudor. In 1538 she married the Duke of Feria. (Acquired by Carlos IV, it proceeds from Aranjuez.)

Num. **2116,** *Lady with a Cross on her Neck.* This adorned lady has not yet been identified. From her neck hangs a Cross of the Portuguese Order of Christ.

Num. **2117,** *Margarita de Parma* was the daughter of our Emperor Carlos V and of a lady named Juana van der Gheyst. She was born in Audenarde in January 1521 and died in Ortonna in 1586.

Num. **2117** bis: *Doña Margarita of Portugal* was the daughter of Don Duarte, Juan III's brother. She married Alessandro Farnesio. This tablet and the previous one proceed from a triptych. (Both of them figured in the Manor house of Duke of Arco.)

Num. **2118,** *Felipe II.* Num. **2119,** *The Lady with the Golden Chains.* She has not yet been identified.

Van Scorel, Jan. *Dutch painter born in Scorel ih 1495 he died in Utrecht in 1562.*

Num. **2580,** *A Humanist.* It is a superb portrait, a very noble face with 'a serene glance toward the spectator. The left hand leans on a dog and the right one points to the Babel's Tower abandoned after the dispersion. It is such an expressive figure that it seems to wait our answer to its question.

Marinus Claeszon von Reymerswaele. *Dutch painter, born in Zealand at the end of the 15th century, he died in 1567.*

Num. **2567,** *The Money Changer and his Wife,* We see a certain monotony in the coloring and a hardness in the folds. Nevertheless the picture is admisibly designed and evidently realistic in all its parts and details. Very noticeable are the filcher hands characteristic of the money changers in their attitude of taking and clasping wealth. (Legacy of the Duke of Tarifa, it entered the Museum in 1934.)

Room LX A.—FLEMISH OF THE 17th CENTURY

Again we meet **Rubens, Van Dyck,** and contemporaries as **Crayer** and **Sechers,** who do not add anything new to what we have seen up to now. The main interest belongs to **Otto Venius** with his beautiful tablet in which he portrayed the Dukes of Ciudad Real.

Otto Venius *(Leyden, 1558; Brusels, 1629), Rubens's master.*

Numbers **1858** and **1859,** *Don Alonso de Idiáquez and his Wife Doña Juana de Robles.* They are two doors of a triptych. The two praying figures are accompanied by their homonymous Saints: St. Alphonsus and St. John the Baptist. Allende-Salazar and Sánchez Cantón give us the principal facts about these two personages. Don Alonso was born in San Sebastian in 1565, the son of Juan de Idiáquez, Felipe II's minister. He possessed the titles of Ist Duke of Ciudad Real and Ist Count of Aramayona, Great Knight Commander of the Order of Santiago, Vice-roy and Captain General of Navarre, Grand-master of Camp, General and Castellan of Milan, etc., etc. In Flanders he married Doña Juana de Robles, Baroness of Villy and Moleycierre, daughter of Don Gaspar de Robles, Knight Commander of Horcajo, Colonnel of Germans and Governor of Friesland, who died in the siege of Antwerp. (The origin of these works is unknown. They entered the Museum in 1870.)

Anonymous Flemish. Num. **2884,** *Judith and Holophernes.* A very beatiful tablet of golden tinge and two carnations; the pale one of Judith and the blushing of her maid-servant.

A. Cronenburch. *This painter, born in Friesland (Netherland) painted about the end of the 16th century.*

The four tablets, with portraits whose background are always the same grey stones with lion heads as motif, are wonderful for the purity of the drawing. Certain delicate details, such as a yellow flower, a few carnations, etc., are a good proof of the artist's exquisite sensitiveness.

Num. **2074,** *Two Netherlander Ladies.* Num. **2075,** *Portrait of a lady and a child* (Pl. 42).

Num. **2076,** *Portrait of a Lady with bound Hands.* Num. **2073,** *Portrait of a Netherlander Lady.*

M. de Coxcyen. Numbers **1468, 1469** and **1470,** *Triptych on the Death of the Virgin.* The Virgin is expiring with a smile and an Angel is waiting to take Her to Heaven. The Apostles appear to be somewhat pompous. The birth of Mary is richly intonated, but the scene is rather conventional. The appearance is very charming, though the figures in the foreground are entirely out of the situation. The whole triptych is very richly colored.

Jan van Scorel. Num. **1515,** *The Deluge.* A crowd of miniature people, with a great display of nudes, are climbing up the trees and the mountains to free themselves from the sweeping waters.

Marino Claeszon van Reymerswaele. Num. **2100,** *St. Jerome.* On the book placed on the lectern the *Great Assize* by Van der Weyden is visible. (This tablet was in the Alcázar in 1636.) Num. **2101,** *The Virgin and the Child.*

Jan Sanders van Hemesen. Num. **1542,** *The Virgin and the Child.* A large-sized canvas with figures painted in hard, tanned colours. The Virgin, dressed in a red cloak and green gown, without the usual face of the Virgins, is sitting and leaning upon a tree. The Child, both legs parted, is caressing His Mother.

Hollandish School. Num. **1960,** *Portrait of a Man.* Painted down to the knees. A splendid head with a bearded face.

Anonymous disciple of Antonio Moro. Num. **2881,** *Portrait of a Young Man.*

Room LXI.—MURILLO

Our Prado Museum is so rich with works of **Murillo** that not being able to have sheltering in the Great Central Gallery, this beautiful room has been reserved instead. It is certain that the best hang in that Room, but the ones here are quite worthy of having hung by the side.

Murillo. Num. **960**, *The Holy Family of the Little Bird* (Pl. 43). Thus it is called because of a little bird which characterizes it and that the Child has in His right hand. Everything in this scene reveals a sweet intimacy. It could easily be the Holy Family or that of a minstrel from Sevilla in his shop. Saint Joseph has left his carpenter's bench and rests seated, the Virgin is reeling a skein of thread. The Child amuses himself showing the little bird to the dog. For this idea and a similar one Murillo has been called vulgar; an unjust appreciation since he always painted what he wanted, and thus, as episodes like this modestly described, he knew how to give sumptuousness to his marvellous Conceptions.

Something similar occurs with Num. **973**, *The Conception*, half body, about which there is a popular story without basis. It is well understood that a young girl from Seville, of unusual beauty served as model, and nevertheless the artist has known how to ennoble her, even to giving her the lights of divinity.

On the other hand, nobody can deny that in Num. **981**, *Vision of Saint Francis in Porciuncula*, true celestial atmosphere exists, as much in Crist and the Virgin as in the Saint kneeling in ecstasy. The angels shed the roses into which the spines of the brambles had changed, and splendid red skies inundate all the composition.

It does not cease to be charming even though there is an anachronism in Mary's dress, Num. **968**, *Saint Anne and the Virgin*, already of the last epoch of the painter.

The aggregate of Murillo's pictures is wonderful upon sight, and if we remember that he was self-taught in the essential, and that some creations of his have lasted throughout many centuries and maintain their pristine freshness, we will have more than sufficient motives in order to dedicate a place of honor in great Spanish painting to him.

Num. **975**, *The Virgin of the Rosary*. This is one of the most beautiful Mothers in the iconography of all times. The conjunct Mother-Son is extremely happy and harmonious. None of the figures surpasses the other. So, if the Mother is imposing for her majesty, the Son is captivating for His vehement, «stuck», perforative glance that Murillo knew how to give to the children. Instead, *The Virgin and Jesus* under num. **976** must have been painted during the first epoch of the artist if we may judge properly some hardness in the execution that we can notice in the face of the Divine Child.

Num. **987**, *Saint Jerome*. A full figure of natural size. It is a beautiful work of rich carnation corresponding to the age of the Saint and painted, according to Meyer, between 1650-1652, that is to say when Murillo was about 32 or 33 years old.

Num. **996,** *Rebecca and Eliezer.* Extremely graceful in colour and composition is this group of figures, who appear standing beside the curb-stone of a well. If we want to realize the facilities that Murillo must have had to find in the Seville of his time those fashionable and graceful models, it is enough to appreciate the elegance of the four water-carrier women.

Num. **961,** Is also worthy of praise: *The Adoration of the Shepherds* (Pl. 44). Besides the masterly realism of the figures, the picture is full with those details that Murillo could use for extremely ornamental purposes, such as the lamb, the hen, the eggs, etc.

Very beautiful and sensitive is *The Mother of Sorrows* (num. **977**), as vell as *Ecce Homo* (num. **966**), *Saint Ferdinand* (num. **983**) and *Christ on the Cross* where Jesus is shown nailed with three nails as it should be.

Room LXI A.—RIBERA

This Room is also magnificent, destined to bring together all the works of Españoleto which could not be given a place in the Great Central Gallery. The collection of works of the painter born in Játiva which we have in the Prado Museum cannot be achieved by any other Museum in the world; so although it is certain that almost all this was executed in Naples, on the other hand the Spanish demands were so frequent and numerous that the best works of Ribera arrived at our shores.

Num. **1079,** *Saint Andrew* is represented down to the knees with a very forshortened face and prodigious hands. A fish on the table alludes to the work of a fisherman. The cross where he suffered martyrdom is visible in the penumbra.

Num. **1073,** *Saint Peter in Vinculis.* The saint appears lying down on the ground with unfastened shackles. An angel, beautifully dressed in violet and yellow inks, is showing him the way out. The lighting and shading of the picture impress a hardness of strong contrast against a gloomy background.

Num. **1072,** *Saint Peter Apostle* bolding two keys with his right hand.

Num. **1121,** *Archimedes*, holding two compasses with his hand looks like a laughing and breast-uncovered beggar.

Num. **1102,** *Saint Joseph with Jesus Child.* The hardness of the contrast reaches the highest point in this picture. The face and the hands are the only lighted touches.

Num. **1124,** *Women in combat,* in which two brave women fight in the presence of soldier spectators. Certain event occurred in Naples before the Marquis of Vasto, between two women, Isabelita de Carazzi and Diambra de Petinella, who fought over the love of Fabio de Ceresola.

Num. **1095,** *Saint Sebastian,* Excellent half nude without excessive hardness and with a unique amber-like modelling that makes evident the athletic type. The correct diagonals formed by the branches of the tree and the arms should be noticed.

Num. **1120,** *Æsop* is another beggar from the Posilipo, with torn garments. Is he writing one of his fables? Num. **1115,** *Saint Jerome.*

Num. **2442,** *St. Diego of Alcalá.* This new version of the miracle of St. Casilda presents the saint admiring and showing the flowers that have been transformed from food. (Acquired from Don Emilio de Sola in 1932.)

Num. **2594,** *St. Luke contemplating the Crucifix.* One of the most pathetic paintings by Zurbarán. We see an emaciated Christ with His crossed feet fastened to the cross with four nails. This is definitely rare in the Spanish tradition because generally three nails are employed. St. Luke is represented by the painter holding the palette and brushes while painting Christ. According to patristic tradition St. Luke was a painter but without doubt in this case his figure is actually a self portrait of Zurbarán. His face could not possibly be more attentive and expressive. This characteristically shaded canvas is one with the strongest light and dark contrast. (Acquired by Don Cristóbal Colón in 1936 with funds from the Count of Cartagena legacy.)

Num. **2803,** *Still life.* There is a sharp constrast upon the dark background of various bronze, clay, and porcelain pots. This almost perfect study of the natural was one of his early works. (A gift of Cambó in 1940.)

Num. **2888,** *Flower-pot.* Acquired by the Ministry of National Education in 1946.

Num. **1111,** *Saint Chistopher.* Num. **1077,** *Saint Andrew.* Number **1070,** *The Immaculate Conception,* with blue mantel and white gown. The shape is not so graceful as the usual by Murillo.

Num. **1071,** *Saint Peter.* Num. **1112,** *The Blind Sculptor Gambassi* is feeling the head of Apollo; it is a very hard picture, although the hands that are feeling the head seem to «speak».

Room LXII.—MURILLO AND OTHER PAINTERS

There are also four little canvases by Murillo in this room, with the story of the *Prodigal Son*, that served for the definite pictures of the Beit Collection in London.

In num. **997,** One sees the son receiving his heritage, and in the three that follow, the farewell to the paternal home, his licentious life among the court people, and his ultimate destiny as hog-keeper.

We also find some *Landscapes;* a *Self-Portrait*, a copy by Murillo, and a second copy made by A. M. de Tobar.

Valdés Leal. Num. **1160,** *The Presentation of the Virgin in the Temple*, is a theme of pictorial Italian tradition (Tiziano, Crespi, etc.), that represents the girl Mary being presented in the temple to dedicate herself to God. The priest receives her while her parents, Saint Joachim and Saint Anne, with other persons comment upon the action. Some believe the person holding the water-stand to be Valdés Leal himself.

Iriarte, Ignacio. *He was born in Azcoitia (Guipúzcoa) in 1621 and died in Seville in 1685.*

Numbers **2970** and **837,** Two *Landscapes*, one with shepherds and the other with a battered Roman building.

Sevilla Romero, Juan de. *Born in Granada in 1643, died in the same place in 1695.*

Num. **2509,** *Epulon and the poor Lazarus*. The latter is looking at the rich man sitting at the table together with his family. A manservant is menacing the beggar. In the background there is a canvas representing the death of a Just man.

Room LXII A.—RIBERA

Again we find the *Apostles, Jeromes, Hermits*, and *Penitent Magdalenes*.

But we also have in this Room some important canvases such as num. **2506,** *Old Userer*, a middle-sized picture of the so-called *de genre* that the artist painted so easily. It is a half-body figure representing an old woman who is weighing gold coins on a scale. The expression of her corrugated and malicious face is self-speaking. The picture is signed on the lower left angle.

Numbers **1122** and **1123** are two fragments of a beautiful canvas named *A Fable of Bacchus*, painted by Ribera in the best epoch of his life. The picture was for some time in the Alcázar of Madrid but unfortunately it suffered great damages in the fire of 1734. Only three fragments could be saved, two of which are hung in this Room. The third piece belongs to a foreign collection. The first fragment is a feminine half figure in profile. She has a meditative face and a visible arm that, by itself, is a masterpiece. The second one shows the head of an old man, crowned with ivy, representing Bacchus. Ribera consulted a relief in Naples titled «Dionisos in the House of the Dramatic Poet», in order to paint this picture. A copy of this canvas is kept in a private collection in Paris.

Room LXIII.—CANO AND CARREÑO

Alonso Cano. Numbers **629** and **2637**, *Christ Dead, Sustained by an Angel*. If this painter prevailed in his incomparable *Conception* and, in general, in his presentation of Mary, this Christ dead, and almost bathed in moonlight is not inferior in greatness. It reveals the sculptural qualities of the gifted artist. The movement of the left leg harmonizes perfectly with the inclination of the head, avoiding any difficult symmetry. Grey lights, silvered upon the tenuous modelling of the ghost-like body, produce the impression of mystery and anguish that the painter definitely desired. (Num. **629** was acquired in the auction of the Marquis de la Ensenada, in 1769. Num. **2637**, is from the Bosch Legacy.)

Carreño. Num. **2800**, *The Naked Monster*. The choice of certain deformed beings has been very extended from Antonio Moro to Zuloaga passing through Ribera, Herrera *the Young*, Velázquez, Carreño, etc. With the existences of museums and private collections, it can form an interesting Spanish Gallery of monsters, which besides would have an undoubted historical value. This frightening girl was called Eugenia Martínez Vallejo, from Las Bárcenas, and her weight when Carreño portrayed her at six years was «seis arrobas» (150 pounds). Carlos II ordered Carreño to do two portraits one of them showing her decently dressed «for Palace use» and the other naked «with the accustomed accuracy of his brush work». In fact she is described with a true vigor of brush work and with an absolute modern fluency. The naked one, in spite of her fatty exuberances, is not repugnant and is represented (as Bacchus) with grapes and vineleaves. The first of the two, the dressed one figured at first in the Alcázar and later in the Zarzuela. The other one was also in the Zarzuela but Fernando VII gave it to the painter of the chamber, Juan Gálvez, who later sold it to Prince Don Sebastián Gabriel de Borbón (figuring in the Pau Collection) which the primogenital Duke of Marchena inherited. Finally it was given to the Museum in 1929 by Don José González de la Peña, Barón de Forma, resident in Anglet (France).

Num. **645,** *Pedro Iwanowitz Potemkin, Ambassador from Russia,* is a proof that when the case demanded it Carreño also had a brilliant palette. One simply cannot deny that a certain influence of Rubens is present. This ambassador was in Spain two times, in the epoch of Carlos II, and probably the portrait was done during the second, in 1681.

Num. **647,** *The Buffoon Francisco Bazán.* Another ill-fated «pleasure giver». (From the Alcázar it passed to the Retiro.)

Room LXIII A.—SPANIARDS OF THE 17th CENTURY

Castillo, Antonio del. *Born and died in beautiful Córdova (1603-1663). He was the son and disciple of Agustín del Castillo. His apprenticeship was with Zurbarán in Seville. A very meticulous painter, and a lover of the natural he was also gifted with an irritable character. It is told that when his disciple, Juan de Alfaro, was assigned the decoration of the cloister of Saint Francis he marked all the pictures visibly with; «Alfaro pinxit». Castillo was mortified, and having received a commission to paint in the said cloister, created a magnificent work which he signed; «Non pinxit Alfaro». It is also said that he died a hypochondriac due to the envy which Murillo's works produced on him when he tried to equal him in vain.*

Numbers **952** and **953,** *History of Joseph.* They are two of six canvases in which the artist resumed the history of the son of Jacob. In the first, one sees the scene in which Joseph is sold by his brothers to the Israelites, and in the second, the defense of his chastity, with the background a prison in which he explains the meaning of his dreams to the bread-maker and the cup-bearer. (The six canvases were acquired in 1836 for the incredible sum of 9.675 pesetas.)

Esteban March, who died in 1660, is a disciple of Ribera. If he excels in some particulars it is due to the mistakes of his master, as for instance in num. **878,** *Old Drinker.* However, he is the author of some appreciated pictures, such as num. **880,** *Old Woman with Jingles in her Hand,* a de genre scene where he was lucky in copying the master. Num. **882,** *Saint Onophre.* Num. **817,** *Old Woman with a Bottle in her Hand.*

Room LXIV.—SPANISH PAINTERS OF THE 17th CENTURY

Mazo, Juan Bautista. Num. **888,** *The Empress Doña Margarita de Austria.* It is an excellent portrait, perhaps the best by Mazo. She was the daughter of Felipe IV and Doña Mariana de Austria born in 1561 and married to Emperor Leopold fifteen years later, dying in 1673. She is in mourning for the death of her father the king. The legend that appears below the seat is apochryphal and painted much later. In the background in another room one discovers her younger brother Carlos II el Hechizado (the Bewitched) with the dwarf Maribárbola and two other persons. According to Von Loga this portrait was done the same year that the Princess left Spain to marry the Emperor. As Allende-Salazar and Sánchez Cantón tell us: «Only *The Meninas* surpass this picture in giving us a faithful image from an everyday scene of the life of the 17th century Spanish Court, which was never very festive but even more so upon the death of Felipe IV. And the nun-like spirit of Doña Mariana served to add even more gloom to the Alcázar of Madrid.» Doña Margarita is the Princess in the picture of *Las Meninas* by Velázquez. (It entered the Museum in 1847.)

Num. **1221,** *Prince Don Baltasar Carlos.* He was born in 1629 Prince of Asturias and son of Felipe IV and died in 1646. In this portrait he is sixteen. It is one of the best portraits by Mazo, in fact it was believed by Velázquez. (It came from the Academy of San Fernando in 1827.)

Cerezo, Mateo. Num. **2244,** *Saint Augustin* appears kneeling and dressed in the garments of his Order. He is looking at the apparition of the Virgin and the Child. At his feet is the mitre, as, Bishop of Hippona. The signature by the mitre runs: don Matheo Zerezo, ft. 1663. This picture was included in the exhibition of Spanish Painting that took place in London.

Jusepe Leonardo. Num. **860,** *The Virgin's Birth.* Three women attend her saintly parents, others the new-born child. Saint Joachim enters through, a door followed by a child. A moving and interesting composition, it is very traditional in its painting but treats the figures with a grace and charming ferminity. It shows that the artist was some what more than a painter of battles, and that upon deciding to deal with a secene of sweet intimacy he knew how to come out triumphant among other contemporary artists.

Claudio Coello. Num. **2583,** *The Child Jesus in the Door of the Temple* (Pl. 45). It is doubted in effect, if the figures be Jesus Christ, the Virgin and Saint Joseph who converse, or if they deal with Saint John who is bidding farewell to his parents, Zachary and Elizabeth. The suavity of the somewhat sought-after coloring of the faces makes one think, as in the past, if the canvas be the work of Carlo Dolci, of whom our Museum has nothing. While it was in the possession of its owner, the Marquis of las Marismas, it was believed to be original of the Italian painter; and as such Conquy engraved it. With the same attribution it was sold in the Hotel Drouot, of Paris. Later it passed through the hands of the Princess Orloff and of Don Apolinar Sánchez Villalba, from whom it was acquired in 1935. Then it was cleaned and the signature «Claudio Coello MDCLX» appeared.

A Charles II by Carreño also hangs in this Room. There is another *Charles II* by an anonymous author (num. **2504**).

Room LXV.—SPANISH PAINTERS

Collantes, Francisco. *Born and died in Madrid (1599-1656), a disciple of Carduccio.*

Num. **666,** *Vision of Ezekiel.* This canvas has a narrative greatness and not just a little originality within the beautiful production of our painting. In the hour of the resurrection of the flesh, that the prophet sees thus before, the skeletons galvanize and come forth from their sepulchres in a desolate landscape of ruins. It is autographed in a semi-open sepulchre to the right. Once one of the fifty pictures taken by Joseph Bonaparte, in order to form the Napoleon Museum in Paris, the French returned it in 1816. (Proceeding from the Academy, it intered in 1827.)

Num. **1020,** *The return to the sheep-fold.* A very beautiful painting by Orrente, it reminds of the Basano's similar themes.

We have to mention number **2442,** by Zurbaran, *Saint Diego os Alcalá* who shows to Father Guardián how the flowers has become food, like in the miracle of Saint Casilda.

It is also noticeable num. **701,** *Saint John,* a painting by J. G. de Espinosa, in diagonal, lighted artificially and with a more mystic than ascetic look.

Num. **2836,** *Saint Monica.* num. **2837,** *Tearful Saint.* Both are profile, both in mourning, both tearful, the elder and the younger. These canvases, not of great dimensions, figure in the altar-piece of Yepes and were finished two years after Greco's death. They suffered deteriorations in 1936, and were later restored.

Room LXVI.—TENIERS

At present let us meet **David Teniers II** of whom our Museum own a large repertory of paintings. The Teniers formed a dynasty of painters extending from the 16th century to nearly the 17th. There were two named Jules, one Abraham, one Theodore and various Davids, the second of the latter was also named «David Teniers, *the Young*» and was the most eminent figure of this large family.

David Teniers II or **the Young**, *was born in Antwerp in 1610, and was the disciple of his father, David Teniers I, or the Old. He married Ana Brueghel, the daughter of John Brueghel de Velours. He was a good friend of Rubens by whose mediation he obtained from the Archduke Leopold the post of «Preserver of the Gallery». He painted for Felipe IV, Christine of Sweden, Charles I of England and other magnates. It is also said that he was professor of drawings to Don Juan de Austria.*

His pictures were not of large size and he liked to represent the gaiety of smokers, drinkers, players; the tumult of the kermess with their meetings, recreations and dances and the quiet life of the hamlet in its country labors. It was the art he had learned in Holland with Van Ostade. At forty six he was widower with seven sons; later married again he had four more. With the help of the elders he became rich (to the extreme that he built a palace with three towers).

The last years of this painter were sad. Upon his second wife's death and afterwards that of his eldest son who was his principal assistant, his other greedy sons and grand-sons litigated with him, who was already old and infirm, and they all finished with the patrimony of the family. Teniers died et eighty years in the deepest misery.

The best collection of the Teniers are distributed in Madrid and St. Petersbourg. In the Prado we number more than fifty pictures of the Teniers's family. In the Ermitage there are about forty.

We own two canvases by Abraham which are, number **1783**, *A Guard-room* and number **1784**, *A Guard-room* (the title is repeated); and David II's lot with religious themes such as numbers **1820**, **1821** and **1822** about the *Temptations of Saint Anthony Abbot*, in which we find the propicious woman, the procuress with horns, and the small monsters representing sins; pictures of trifling genre such as numbers **1794** and **1796**, *Smokers and Drinking People;* picaresque genre such as numbers **1799** and **1800**, *The Old Man and the Maid;* witty as the four monkeys; documental as those entitled *Surgical Operation* and *The Alchemist* and for ending the folk-lore as we detect in the *Feast of the Villagers* and in the curious one *Le Roi boit* (The King drinks!) a familiar scene which the Flemish enjoy very much.

Num. **1813,** Is very interesting: *The Archduke Leopold William in His Picture Gallery in Brussels.* The Archduke appears with four gentlemen; one of them is the young Teniers. They are in the Gallery enriched with very clearly reproduced works by Tiziano, Raffaello, Ribera, il Giorgione, Van Dyck, Veronese and other important artists.

Here hangs the *History of Reynaldo and Armida*, from «Jerusalem Liberted», represented in twelve pictures 27 × 39 centimeters, attributed to the brush of David Teniers I, the Old. They are finely miniature-sized and very pleasant of color. (From the Collection of Isabel Farnesio in La Granja.)

Room LXVII.—JAN BRUEGHEL «DE VELOURS»

This room is almost entirely dedicated to **Jan Brueghel de Velours.** The ample dynasty of the Brueghel starts with Peter Brueghel, *the Old.* He left two sons: Peter Brueghel d'Enfer, so called due to the deviltries displayed in his canvases, and John Brueghel *de Velours*, because of the velvet-like delicacy given to his decorative subjects. De Velours always counted on Rubens's frienship and protection, to the extreme that he collaborated with him in a large number of canvases.

Jan Brueghel «de Velours». *Flemish painter born in Brussels in 1568 and died in Antwerp in 1625. When his father died he was only one year old and his grand-mother, the paintress Mary de Bessemers, educated him. He learned from her that delicacy with the brush which distinguished him among all the artists of his epoch which was soon to gain him the nickname of «velvetlike». He later became Peter Goekindt's disciple. Upon his return from his travels through Italy he resided in Flanders and in 1610 was named painter of Chamber of the Archdukes Albert and Elizabeth Clara Eugenia. When he died Rubens became the tutor of his sons. One of them was the painter Jan II the Young and another, Anna, married David Teniers. The work of de Velours in the Prado is very abundant; there are more than fifty pictures.*

Numbers from **1394** to **1398,** *Five Human Senses.* The mythological themes having been exhausted by Rubens, who was an unexcelled master in these subjects, it became necessary to have recourse to these themes in which genre and allegory could be mixed in an harmonious synthesis. Brueghel painted these five tablets of equal size, which are the plastic representations of the feelings excited by the five physical senses. In the representation of sight there are pictures, statues, optic instruments, a nymph contemplating *The Cure of a Blindman*, a monkey with eye-glasses..., etc. In the auditory we see musical instruments, watches, bells, a nymph singing with a lute, a distant concert, etc. The olfactory is shown with flaks of perfume, abundance of flowers, perfume censers, a nymph smelling a bouquet offered to her by a cupid, and in the background a garden... To the gustatory correspond all the victuals on the floor; pictures representing banquets, a nymph who is eating from a well-supplied table while a satyr pours wine for her; in the background there is poultry-yard a kitchen. For touch the painter has represented a pleasant scene, the kiss of Venus and Cupid, and other themes expressing sorrow, paintings of torments, a man whipping a donkey, etc.

Everything is easy and candid, but maybe the charm is in this untrascendental ingeniousness which only looks for a smile of agreement. As a miniature-sized painting it is perfect. All these tablets were presented by the Duke of Pfalz-Neuburg to the Cardinal-Infante, who gave them to the Duke of Medina de las Torres and he in turn to Felipe IV. Brueghel continued to repeat these themes in the canvases numbers **1403** and **1404,** which came from Flanders for Queen Isabel.

Numbers **1416** and **1417,** *Garlands.* It was the fashion of the epoch (observe num. **1909** by Seghers) although with Italian precedents, to represent a figure of the Virgin alone, with the Child, or with angels framed with a garland of flowers, fruits, birds, butterflies, etc. Sometimes Rubens or another painter did the figures, reserving the garland for Brueghel (or another) to let him boast the excellencies of his thin brush work. We cannot deny it certain merit, but of course the main part is the patience.

Save some landscapes, we point out numbers **1438, 1439,** and **1441,** with *Country Scenes* which are according to Brueghel the Olds's tradition and have the movement and gaiety of popular scenes. Sometimes the Archdukes appeared to participate in the general joy, and so we see them at times walking and frequently sitting at the foot of a tree or under a canopy. Some of these canvases were sent to Spain by Isabel Clara Eugenia and figured in the Alcázar.

Room LXVIII.—(Corridor). SPANISH PAINTERS OF THE 16th CENTURY

We have already met some of these artists in the main floor where we have seen their most important works. Thus we shall give a rapid glance to those figuring in this Room. However, let us now contact for the first time other painters of the same epoch whose principal pictures will be described.

Correa, Juan. *We have no notices about his birth and death dates, and only know that he painted during the 16th century. During his stay in Toledo he painted for the Cathedral from about 1539 to 1552. He painted the tablets for the altar-piece of the Monasterio de Guisando and those of the convent of the priest of Saint Bernard in San Martín de Valdeiglesias, which belonged to the Church of the Tránsito in Toledo.*

Num. **671,** The Death of the Virgin (Pl. 47). Undoubtedly we are before his best work which induces us to think that he knew the early Flemish. The apostles surround the Virgin; some read, others meditate and Saint Peter offers a candle. To the left and kneeling is the donor, D. Francisco de Rojas, Knight of Calatrava, painted with patient minuteness. In front we see a scene of the Virgin's death; on the other sides are the armorial ensigns of Rojas and Ayala. Acording to the subject the picture is treated with a great intimacy and devotion. (It proceeds from the Church of the Tránsito in Toledo.)

Navarrete el Mudo *(The Dumb), named John, was born in Logroño around 1526 and died in Toledo in 1579. He was dumb from brith. Still young he went to Italy where he especially studied Venetians. He has been called «The Spanish Tizian» nevertheless, his general coloring is cold. Felipe II encharged him with a series of the Apostles for El Escorial but the work remained unfinished. Father Sigüenza held him in the high esteem which he deserved and if death had not seized him in his full maturity he would have left wonderful works without doubt*

Num. **1012,** The Baptism of Christ is a small sized tablet with Jesus, the Baptist and four angels, and was commissioned by Felipe II although this work does not characterize well the personality of the artist. He is to be best studied in El Escorial.

Master of the eleven thousand virgins. *A master from Segovia; of unknown name, who painted about 1490.*

Num. **1294,** The Descent of the Virgin to reward St. Alphonsus. The saint, kneeling, is taking the chasuble given him by the Virgin in reward ot his having sung the glories of Mary. The Virgin is followed by a crowd of maids. At the bottom, on the right, two page-boys tumble down in surprise.

Anonymous Spaniard. Num. **528,** *A 54 year-old Gentleman.* Dressed in black, with gorget and holding a small book.

Room LXIX.—(Entrance to the «Cafeteria»)

Room LXX.—(Corridor)

Juan de Pareja. *This Pareja was a mulatto of reddish skin and tightly curled hair who served Velázquez in Seville. He did not have him in the studio as an apprentice but as a servant who mixed the colors and cleaned the brushes. The biographers of Pareja call him the «slave» of Velázquez, because his parents had come to Spain as such. So it is said, without the consideration that slavery had been abolished a century or a century and a half before. Velázquez took him to Madrid so that he might serve him with the same duties, and he also took him to Italy where he made the portrait which the Count of Radmor possesses in his castle in Salisbury.*

It is related that at the age of 45 he revealed himself as a painter. That is to say, that without Velázquez having realised that his servant could handle the palette and brushes, he surprised him with a picture magnificently painted. It is even added that, seen by Philip IV, he ordered Velázquez to set him «free»

All this sounds like rumour but it is evident that Pareja, seeing his master paint over so many years, acquired an undeniable skill which was surprising at times. Anybody can see that these abilities did not pass unnoticed by Velázquez, and knowing the kindness of his character, it is to be believed that he encouraged them, giving him advice and teaching. The constant dedication of Pareja to his master is manifested in the fact that when Velázquez died, he continued serving his widow and Mazo to the end of his days. He was born in Seville in 1610 and died in Madrid at seventy years of age.

According to Cea Bermúdez, some of his best canvases were attributed to Velázquez and Mazo.

Num. **1041,** *Saint Mathew's vocation.* It is a painting of fine proportion very beautiful, even though without the least rigidity of composition. Saint Mathew appears seated in a luxurious room, carrying out his function of tax-collector. Next to the personages of the time are others with breaches and soft hats conforming to the period of the painter. In this detail, as in the presentation of the figure of Christ, it appears that the painter has been inspired by

Veronés. The figure of the page at the back is very pleasing, who having taken a folio from the shelf, stops to listen with great attention to the convocation to Jesus. Another personage, next to this one in the scene and directing his look at the spectator, is Juan de Pareja himself. His name written on the paper that he carries in his hand confirms this. The painting dates from 1661 and forms part of the collection that Isabel Farnesio had in La Granja.

Antonio Arias. *Born and died in Madrid (1620-1684). He painted, with Carducho, some wall frescoes for the Palace of Buen Retiro.*

Num. **598,** *Caesar's Coin.* An episode narrated in Ch. XX of the Gospel of Saint Luke. Signed in the lower left corner, 1646. It is one of the first paintings which entered the Museum at its very beginnings.

(Without number: *Saint Bruno renounces the Archbishopric of Regio,* by **Vincencio Carducho.**

Palomino. *Of Christian name Antonio, born in Bujalance (Córdoba) an died in Madrid (1665-1726). A disciple in Córdoba of* **Valdés Leal,** *he also completed at the same time the career of lawyer. Juan de Alfaro encouraged him to go to the Court. Arriving in Madrid, he completed the paintings that Alfaro had left incomplete. He married doña Catalina Bárbara Pérez, and was highly estimated by Claudio Coello and Carreño. By their influence, he painted the ceiling of the Palace, after which Carlos II named him «Pintor del Rey». («King's Painter».) Lucas Jordán arrived at Madrid and our painter helped him, giving him themes for the Italian to expand upon and reproduce. Palomino painted in many Spanish cities. He has been called «the Spanish Vasari», for having written the «Museo Pictórico» about the lives of the Spanish painters. His wife dead, he made himself a priest, though he wore the long suit for a short time because he died the year following his ordenation. The literary work of Palomino has been translated into various languages.*

Num. **1026,** *The Immaculate Conception.* To the right, the dragon biting the apple. The drawing is correct, the colouring dull and the figure is no longer somewhat vulgar. It is signed in the Moon, under the garland of flowers. This picture was bought by Fernando VII from the widow of the Napolese painter for 8000 *reales*.

Orrente, Pedro de. *He was born in Montealegre (Albacete) about 1570 and died in Valencia in 1645. He has been called the «Spanish Bassano», not because he was in Italy where he might have been able to study the Venetian master, but because he admired and copied some of his paintings which arrived in our country. He travelled over almost all Spain, stopped in Toledo where he worked together with El Greco and was immediately considered to be his disciple and drew and painted a great deal. His animal drawings are very much appreciated.*

Num. **1017,** *Journey of the Loth family* (?). It is a view of the patriarch Abraham's caravan travelling across the desert. (It was in the Palace of Buen Retiro.)

Num. **1015**, *The Adoration of the Shepherds.* At the entrance of the cave of Bethlem, tinged by the slight dawn light, the Virgin Mary shows the Divine Child to the shepherds. One of them approaches with a lamb slung across his shoulders; a woman who kneels with her hand on a basket of gifts calls to the other shepherds who come near preceeded by a dog. The ox warms the feet of the recently born with its breath, which in its turn is contemplated by St. Joseph. Orrente has made a well managed show of light and dark. The tonality is burnished; the action a little scattered; there are many things... But, nevertheless, it is a painting which Caravaggio would not scorn. (In 1772, the painting was in the Madrid Palace.)

Bocanegra, *Anastasio, died in Granada, 1668. He was a follower of Alonso Cano. A painter of second order but full of vanity from the time he was named; «The Kign's Painter», in 1676, which did nothing else to him than obstruct his life and even to precipitate his death. He has paintings in Paris. St. Petersburgh and other important capitals.*

Num. **619,** *The Virgin and Child Jesus with Saint Elisabeth and St. John.* The precursor kisses the hand of Jesus. (Acquired for 3000 pesetas in 1873 from doña María Carmen Cabrero de Larrañaga.)

Room LXXI.—THE LADY OF ELCHE

Among other worthy pieces willed by the Mexican D. Mario de Zayas, excels the famous *Dama de Elche* (Pl. 48) (Lady of Elche) so called because it was discovered near this Alicantine town. It was acquired by the French archeologist, Pierre Paris, who gave it to the Louvre Museum where it remained many years until it was rescued for the national patrimony through exchange. It is anterior to the 5th century B. C. and belongs to Iberic art. It is made of a tenuously polychromed lime and appears marvellously adorned with mitre, roundlets and neck-laces.

Room LXXII.—SPANIARDS OF THE 16th AND 17th CENTURIES

This room is distinguishable by the *Flower pots* of **Arellano** and **Bartolomé Pérez** and apart from them we also meet the painter **Rodrigo de Villandrando.**

Arellano, Juan de. *He was born in Santorcaz (Madrid), in 1614 and died in the capital in 1676. At thirty-six he entered the workshop of Juan Solís, where he copied the flower pots by the Italian, Mario Nuzzi, «Mario de Fiore», which enlivened his fondness for this popular art of the 17th century. He was followed in this genre by his son, José and his son-in-law, Bartolomé Pérez who excelled the former and at times even his own master. Those of Juan still conserve the fresh tints of the original painting; but in general they have darkened, maybe due to the intense stamping of the canvas.*

Villandrando, Rodrigo de. *We ignore almost everything about his life, and his death is registered as on September 4, 1628. He belongs to Pantoja's tradition, and was also a courtier painter.*

Num. **1234,** *Felipe IV.* He appears standing, dressed in white with golden embroideries, a green cape, and with his hand on the head of the dwarf, «Soplillo», sent from Flanders by Isabel Clara Eugenia. (It figured in the inventory of the Alcázar.)

Núm. **1234** *b), Isabel of France, or Bourbon, Wife of Felipe IV.* It matches the previous and the queen is also dressed in white and goldf. (D. Valentín Carderera's legacy.)

Sánchez Coello. Num. **1138,** *The Princesses Isabel Clara Eugenia and Catalina Micaela,* daughters of Felipe II and Isabel of Valois, his third wife. Isabel gives her sister a crown of flovers.

Pantoja. Num. **2562,** *Felipe III.* Son of Felipe II and father of Felipe IV, he was born in 1578 and died in 1621. He is portrayed with half armature and staff. (Duke of Tarifa's legacy.)

Num. **2563,** *The Queen Doña Margarita,* wife of Felipe III dressed in white with pearls. (Item.)

Room LXXIII.—THE TREASURE OF THE DAUPHIN

This treasure is called of the *Dauphin* because Felipe V inherited it from his father, the Dauphin of France —the primogenial of Louis XIV— who never reigned. Bernardino de Pantorba tells us: «It seems that the king of Spain received that lot of jewels without showing a great interest and ordered that they be kept in the Palace of La Granja, where they remained for many years. Following the monarch's orders, in 1734 an inventory was made noting 86 jewels of hard stones with settings of gold, enamel, precious stones and cameos. Today we have 71, to which it must be added the pieces of rock crystal work which are 49, making a total of 120 jewels, due to Italian and French artisans of the 16th and 17th centuries».

Room LXXIV.—(Rotunda). SPANISH PAINTERS OF THE 17th CENTURY

Antolínez. Num. **2443,** *The Immaculate Conception.* Excessively notched and crude of colour. Angels, palm-trees, roses, crowns, white lilies..., a «totum revolutum».

Valdés Leal, Juan de. *This painter was born in Seville in 1662 and died in item in 1690. According to some biographers, he was a disciple of Antonio del Castillo and others point out Herrera el Viejo (the Old) as his master. If he was the latter's disciple, he inherited his naughty character and pessimism, which in Valdés was desolating; Maybe because of the reverse of fortune his character was altered and balanced, which at times lifted him to masterly peaks and others drew him to the most atrocious vulgarities. Incorrect in the sketch and valiant in the coloring, he excels in the impassioned and vigorous compositions. He married Doña Isabel Martínez Miralls, with whom he had five children, one of them called Lucas, who was a painter. His most popular works are* In Ictus Oculi *and* Finis Gloriae Mundi *which hang in the Hospital de la Caridad in Seville.*

Num. **2582,** *A Martyr of the Order of St. Jerome.* This Saint so balanced and so placid with his three crown's palm and his book, displays the complex personality of the painter. Here he shows himself grave and restrained, careful of the sketch and of the meditative expression in contrast with pompous and dramatical compositions of the same epoch. (Marshall Soult took the painting off to Paris with the following one; it belonged to Louis Philippe's collection and passed through several hands. In 1935 the Patronage of the Museum bought it.)

Num. **2593,** *Saint Jerome,* is a magnificent picture in which we see the Saint with Cardinal's clothing, and two angels carrying the hat. At his feet is the lion. (It was acquired from Agnew's House, in London, by means of the Count of Cartagena's legacy.)

Claudio Coello. Num. **662,** *St. Dominic of Guzmán.* Num. **663,** *St. Rose of Lima.*

Anonymous Italian. Num. **2561,** *D. Luis de la Cerda, IX Duke of Medinaceli.* It is a beautiful Napolitan painting of the General of the Naples' galleys, who died prisoner in the castle of Pamplona in 1711.

Romm LXXV.—RUBENS AND CONTEM-PORARIES

Leaving out two pictures about religious subjects, belonging to the series of the Apostles distributed in different Room, **Rubens** still offters the spectator an exhibition of his copious imagination of mythological themes.

Erasmo Quellyn. *Born in Amberes, 1607, and died in same, 1678.*
Num. **1630,** *Death of Eurydice.* Eurydice, bitten by an asp in the foot, falls dead in the arms of her husband, Orpheus. Signed on the lower edge. (Painted for the «Torre de la Parada».)

J. P. Gowi. *He died in Amberes during the first half of the XVII century.*
Num. **1540,** *The fall of Icaro son of Dedalus.* His father made him some wings but he wanted to fly so high with them that the sun destroyed them and he fell into the Aegean Sea. It is signed and was painted after a sketch by Rubens.

Rubens. Num. **1543,** *The judgement of Solomon.* This painting is considered to be of Rubens, but it has also been attributed to Bockporst and to Jordaens. It is the biblical episode of the two mothers, one child dead and the other alive.

Num. **1675,** *The goddess Flora.* The figure of the Queen of the flowers is of Rubens and the flowers are by Jan Brueghel, his follower.

Num. **1658,** *Lapiths and Centaurs.* By Rubens, Hypodamia, desired by Mars, married Piritoo, king of the Lapiths and during the wedding banquet, Mars launched the centaurs against the Lapiths. This is the episode which the canvas depicts.

Num. **1660,** *The Banquet of Tereus.* The mythological fable tells us that Pandion, the king of Attica, being grateful to Tereus, king of Tracia, because of his assistance in the war, gave him one of his two daughters named Procne, in marriage (from whose union they had a son called Itis). But Tereus loved the other daughter, Philomela, and in order to attain her, he left his wife in a forest leading others to think that she died. One day Philomela found her sister and referred her as being ignorant and that she had abandoned herself to Tereus. Then Procne killed her son, Itis, and had his flesh served to her husband. The Rubens' scene represents Procne, followed by Philomela showing the head of Itis to Tereus to make him understand that the meat he had eaten was that of his son. (Painted for the Torre de la Parada.)

Num. **1659,** *The Abduction of Proserpine.* By Rubens. She was

the daughter of Jupiter and Ceres, and was attended by Pluto, god
of the hells but Ceres refused him. However during Jupiter's absence,
Proserpine was taken off one day when she was in a garden picking
flowers with some friends. She became the goddess of hell together
with Pluto until the day her mother rescued her. In the composition
we see Pluto on a cart carrying Proserpine in his arms while Minerva,
Venus and Diana try to detain him. (It was painted for the Torre
de la Parada.)

J. Cossiers. *Born and died in Antwerp (1600-1671).*

Num. **1464,** *Prometeo.*

Paeter Simons. *Native of Antwerp. Died 1629.*

Num. **1971,** *Cephalus and Procris.* Cephalus rests, keeping a javelin in his right hand. His wife Procris rests at his side also.

Jack Eyck. *Born in Antwerp (1612-1668).*

Num. **1714,** *Apollo pursuing Daphne.* Scarcely does Apollo reach
her and the nymph changes into a laurel.

Num. **1711,** *Hercules killing the dragon.* A copy of a painting by
Rubens, made by Juan Bautista del Mazo.

Num. **1667,** *Orpheus and Eurydice.* Eurydice wife of Orpheus,
died due to a snake bite, and the latter descended to hell to rescue
her. Pluto and Proserpine, the masters of hell, impressed by the
weeping of the lyre player returned his beloved imposing but one
condiction: that Orpheus would walk ahead and would not turn
his head to look at Eurydice until arriving at the earth. This is the
theme described by Rubens developed with the gracefulness and
elegance that he knew how to give to his mythological figures.
(It was in the Academy.)

Num. **1715,** *Andromeda.* Copy by Rubens.

Num. **1668,** *Birth of the Milky Way.* By Rubens. A little jet
of Juno's milk, who nurses her son Hercules, is the origin of the
great nebulose. Jupiter, the father, is also represented. The symbol
of Juno is the peacock, and the eagle and rays are those of Jupiter.
(Painted for the Torre de la Parada.)

Num. **1551,** *Apollo the Conqueror of Marsyas.* By Jordaens. Midas,
King of Frigia, in a musical match in which Apollo and Pan compete,
gave the prize to the latter. Apollo as a punishment to the injustice,
made the ears of Midas grow as long as those of an ass. Marsyas, a
fluteplayer, defied Apollo who played the lyre; the prize would
consist in the conquered remaining at the conqueror's mercy. The
Muses conceded the victory to Apollo, who tied Marsyas to a pine-
tree and flayèd him alive. In this composition we see Marsyas playing
the flute, Midas with his enormous ears and Jupiter crowning Apollo.
The picture is painted according to a sketch by Rubens. In the
background appears a copy of *The Meninas* by Mazo.

Rubens and Snyders. Num. **1664,** *Ceres and two Nymphs.* The figures are by Rubens; the animals and fruits by Snyders. Rubens did not like other subjects than the representation of the human figure, and when he was commissioned to do landscapes, animals, fruits, flowers, etc., he usually gave his disciples and collaborators the work (Jan Brueghel de Velours, other times Snyders, etc.). Ceres receiving the cornucopia, the nymph playing with a monkey and the other in the background show the opulent flesh tones which characterize the genial painter from Antwerp. The decoration does not distract from the figures. It was probably painted between 1620 and 1628, according to Schäffer. (This canvas was also kept in the Academy of San Fernando from where it came to the Museum in 1827.)

Cornelis de Vos. *A Dutch painter, born in Hulst about 1585 and died in Antwerp in 1651. He was a good friend of Van Dyck's and Snyders, who painted in Rubens's workshop, and although trying to withdraw himself from the latter's school, he painted according to the old Flemish school. Rubens's influence is noticeable in his works especially in the subjects choiced and in the treatment of them.*

Num. **1862,** *The Birth of Venus.* This canvas is precisely upon a Peter Paul Rubens's sketch. The goddess born from the sea's spume already steps upon the beach sand followed by two tritons and a mermaid who offers her a necklace. There also are two cupids in flight.

Num. **1345,** *The fall of Phaeton,* by Jan Eyck.

Num. **1631,** *Jasón, Chief of the argonauts.*

Rooms LXXVI and LXXVII.—(Bureaux)

Room LXXVIII.—(Bureaux)

Room LXXIX.—(Staircase). VARIOUS

Most of the painters in this room belong to Italian schools. With some of first rank as **Sebastiano del Piombo** and **Palma** *il Giovanni (the Young)* and others who came into Spain under our king's protection, such as **Giaquinto, Lucca Giordano, Carducci,** etc., there are also several French and Flemish painters of the 16th century.

Lucca Giordano. *Naples 1632-1705. He was Ribera's and Pietro di Cortona's disciple and in his time was nicknamed «Lucca fa priesto». that is to say «Luke hurry up», because of his astonishing fluency in covering meters and meters of the canvas. It is told that in a boasting* *of rapidity he painted in a day and a half a huge altar-piece panel for the Society of Jesus's Church in Naples, entitled* Francisco Xavier Baptising the Japanese, *without knowing how the Japanese and the Navarre's missionaries were. He sold the copies from the Venetians at very high prices, and when his fame arrived in Spain, in 1692 Carlos II the Bewitched sent for him for the decoration of some royal rooms and relatively in a short time, he fulfilled several domes, for example; those of El Escorial, the Royal and the Buen Retiro palaces, the Church of Atocha, the Toledo Cathedral. In these times Claudio Coello died victim of vexations and melancholy. During his stay in Spain he became richer than he was, and upon the king's death he returned to Italy and travelled throughout the whole peninsula painting mansions. His painting is superficial, pompous and full of mannerism. It represents allegorical figures, obese angels, etc., whose repetition ends up in boring the spectator. It is quite a monotonous scenography in the coloring, very tireful, and that only a court in decadence in all its aspects, could like. However, in the small canvases which are treated more attentively, he attains some successes that are undeniable.*

Num. **183,** *The Conquest of a Fortress.* This is not canvas well-characterizing the painter.

Num. **190,** *Rubens Painting; Allegory of Peace.* In this canvas larger than the previous, he moves more comfortably. The Antwerp's painter is sitting upon an allegorical figure which is said to be the representation of Discordance; he is depicting a matrone driving and Furor. The rest is an allegory trying to equal those with which Rubens liked to surround his historical personages. (It was acquired at the sale of Ensenada.)

Num. **196,** *Æneas, Fugitive with his Family,* reproduces an episode of the Æneid and does not lack expression nor energy. (In 1700 it was in the Zarzuela, and in 1772 in the Palace.)

Bourdon, Sebastien. *(Montpellier, 1616; París, 1671).*

Num. **1503,** *Christine of Sweden on Horseback.* Let us pause momentarily before this picture, more for its historical than artistic interest. The fantastic daughter of Gustave Adolf, protestant, as her daughter, who renounced the throne and became a Catholic. She ordered Monadelchi killed and worried the ecclesiastical dignitaries in Rome at the end. She appears in this portrait in a hunting scene on horseback followed by several dogs, and a page who carries the falcon. The portrait was sent to Felipe IV by order of Christine herself. (It then passed to the Alcázar of the Retiro.)

Cavedone, G. *An Italian painter born in Sassuolo (Modena) in 1577 and died in Bologna in 1660. Escaping from his father's terror he entered the service of a Bolognese gentleman, very fond of Art, who introduced him to Annibale Carracci, being admitted in the latter's*

Academy. Then he travelled through Venice in order to study its masters and returned to Bologne where he was commissioned for many works and spent plenty of money; but misfortune gloated over him, because his wife was accused of being a witch and suffered torments. This fact and his daughter's death determined in him a sickness and miserable state which weakened him.

Num. **95,** *The Shepherds Adoration.* We see the Virgin ans Saint Joseph with the Child at the stable and three shepherds approaching in order to adore Jesus. It is easy to appreciate Carracci's influence. Carlos IV acquired this canvas.

Parmigianino, *is Francesco Maria Mazzola, an Italian painter who took the name of his fatherland, Parma, where he was born in 1503. He died in item in 1540.*

Num. **281,** *Cupid,* is a replica of the one belonging to Vienna's Gallery. The figure of the Child of Love is well-shaped, and gracious in his attitude of curving the arch. (In 1636 it was in the Alcázar of Madrid.)

A. Vaccaro. *Was born and died in Naples (1598-1670). A follower of Caravaggio and of Domenichino.*

Num. **473,** *Death of Cleopatra.* With clothes of the period of the painter, she has uncovered her right breast to bring an asp to it. According to H. de Vos, the attribution to Vaccaro is doubtful.

Num. **466,** *The penitent Magdalen.* The signature is in the bottom right hand corner, and consists of and a*A* and a *V* joined together.

T. Van Thulden. *A native of Bois-le-Duc (1606-1669).*

Num. **1844,** *Orpheus. Playing the lyre,* the sounds of which the animals listen to, who surround him. It was shown in the Torre de la Parada, where it was taken for an original by Rubens. The animals are painted by Snyders.

Ranc. Num. **2326,** *Philip V on horseback.* Son of the Great Dauphin of France and first Spanish king of the Bourbon dynasty. The rider is half armed; in the upper part flies Victory with a palm in her hand. Under the horse a pitched battle is noted. This picture suffered a great deal during the fire of Alcázar, in 1734.

Pictures of Cignarolli, num. **99,** Cargiulo, num. **238,** Vaccaro, number **462,** etc.

UPPER FLOOR

Room LXXX.—MENGS

With the exception of one picture of Kauffmann, all the rest that covers the walls of this room are by **Mengs,** a painter who came to Spain called for by Carlos III. In his times he was very famous, thanks to his prim, stuccoing and acedemic painting, with a great readiness for the reproduction of silks, satins, gauzes, laces and jewels. His portraits are more or less «exhibitions» and they do not deal with problems of color nor of light: all they do is, in a suave and praising manner, show classical purity in which the essential is the similarity. Other than these, there are five religious pictures that are not any marvel, the rest being royal portraits. His self-portrait is also included.

Mengs, Anthony Raphael. *Born in Aussing (Bohemia) in 1728. Since he had a great ability for sketching from his chilhood, his father tried to cultivate his vocation and took him to Rome, where he studied assiduously. His apprenticeship finished, he went to Dresden and was named painter of the Chamber of August III. He returned to the Eternal City, married Margarita Guazzi and through her efforts was converted to Catholicism. After decorating some palaces he left for Naples, where Carlos III met him, inviting him to come to Spain. The Bohemian painter accepted and arrived in Madrid in 1761, remaining eight years, at the end of which he was called to Rome by Pope Clement XIV, who wanted him to decorate a room in the Vatican. As the painter suffered from tuberculosis, he accepted the offer with the hope that the Roman climate would favor his health. He decorated the said room, for which work he did not want to charge anything, «because he was in the service of the King of Spain». Upon returning to Madrid he remained in the Spanish capital from 1774 to 1776, taking advantage of this time in order to finish a room of the great dining room in the Palace of Orient with the* Deification of Trajan. *Once again suffering from his sickness and with the worry of his wife and seven children, he asked permission to go once more to Rome, to which the King gave his consent and even granted a pension on which they might live. Soon after his wife died and not being able to live without her, he promptly followed her to the grave. He died in 1770, in such misery that his* *burial was scarcely taken care of. As for his children, they were, cared for by Carlos III, until they could earn a living for themselves. Mengs was loved by everybody because of his amiability and his modesty, and he was both friend and protector of Goya in the first phases of the Aragonese painter's life. He also protected other contemporary Spaniards and acquired works that today decorate our Museum and conserved others that would have ended up in flames had it not been for his authority. Spain should indeed be grateful to Mengs.*

Num. **2197**, *Self-Portrait*, shows him dressed in an artist's smock, brushes in hand; his face wasted away, his forehead unobstructed, his eyes vibrant and with long hair. This portrait shows more spontaneity than the rest in this room.

Num. **2201**, *Queen María Amalia of Saxony*. Daughter of August of Poland, Elector of Saxony and of María Josefa of Austria she was born in the year 1724, married the future Charles III in 1738 and died in Madrid in the year 1760. She appears seated holding a book in her left hand.

Num. **2186**, *Marie Joseph of Lorraine*. Archduchess of Austria, daughter of Francisco I and María Teresa, she was engaged to Fernando IV of Naples, but died before the marriage. She holds a closed fan in her right hand.

Num. **2187**, *The Prince Don Antonio Pascual of Bourbon*, son of Carlos III and María Amalia of Saxony. He was born in Naples in 1755, married his niece María Amalia, and died in Madrid in 1817. It is the same person whom Goya painted in num. **733** of Room XXXII. From his neck hangs the Toison.

Num. **2188**, *Carlos IV, as Prince of Asturias*, as primogenial son of Carlos III and Marie Joseph Amalia of Saxony, he was born in Portici in 1748, married Maria Luisa of Parma in 1765 and began to reign in 1788, dying in Naples in 1819. In hunting dress, with rifle and dog, he wears the Toison and the sashes of the Saint Spirit and Saint Jenaro.

Num. **2189** and **2586**, *María Luisa of Parma*. Princess of Asturias by her marriage with the previous. Daughter of Felipe, Duke of Parma, and of Luisa Isabel of France, she was born in Parma in 1751 and died in Rome in 1819. In the first she appears portrayed with two carnations in her right hand a closed fan in the left; in the second, that remains unfinished, she wears a bow of roses at her neck. (Willed by the Duke of Tarifa.)

Num. **2190**, *Ferdinando IV, King of Naples*, son of Carlos III and María Amalia of Saxony, to whom we have referred while viewing **2186**. He was king of Naples, born in Naples in 1751, married Carolina of Lorraine in 1768, and died in Naples in 1825. We see him standing with sceptre in his right hand.

Num. **2191**, *The Archduke Francis of Austria*. Son of Leopold of Tuscany and María Luisa, grandson of Carlos III: he became Emperor of Germany with the title of Francais II and father-in law, of Napoleon the Great. He died in 1835. Precious portrait of the child, one of the best of Mengs, wearing the Toison on his chest.

Num. **2192,** *The Archduke Ferdinand and María Ana of Austria*. Children, brothers of the previous. The first was born in 1769, and succeeded his father as Duke of Tuscany, and died in 1824. The second, born in 1770, died in 1809. Ferdinand shows the Toison and María Ana holds an ivory toy in her right hand.

Num. **2193**, *The Archduchess Teresa of Austria*. First daughter of the above-mentioned Duchess of Tuscany, born in 1767, married to Antonio Clemente Teodoro, who was king of Saxony, she died in 1827. She is seen entertaining herself with a parrot in a cage.

Num. **2194,** *María Carolina of Lorraine*. She died before María Josefa (to whom we have previously referred) was married. Her sister María Carolina married Fernando IV, King of Naples in 1768. She was born in Shoenbrun in 1752 and died in 1814. This portrait was obtained from a miniature equal to the one of her sister.

Num. **2195**, *Prince Xavier of Bourbon*, son of Carlos III and María Amalia of Saxony, born in 1757 and died in Aranjuez at fourteen. She wears the sash of Saint Jenaro and the Toison.

Num. **2196**, *Prince Don Gabriel of Bourbon*. Brother of the previous, he was born in Naples in 1752, was Prior of Malta, and died in El Escorial in 1788. It is known that he was translator of Salustius.

Num. **2198,** *Leopold of Lorraine*, Great Duke of Tuscany and later Emperor, he was the son of the Empress María Teresa, born in 1747, married María Luisa, daughter of Carlos III, and died in 1792. He is the father of the young princess cited in numbers **2191** and **2192**.

Num. **2199,** *María Luisa of Bourbon*. Wife of the previous, she was born in Naples in 1745 and died in Vienna in 1792.

Num. **2200,** *Carlos III*. Son of Felipe V and Isabel Farnesio, born in Madrid in 1716; he inherited the Dukedom of Parma, the kingdom of the Two Sicilies, and in 1759 the Crown of Spain. He died in Madrid in 1788. He wears the staff of command in his right hand. Toison, Saint Spirit and Saint Jenaro. It is supposed that this portrait was painted soon after the arrival of Mengs in Spain.

Kauffmann, Angélica. *German painter, born in Schwarzenberg (Switzerland), in 1741, and died in Rome in 1807. Daughter of a painter who, in order that she could enter the Academy, dressed her up as boy. Still adolescent, he took her to Milan, already with a name as a portrait painter.*

Very much loved by the English painter, Dance, she nevertheless preferred to continue her painter's pilgrimage, travelling about all over

Italy. Called to London, she was received in triumph. And at this point,
her marriage tragedy took place; having got married in secret to the
Count of Horn, she discovered the terrible mistake she had made; her
suitor, now her husband, was not the real Count, but his servant, dressed
in his master's clothes. However, she resigned herself to the situation
until the illtreatment of her husband made it impossible for her to continue.

Finally, through a large sum of money which she paid to him, he
let her have a divorce, and shortly afterwards she narried the Italian
painter, Antonio Zuchi, for whom she left London to set up house per-
manently in Rome. During her stay in London, as Angélica was very
beautiful and interesting, the great Reynolds painted as many as three
portraits of her.

Num. **2473,** *Anna von Muralt.* Like all the pictures painted by
this artist, it is extremely full of mannerisms, «nice», feminine, pleasant
colours are used. There is a landscape background and, on a little
stone seat, a bunch of flowers. (Errasu legacy.)

Room LXXXI

Contains sketches and pastel drawings by various artists
such as tiépolo, Francisco Bayeu, Vicente López, Bernino,
José del Castillo, etc.

Room LXXXII

In this room is the Errazu legacy, which consists of
pictures of the Romantic period, signed by the Madrazo,
Esquivel, López Piquer, Fortuny, etc. There is no need to
say that, in general, it is the painting which corresponds
to the period, very academic, correct and finished, perfectly
drawn and pure in colour, showing the very least possible
preoccupation with the natural.

Among the paintings by Raimundo de Madrazo, there
is a beautiful head portrait of the Queen Regent, María
Cristina of Hapsburg; among the works of Mariano Fortuny
are some Moroccan themes which he treated during his stay
in Africa, a Faust fantasy and a delicious nude in miniature;
some landscapes by Martín Rico; a portrait painted by Meissonnier; a life-size female nude by Baudry, which belonged
to Napoleón III, and the full-length portrait of the donor,
Ramón de Errazu, painted by Madrazo.

Room LXXXIII

This whole room is devoted to Spanish painters of the 17th century, some of which reach the first years of the 18th.

Mazo, Juan Bautista del. Num. **899,** *The death of Adonis.* This canvas is probably by Agüero, and forms a series with another three in the same room, all of which are on mythological themes.

Cano, Alonso. Without num.: *Christ crucified.* The «Christ» is lifesize, of sculptured finish, well-modelled and standing out against a dark background. The figure is a pathetic one which reveals the extreme sensibility of the artist.

Murillo. Num. **971,** *The Immaculate Conception,* a traditional painting by the Sevillan artist, it is small and extremely beautiful.

Escalante, Juan Antonio. *Born in Cordoba 1630, and died in Madrid, 1670. He was a pupil of Francisco Rizi. He copied many works by Tintoretto, the brilliant hues of which denounce the influence. Most of his paintings are bright. He painted for a great many churches, among them that of the Carmelitas Descalzas, in Madrid, and that of the convent of El Puig, near Valencia. Hist best canvas is the* Most Pure Conception, *in the Budapest museum, on the walls of which many Spanish works are hung.*

Num. **697,** *Christ stretched out.* The bracket of the cross is close to a skull. It is an impressive nude, with hot and dull red, which stand out little against the shroud. As always he shows violent contrasts, somewhat revealed in this case by the intonation of the head.

Villafranca, Pedro de. *Born in Alcolea (La Mancha). Was chiefly an engraver and there are known to exist two prints of his (1632 and 1678).*

Num. **1232,** *Philip IV.* Life size, he is standing up, dressed in black with cape, ruff, the Golden Fleece, hat in his left hand and in the right a sheet of paper which says: «Señor Don Juan de Góngora». The head is copied from Velázquez. This Góngora (not to be confused with the poet, whose Christian name is Luis) was President of the Finance Council during the protection of Luis de Haro.

Anonimous Sevillan. Num. **1134,** *The Water of the Rock.* Biblical scene which evokes the moment in which water gushes out of the rock struck by Moses with is rod. The thirsty Israelites hasten to drink. This large-size picture has been attributed to many painters: according to some it is by Roelas, according to others, Llano Valdés. The most likely solution is that it was executed by R. Longui, who believed it to be by Giovachino Assereto, according to a sketch found in the Renek Collection, in Berlín. (In belonged to Elizabeth Farnesio.)

Carreño. Num. **642,** *Charles II.* This is a replica of the one which, with the same number, is hanging in the Central Gallery, Room XXIX.

March. Num. **881,** *Saint Jerome.* As in most of his pictures, he goes on being reminiscent of Ribera.

Gilarte, Mateo. *Born in Valencia about 1620 and died in Murcia, 1690. Pupil of the Academy of Valencia, he established himself in Murcia and was a great friend of the painter, Juan de Toledo, so much so, in fact, that they set up a studio together. It is said that his daughter Magdalena inherited his talents.*

Num. **714,** *The Birth of the Virgin.* Saint Anne on the couch is, like the Virgin, attended by several women. Saint Joseph is present. At the top, a celestial opening in the background. As a painting, it has little contrast, although there are some skilful strokes of light. It is signed on the left. A notice says that it was presented by Bernardo de Salafranca and Zúñiga, alderman of Murcia, to the Congregation of the Assumption. (It has been brought from Saint Francis the Great, Madrid.)

Arias, Antonio. *Born and died in Madrid, 1620-1684. Pupil of Pedro de las Cuevas, he was one of the best painters in Madrid. In spite of having been well favoured and of irreprochable habits, he died destitute in the Hospital. He left a daughter who showed a keen interest in painting.*

Num. **599,** *The Virgin and the Child.* The Virgin, sitting in the country, offers her breast to Child, who, distracted, turns his face away. Signed in the bottom right-hand corner. (It was brought from the Museum of the Trinity.)

Agüero. Num. **897,** *Letona and the Peasant turned into Frogs.* Overwhelmed by the largeness of the landscape are seen the miniature figures of Latona with her children Apollo and Diana. The main feature is the lagoon where the Lycians have been converted into frogs, as a punishment for not having allowed Letona to use the water.

Num. **895,** *Dido and Aeneas.* Similar to the last picture, it consist of a landscape with the two small figures of Aeneas saying goodbye to Dido before going on board the beautiful vessel which is to be seen on the quay.

Madrid school in the 17th century. Num. **1317,** a: *Portrait of John Joseph of Austria.* This portrait by a painter whose attribution is unknown is interesting because it shows us what the bastard son of Philiph IV and the actress called La Calderona were like.

Coello, Claudio. Num. **992,** *Portrait of P. Cabanillas.* Half-size portrait. The subject is dressed in brown. (It belonged to Elizabeth Farnesio.)

Velázquez School. Num. **1233,** *Portrait of Prince Baltasar Car-*

los. He appears as a hunter, with his cap on a cushion. A spring landscape is seen from the balcony.

El Greco School. Num. **831**, *Saint Eugene.* A large picture in which the influence of El Greco is manifest.

Agüero. Num. **896**, *The Departure of Aenas from Carthage.* As the other pictures which form this group, the main feature of this extensive canvas is not Aeneas but the landscape. This series of canvases, which were in Aranjuez, were formerly considered works of Mazo, but Elías Tormo holds that the undoubted author is Agüero.

Room LXXXIV

Mariano Maella. *Born in Valencia, 1739, the son of a father of the same name, who was also a painter. He went to Madrid at an early age to enter the studio of Philip Castro and afterwards the Royal Academy of San Fernando. The Academy records inform us that he was «amply rewarded». His father, a painter of minor importance, and not having much faith in his son's success, proposed that he should go to America or take up business as a career; but the boy preferred to leave for Rome, where he painted for some time.*

On his return to Madrid, he was sought out quite a lot by Francisco Bayeu, who commisioned him to do a great many works, even making him a collaborator in the chapel of Saint Ildephonse. He also painted for Toledo, Aranjuez, and the Prince's Cottage in the Escorial.

Num. **2440**, *Carlota Joaquina, Infanta of Spain and Queen of Portugal.* Daughter of Charles IV, born in 1775. Was given in marriage to the future John IV of Portugal when she was ten years old, and died fifty five years later. Dressed in pink and beside a table on which a cage can be seen; she has placed the canary on the index finger of her right hand. It is quite a dull picture, inferior to any of Goya's. Goya eclipsed Maella, as he did all the painters of his time.

Num. **2451**, *The Sausage Seller,* by **Ramón Bayeu.** A sausage and ham seller. At the back, a water-carrier. It is a canvas painted in very clearly defined tones, because it is designed cartoon-fashion for the tapestry factory.

Canaletto, Giovanni. *An Italian painter born in Venice, 1697, and died in the same city, in 1768. His Venetian landscapes, executed down to the last detail, are simply enchanting.*

Num. **2465**, *The Great Canal in Venice with the Rialto Bridge.* On the left is the Fondaso de Tedeschi and on the right the Palazzo Camarlenghi. Several gondolas move through the canal. It is a small picture, but very beautiful. Some doubt that the painting is by Canaletto. (Laffite legacy.)

Num. **1044,** *The Royal Pairs* by Luis **Paret.** The theme is an equine celebration held in Aranjuez in 1773. Running in front of the pairs are Prince Charles (later Charles IV); the Infante Gabriel (son of Charles III); the Infante of Luis Antonio (son of Philip V), and the Duke of Medinasidonia. From the second box, on the façade of the Palace, the celebration is being witnessed by Charles III and Princess María Luisa of Parma.

Num. **1045,** *Oath of Fernando VII as Prince of Asturias,* by **Luis Paret.** The ceremony is held in the church of Saint Jerome the Royal, in Madrid, in 1789. Two moments are illustrated: the Prince takes the oath before Cardinal Lorenzana: then kisses the hand of his father Charles IV, who is on his throne beside his wife María Luisa of Parma and his son Charles María Isidro. This picture, like the last one, is signed by the artist.

Num. **2477,** *Fiesta in a Garden,* by **Amiconi.** Musicians, a couple dancing, the servants preparing refreshments, groups in the backgroung, spring foliage. A small picture, very pleasantly carried out, whose attribution is not absolutely sure.

In this room are shown some canvases of scenes from the *Passion of the Lord,* by **Domingo Tiépolo,** son of the great Juan Bautista whose works in Spain he carried on. He painted them for Saint Philip Neri, of Madrid, from where they were taken to the Museum of the Trinity and on to the Prado.

Joli, Antonio. *Born in Modena about 1700. Architect and painter, he was a pupil of Pannini and painted in Spain, Germany and England. He was finally made painter of Charles III, king of Naples.*

Num. **232,** *The Embarkation of Charles III in Naples.* The Marquis of Tanucci is seen in a coach in the foreground. The gulf seems to be full of ships. A placard on the wall records the ephemeris, 6th October, 1759.

Num. **233,** *The Embarkation of Charles III in Naples.* A large picture, like the last one, with the fleet commanded by the Marquis of Victoria. Here the notice is written on the sail of a launch, on the right. (This picture and the preceding one come from the Museum of the Trinity.)

Room LXXXV.—ITALIAN PAINTERS OF THE 16th AND 17th CENTURIES

In this room, together with some of the **Bassano,** there are other painters of the Venetian School.

Bassano, Japoco (See Room X A). Numbers **27** and **28,** *The Expulsion of the Merchants from the Temple.* The same theme is seen with a different composition. The last version was saved from the fire of 1734 in the Alcázar, but even so the damage is visible.

Bassano, Francesco. Num. **33,** *The Adoration of the Kings.* Num. **34,** *The Last Supper.* Num. **43,** *The Virgin Mary in Heaven.* The influence of the painter's father can be seen in all three.

Puligo, *named Domenice Ubaldini, born in Florence, 1492, and died in the same town in 1527. Pupil of Guirlandaio and assistant to Andrea del Sarto, whose influence is notable.*

Num. **294,** *The Holy Family.* An extremely intimate scene in which the Virgin, caressed by the music of an angel and in the presence of Saint John breast-feeds the Holy Child. A curious detail is the cup of water with the linnet.

Campi, *named Vicencio. Was born and died in Cremona 1536-1591.*

Num. **59 a,** *The Crucifixion.* With the figure of Christ bravely shortened.

Parrasio. Num. **284,** *Christ reclining adored by Pope Saint Pious V.* Small picture in which an angel lifts the left arm of Jesus. Underneath the skeleton of Adam. Signed on the femur of the skeleton. The figure of the Pope is his authentic likeness. (Given by Philip II to the Escorial.)

Num. **348,** *Christ with the Croos on His Shoulders,* by **Sebastiano del Piombo.** Small picture, admirably executed, and which is interesting in that it is painted on slate.

Cangiaso, *o Cambiaso, Lucas. Was born in Moneglia in 1527 and died in the Escorial, in 1585. Pupil of his father, Juan. After having painted around Florence and Rome, he accepted Philip II's invitation to paint in the Escorial. He made the journey after the death of his wife and decorated the choir left. On one occasion he asked the king to intercede with Pope Gregory XII to grant him special permission in order that he could marry his sister-in-law. It appears that this annoyed Philip II, and it is even said that an indignant refusal determined the death of the artist. When he died, it has been ascertained that the Spanish monarch ordered many of his works to be destroyed.*

Num. **60,** *The Holy Family.* The strange and sometimes absurd character which Cambiaso's canvases so often have is not reflected in this one. (It was acquired by Charles IV.)

Portelli, Carlos. *Belongs to the Florentine School; he was born in Loro and died in Florence in 1574.*

Num. **476,** *Charity,* with beautiful studies of children. In the preceding epoch this canvas was believed to be by Jorge Vasari. It was Voss who gave it its present attribution. (Also acquired by Charles IV.)

Volterra, *named Daniel Ricciarelli. He was born in Volterra about*

1509 and died in Rome, 1566. This is the painter who, on the death of Michelangelo, placed gauzes over some of the nudes in the Final Judgement *in the Sixtine Chapel, as Pope Paul IV had proposed that the famous fresco should be made to disappear. Pupil of Sodoma and of Peruzzi, he finished some works of Perino del Vaga in the Vatican; he was a friend of Michelangelo, who lent him drawings for his works, and, as sculptor, provided him with the bronze horse for Henry II's statue, commissioned by Katharine Medici.*

Num. **522,** *The Annunciation.* It is the traditional theme of the Florentine School, with the presence of the Eternal Father and the dove of the Holy Ghost in a celestial break-through. (The attributions is made by Voss.)

La Tintoretta. Num. **383,** *Young Venetian Girl.* (Note in the Artists' index what we say about this daughter of Tintoretto.) It is a half-size portrait in which the subject is adorned with a pearl necklace. The attribution is made by Berenson.

Campi, Antonio. *Born in Cremona and died abut 1591.*

Num. **59,** *Saint Jerome meditating.* He appears seated with a pen in his hand a lion at his feet. It was first painted on a panel from which the painting was transferred on to the canvas. The signature is underneath the Saint's left foot. (It was painted for Philip II.)

Procaccini, Camilo. *Italian painter, born in Bolonia in 1550 and died in Milán 1629.*

Num. **293,** *The Virgin embracing the Child.* A moving and impressive picture made so by the Virgin Mary's affectionate embrace of her divine Son. By its character it belongs more to the Lombrad School than to the Bolonese.

Room LXXXVI

The whole room is devoted to a collection of beautiful, large-size paintings by Italian artists.

Stanzione, *named Maximo. Born and died in Naples (1585-1656). Pupil of Caracciolo and of Lanfranco. In Rome he met Guido Reni, whose friend and also pupil he subsequently became, and whom he imitated to such an extent that when he went back to his country, they called him the «Napolitan Guido». There are works by him in the Abbey of San Martino partenopea. When Domenichino died, having left behind him unfinished the work he had been commissioned to do, Ribera and Stanzione finished it between them. He gained a name as a portrait-painter. In Naples he founded an Academy which had numerous pupils. He was a musician, a writer and left a history of Napolitan painting behind him.*

In this room there are several works by «Cavalieri Massimo» which mostly deal with the life of Saint John the Baptist. Num. **256**, *The Birth of the Baptist*. Zacharias, before the altar, hears the angel, who announces the birth of his son. On the left and right, poor and devout groups of people.

Num. **291**, *Saint John says goodbye to his Parents*. It is Saint John as a child who is kneeling at his father's feet. On the right, two shepherds contemplate the scene. The signature, which is incomplete, is in a stone on the right on which a shepherd is leaning.

Num. **257**, *The Preaching of Saint John the Baptist*. Saint John is preaching on a mountain, sorrounded by several listeners.

Num. **258**, *The Beheading of Saint John the Baptist*. The executioner brandishes his blade before the kneeling precursor. On the right, two soldiers. The four compositions are splendid and the semi-nudes extremely virile.

Num. **259**, *Sacrifice to Bacchus*. The god is on a pedestal, and his followers are offering him vine branches and amphoras with wine. The signature is on the pitcher which a woman on the right is taking. Through the Count of Monterrey, Philip IV commissioned the painter to paint twelve canvases, and this might well be one of them.

Gentileschi, Horacio. *Born in Pisa, 1562, and died in London, 1647. Pupil of Leoni and Bacci Lomi. Painted in the Quirinal. Van Dyck, who deeply admired him, summoned him to London, where he went, after staying a while in Paris. In London, he painted a beautiful portrait of the unfortunate Charles I.*

Num. **146**, *The Holy Family and Saint Katharine*. In very bold monochromes. Regarding the attribution, it is not known whether it should be to Gentileschi or to R. Longhi. (From the collection of Elizabeth Farnesio.)

Num. **147**, *Moses saved from the Waters of the Nile*. One of the maidservants is showing the child in the basket. Pharoah's daughter speaks to the infant's own sister on the matter of who should raise him. The scene is presented somewhat dramatically, but is of great beauty, shown especially in the clothing. Signed on the bracelet of the servant who is holding the basket. It is held that this picture was painted in England, by command of Philip IV.

Gentileschi, Artemisa. *Born in Rome, 1597, and died in Naples, 1651. Daughter and pupil of the preceding artist, she accompanied him on his voyage to England. The king ordered some historical pictures from her. She also painted the portraits of several noblemen.*

Num. **149**, *The Birth of Saint John the Baptist*. A very feminine, intimate scene. While Zacharias writes, on account of his being dumb, the name that must be given to his son, several neighbours get ready to wash the newly-born child. R. Longhi was right when he wrote of this canvas: «The most successful interior study among Italian painters of the 17th century». In her choice of colours, Artemisa greatly resembles her father. (It was in the Retiro, from where it was taken to the Palace.) The self-portrait of Angelica is in Room LXXXVII.

Rosa, Salvatore. *Was born in Arenella, near Naples, in 1615, and died in Rome, 1673. Son of a very poor family and being left without a father when he was only seventeen, he had to face the family wants. Having great leanings towards drawing and painting, he met Falcone, who gave him lessons and advice. But he would have gone completely unnoticed if he had not been discovered by Lanfranco, through whom he entered at the service of Cardinal Brancaccio. He took part in the political outcry of Masaniello and finally he had to flee to Rome and later to Florence, where his art triumphed. He was rich and brilliant; he returned to Rome and died at the age of fifty-eight.*

Num. **324,** *Marina seen from the Gulf and Town of Salermo.* A picture more wide than it is long and fairly large, showing the port on the right, a boat in the Gulf and men bathing. It is signed with a monogram, S. R., on the bundle in the foreground. On the right a shield and underneath an inscription which appears to mention Philip IV.

Vaccaro, Andrea. *Was born and died in Naples (1598-1670). Pupil of Jerónimo Imparato and friend of Máximo Stanzione, he formed, together with Salvatore Rosa and others the revolutionary group known as «Companions of Death».*

Num. **468,** *The Meeting of Rebecca and Isaac.* It reproduces the biblical scene by the curbstone of the well. The two figures are beautiful, rich in colour, and resemble Domenichino's art. It is signed on the edge of the fountain. The picture was acquired at Kelly, and in 1772 it was in the Palace.

Num. **469,** *The Passing of Saint Jenaro.* Canvas of a size similar to the preceding one. The Saint, covered with his mitre, is pushed up to heaven by two angels; another carries two decanters with his blood, and the fourth carries the priceless worked finished bishop's crossier. In the background, the Gulf of Naples. It is a briliantly executed picture, signed on the cloud on which is the Saint: an «A» and a «V» intertwined. Secured by Charles IV.

Num. **470,** *Saint Rosalia of Palermo.* The Saint appears in an ecstatic state, between two young angels; others are flying above her, four in all, who are dropping roses. Signed with the above-mentioned intertwined signature in the bottom right-hand corner, under the angel's tunic.

Palma the Young. Num. **271,** *David, the Conqueror of Goliath.* David, a youth, bears the enormous head of Goliath on the right; he is accompanied by soldiers and a cluster of women receive him in triumph. (Bought at the auction of Charles I of England for 100 *libras* by Philip IV.)

Num. **272,** *The Conversion of Saint Paul.* Throwm headlong to the ground by the radiance from heaven, those who are with Saul flee, panicstriken. This picture forms a pair with the preceding one and comes from the same source.

Sacchi, Andrea. *Italian painter, was born in Neptune about 1599, died in Rome, in the year 1661.*

Num. **3,** *The Birth of Saint John the Baptist.* Zacharias, who is standing, articulates the name of his son; several women are looking after the child; in the background, on the couch, Saint Elizabeth. (It belonged to the Marquis of the Ensenada; in 1772 it was in the Palace, in the Infante Javier's room.)

Room LXXXVII

This room is a continuation of the Italian painters of the 16th and 17th centuries.

Carracci, Aníbal. Num. **81,** *Landscape.* It is not one of Aníbal's most characteristic landscapes; even so, it is a delicious one, with deep, thick foliage in the foreground and transparent blues in the background. It is held that only the figures are by Aníbal, and that the landscape itself is by Gian Francesco Bolognese. (Bought by Philip V from the heirs of Maratta. It was in La Granja.)

Parmigianino. *Italian painter, named Francisco María Mazzola, who changed his name for that of his country, Parma, where he was born in 1503. He died there in 1540.*

Num. **282,** *Saint Bárbara.* It is a small picture, but an absolutely enchanting one. The Saint's profile, as a young woman, is extremely beautiful.

Guido Reni. Num. **209,** *Cleopatra killing herself with an Asp.* A favourite theme for this artist. A half-size treatment of Cleopatra with her breast uncovered, putting to it the poisonous ophidian.

Num. **212,** *The Apostle James.* More than half-size portrait, his hands joined as in prayer and he is carrying the staff of a pilgrim. (From the collection that Elizabeth Farnesio had in La Granja.)

Pupil of Tintoretto. Num. **401,** *Cardenal Andrea of Austria.* He is seated and is wearing the red mozetta and cap of cardinal. This Cardinal was the son of Archduke Ferdinand of Tyrol and Phillipa Welser, and governed Flanders in the absence of Archduke Albert. He died in Rome in the year 1600.

Anníbal Carracci. Num. **75,** *The Assumption.* This picture defines the artist's personality better than the preceding one. It is an exquisite piece of work, similar to one on the same theme which figures in the Zwinger de Dresde. The Count of Monterrey brought it with him from italy (It was in the Escorial and was highly praised by P. Santos.)

Artemisa Gentileschi. Num. **148,** *Self-portrait.* Half-size figure, it is painted with two doves. According to Longhi, it was painted about 1630. (From the collection of Elizabeth Farnesio.)

Domenichino. Num. **130,** *The Apparition of two Angels to Saint Jerome.* The Saint is in the cave in Bethlehem with the lion at his side. Landscape background. Several replicas of this canvas are in existence. It was formely attributed to Lucio Massaci. (Acquired by Charles IV.)

Sassoferrato, *named Juan Bautista Salvi. Was born in Sassoferrato, 1605, and died in Rome, 1685. His first master was his father Tarquino; later he entered the studio of Domenichino. He deeply admired Raphael. The Madonnas of Sassoferrato constitute a «style» of this painter. His faces are very beautiful and bear some resemblance to those of his contemporary, Carlos Dolci, and are adorned with an extremely concentrated, clear blue mantle, the upper edge of which throws the eyes in soft shadow. Very occasionally, the mantel is in white. His work of art, the* Virgin of the Rosary, *was painted for the church of Saint Sabina, in Rome, was stolen in this century and found again later.*

Num. **341,** *The Virgin meditating,* with her hands joined more as if in adoration, as in all those of Sassoferrato. (Acquired by Charles IV, it was a feature of the Cottage in El Escorial and later went to Aranjuez, from where it was brought to the Museum.)

Num. **342,** *The Virgin and the Holy Child sleeping.* The two figures are extremely graceful and remind one vaguely of Raphael. There is a similar sample in the Turin Museum. (Acquired in the same way as the latter-mentioned.)

Horacio Gentileschi. Num. **1240,** *The Child Jesus sleeping on the Cross.* The title describes the theme of the canvas. This work was formerly attributed to our Zurbarán, as he, too, was considered a pupil of Guido Reni and later of Murillo in the 18th century. The present attribution was made by H. Voss. (It was acquired in the Ensenada sale in 1767.)

Strozzi, Bernardo. *Born in Genova, 1581, an died in Venice between 1641 and 1644. A man whose life was extremely active, at the age of seventeen he entered the Order of Saint Francis, for which ha was called «il Prete genovese» and also «il capucino genovese». He was temporarily allowed to leave the cloister to look after his old mather; later, however, when she died, he did not want to go back to the convent. Having been detained, he was sentenced to three years' imprisonment,* *with strong protests on his part, so strong, in fact, that they reached the ears of his friends, who climbed the walls to free him. Then the superior transferred him to Monterosso, in the cell of which he left behind some fine frescoes. Finally, one day he escaped and fled to Venice, where he dedicated himself peacefully to his duties as a priest without being molested by anybody.*

Num. **354,** *Verónica*. She holds the linen cloth in her hands: in it, the Face of Nazarene. The countenance of the Veronica is that of a woman which re-appears constantly in the works of Strozzi, almost all of a religious nature. The authors have always wondered what it could be or what it could represent, without having been able to arrive at a satisfactory conclusion. The Face of Christ is beautiful and very expresive. This canvas was fomerly attributed to Velázquez, and a smaller copy of it, in the Museum of Compiegne (France) was held to be by Bernabé de Ayala, who was a pupil of Zurbarán. (From the collection of Elizabeth Farnesio.)

Vaccaro, Andrea. Num. **467,** *Saint Agueda*, who shows her shattered breast. The martyr stands out against a very dark background; her beauty is great but very academic and not very expressive.

Barbalunga, *named Antonio Ricci. Pupil of Domenichino, whose style he imitated so much that sometimes the work of one is confused with that of the other. He established himself in Messina, his native town (he had been born there in 1600) and brought together an extremely large number of works of art, both of good artists and of his pupils. He died in poverty but had gained the reputation of being the greatest painter in Sicily. He lived forty-nine years.*

Num. **17,** *Saint Agueda*. The gem of this maestro. The Saint is in fetters in prison. It is of far higher quality than the one by Vaccaro because of the mournful expression in the face, the richness of the colouring and the realism of the whole figure.

Güercino. Num. **202,** *Saint Augustine meditating on the Trinity*. He is turning his face towards an angel who, with one hand, points out the sea to him and, with the other, a hole in the sand, indicating that it is just as impossible to get the idea of the Trinity into his head as it is for the sea to fit into the hole in the beach. (It was in La Granja, in the collection of Elizabeth Farnesio.)

Num. **200,** *Saint Peter in the Prison*. At the moment when he is about to be freed by an angel, while his guard falls asleep. The whole picture is marvellous and the profile of the angel, incomparable. (It belonged to the Marquis of the Ensenada, at whose auction, it was acquired and taken to the Palace.)

Procaccini, Camilo. *Born in Bolonia, 1546, and died in Milan, 1626. Son of the painter, Hércules the Old. He began by being a pupil of his father. It is believed that he received lessons from Michelangelo*

*and from Raphael. His capacity for invention was amazing and his
use of colour dazzling.*

Num. **292,** *The Holy Family of the raceme.* The three figures are
practically full-size. Voss denies that it is by Procaccini, though he
has not made any alternative attribution.

Bernini, Lorenzo. *Born in Naples (1598-1689). Pupil of his
father, Peter, he was a sculptor and architect, of minor importance as
a painter. He, was favoured by the Popes, especially Urban VIII, and
was summoned to France by Louis XIV; he was heaped with praises
by almost all the sovereigns of his age, lived for eighty-two years and
died a millionaire.*

Num. **2476,** *Self-portrait.* It is an unfinished head, axtraordinarily
life-like if compared with other authentic portraits as this is also
considered. Painted about 1640. (It was acquired in 1929 by the
Guardian of the National Artistic Treasury.)

Manfredi, Bartolommeo. *Was born in Ustiano (Mantua) in
1580 and died in 1617. He began by receiving lessons from Pomerancio,
but his master was Caravaggio. He led a very dissipated life and, according to Zani, he almost always painted unwillingly. He died young
on account of his intemperance.*

Num. **247,** *A Soldier with John the Baptist's Head.* The figure of
the soldiers is half-size and he has a helmet. The painting has darkened considerably, so much so, in fact, that one has almost to guess
that the head of the Precursor is there.

Tintoretto. Num. **385,** *Portrait of an unknown Woman.* It seems
rather to have been painted by his daughter Marietta.

Room LXXXVIII

*Entering the Museum by the Goya door, on
the right is the staircase which forms this room.*

Zelotti, Bautista. *Was born and died in Verona (1526-1578),
Pupil of Antonio Badile, he worked with Veronés, his fellow pupil.
A praiseworthy painter, even though he was second class, he died in
poverty.*

Num. **512,** *Rebecca and Eliecer.* Eliecer puts his presents on the
ground, in the presence of Rebecca, who is beside the well. The signature, apocryphal, is on the right in the lower part of the picture,
and reads: P. Caliar: Ver. F. 1553 (that is to say, Pablo Caliari —the
Veronés— Veronés, completed, fecit 1553). It was saved from the fire
of 1734, although it suffered some damage.

Lanfranco, Juan de Esteban. *Was born in Parma, 1581, and died in Rome, 1647. At a very early age, he entered the service of the Counts of Scotti, who sent him to Ferrara to learn from Agustin Carracci. After having studied at the Correggio, he became a disciple of Anibal Carracci, with whom he worked in the Borghese Palace. Constantly badtempered, he was one of the great persecutors of Domenichino. In 1646 he went to work in Rome, where Pope Urban VIII made him a Knight.*

Num. **236,** *The auspices.* A priest, facing the altar, is holding the entrails of a sacrificed lamb. To the right, a warrior is waiting for the auspices. (It was in El Pardo in 1641.)

Jordan (Giordano) Lucas. Num. **165,** *Bathsheba bathing.* Bathsheba, whose feet are being dried by a maid-servant, is on the edge of the bath, beside a fountain, contemplated by David, who appears on a balcony in the background. This picture was saved from the fire to which we have already alluded, and placed in the Palace in 1772.

Num. **166,** *The Prudent Abigail.* Abigail presents the provisions which she brings for his army to David. On the right, an inane clown. (See the former reference.)

Bassano, Leandro. Num. **44,** *Venice; Embarkation of the Dux.* The Dux with senators and retinue, sets out for the «Bucentauro» which is moored by the bank of the Schiavoni. On the right, Saint George the Great. Signed on the left, under the lower latticed window. (During Philip II's time, it was in Valladolid, from where it was taken to the Retiro.)

Allori, Alejandro. *Was born and died in Florence (1535-1607). Pupil of his uncle, Angel Allori, named «el Bronzino», he perfected his learning in Rome. At the age of seventeen he executed a picture deemed worthy to be hung in the chapel of Alexander of Medici. Returning to his country, he painted a great deal, and was much admired by the Florentine nobility.*

Num. **6,** *The Holy Family and Cardinal Ferdinand de Medici.* The Cardinal is on his knees before the Holy Family accompanied by Saint Anne. He is wearing a Franciscan habit. Ferdinand de Medici (1551-1609) was the son of Cosme, inherited the Duchy of Tuscany from his brother and renounced the dignity of cardinal in 1588. The offering to the Cardinal is evident fron the label worked in the bottom left-hand corner. (Acquired in 1864 by Carlos Mariátegui for the amount of 7500 pesetas for the Museum of the Trinity.)

Falcone, Aniello. *Was born and died in Naples (1600-1656). He was a pupil of our Ribera. Captain of the Company of Death, when Masaniello died he fled to France where he was sheltered by the minister Colbert. He acquired an admirable reputation, amassed a brilliant fortune and was the master of Salvatore Rosa.*

Num. **139,** *Battle of the Romans againt the Berbers.* The movement of the figures reveals the provocative character of the struggle. On the right, three columns of a Corinthian temple. (It was in La Granja in the collection of Philip V.)

Room LXXXIX

This Room mostly consists of «animalias» by **Snyders** and **Fyt,** apart from some landscapes by **Juan Brueghel de Velours.** The animal scenes of the two first artists are very decorative and realistic, as a result of a keen observation of nature. Both painted for Princes and courtiers, whose main distraction was hunting, for which reason they liked to decorate their palaces and pavillions with nature paintings of this type.

Francisco Snyders, *painter from Antwerp (1579-1657), master of the Gilda of Saint Lucas, and married to the sister of the painter Cornelio and Pablo de Vos, was highly esteemed by Rubens, and painted for Philip IV, for Archduke Leopold William and for other sovereignst.*
Juan Fyt, *also from Antwerp (1609-1661) and likewise a teacher at the Gilda of Saint Lucas, went to Italy and stayed some time in Rome. In 1650 he returned to Antwerp, where he was made dean or consul. He was greatly honoured by his fellow countrymen because of his art and his pleasant personal bearing.*
De **Jean Brueghel de Velours** *has already been dealt with in the appropiate place.*

Room XC

Here are to be found further still-life paintings, of a large size, by **Snyders,** and also by **Boel, Pablo de Vos, Van Utrecht** and others.

Pedro Boel *(1622-1674), a painter from Antwerp, was a pupil of Snyders, set up for himself in Paris and worked for Luis XIV on the Gobelin tapestries. He died in the French capital.*
Pablo de Vos, *born in Hults and died in Antwerp (1596-1678), brother of the painter Cornelio, worked for the King of Spain and Emperor of Germany, and especially for the Duke of Aerschot, who was his special patron. Van Dyck painted his portrait.*

Adrián van Utrech, *painter from Antwerp (1599-1652), travelled widely throughout France, Italy and Germany. One of his great patrons was our Philip IV. He married Constanza van Nieulant, daughter of the painter and poet Guillermo; she herself was something of a poet. He was made master of the Cofradia of Saint Lucas, in Antwerp, in 1625.*

Rubens. Num. **2811,** *Saint Augustine meditating on the Mystery of the Trinity.* This theme was also treated by Guercino (Room LXXXVII). It appears to be the original of the same thing in the altar-piece of the Augustines of Monterrey, Salamanca. The theme is the impossibility of our mind, insignificant as it is, to be able to understand such a mystery, just as it impossible for the sea to fit into a hole in the hand. In the last century this work was held to be by Crayer.

Rombouts, Teodoro. *Was born and died in Antwerp (1507-1637). Pupil of Janssens, he visited Rome and Florence where he painted for a few Patricians. On his return to Antwerp, he worked in Gente for the Archduke Ferdinand. In 1628 he was made dean of the Cofradia of painters, in Saint Lucas.*

Num. **1635,** *The Talkative Dentist.* It is one of his best genre paintings. The scene is picturesque to a high degree, with a stong popular flavour. There are two replicas of this work: one in the Museum in Prague and another in that of St. Omer. (In 1674 the painting was in the Pardo.)

Num. **1636,** *The Card-players.* Two courtesans and two soldiers are playing cards in the presence of some other people. (The same reference.)

Teniers I, David. Num. **1818,** *Landscape with Gipsies.* In the centre of the composition, a gipsy is telling an old man's fortune. This was certainly designed for a tapestry. (Collection of Elizabeth Farnesio.)

Quellyn, Erasmo. Num. **1627,** *The Conception.* (Presented by the Marquis of Leganés to Philip IV.) In the Sacristy of the Monastery of the Escorial there is another, similar, picture. At one time it was believed to be by Rubens, but Rooses has denied the value of this attribution.

Momper II. *Was born and died in Antwerp (1564-1635).*

Num. **1592,** *Sea and Mountain Landscape.* The figures in this landscape are painted by Juan Brueghel.

In several windows in this room there are valuable sketches by great mastaers.

Room XCI   closed

Room XCII.—THE LEGACY OF FERNANDEZ-DURAN

The legacy that don Pedro Fernández-Durán made to the Museum in 1930 is contained in Rooms XCII, XCIII, XCIV, XCV and XCVI, in which, apart from some paintings which we shall review, there figure valuable tapestries, furniture, embroideries, pieces of armour, ceramics and drawings, Schools, masters, nationalities appear mixed, because the donor brought them together so, for his pleasure.

Van der Weyden. Num. **2722,** *The Virgin and the Child.* The Virgin appears crowned by an angel. Several Spanish copies are in existence.

De Coffermans, a Flemish painter from Antwerp, who worked in the second half of the 16th century. There is a series of pictures of reduced proportions, such as num. **2723,** which although beautiful in colour, have no originality.

Neefs returns with his interiors of cathedrals which require the help of a magnifying glass.

Of **Maratta** there hangs the *Portraits of Pope Clement XI,* elected to the Consistory due to the forty eight days of having been ordained a priest.

The *Ecce Homo* of **Morales** is one more of those which left his brush: this one is of reduced dimensions.

Num. **2725,** *The Virgin of Carondolet.* It is supposed that it is a copy made by Rubens from the original by Van Orley.

Anonymous Flemish. Num. **2724,** *The unwise and the wise virgins. (The virgins and the lamps.)*—Whilst the wise virgins light their lamps and attend to their tasks, the unwise sing, dance or sleep without looking after the oil. The second part of the parable takes part in the presence of Christ with the overlate repentance of these virgins. A possible author has been thought to be Otto van Venius, who was Rubens's master.

Herrera «The Old», Francisco. *Born in Seville 1576, and died in Madrid, 1656. He commenced painting under the guidance of Luis Fernández. A lover of great apocalyptic themes, of tormented visions, his painting is of rough orchestration, so fantastic that it could be Michaelangelo's, even though more contrasted and incorrect. His character is reflected in his painting; he was acid and unbearable. His wife separated from him, his daughter took refuge in a convent, his son fled to Italy, the other, «the Fair» died in the prime of his life. Embittered by*

his solitude, he left for Madrid, where he painted for the Merced Con-
vent and for El Paular. In Madrid, he died with neither friend nor
family at his side.

Numbers **2773** and **2774**, *Head of an Apostle.* They are two
studies for a composition on the Ascension of the Virgin. At this
moment it is the only piece that can be seen by this painter (the
Museum possesses other works), and naturally, this is only an idea
far from his usual mode of painting.

Room XCIII and XCIV.—(Continuation)

Hemesen, Juan Sanders. *A Flemish painter, born in Hemixen*
(Antwerp) about 1500, and died in Haarlem about 1564. A disciple
of Joos van Cleve.

Num. **1541**, *The surgeon.* Themes of surgeons, operations and
autopsies were very frequent in Holland, and not so much in Flanders. When they arise they do not lack a certain humorous tone.
Remember the *Extraction of the stone from the mad-man* by Bosch.
Also in Hemesen we see the same theme, in a wide public square
in front of the stall of a gabbler. The mother and sister of the patient
help in the operation, the father crossing his fingers and falling
headlong, dismayed. Some people dressed like our workers of today
are not even aware of the event. The expressions of the personages
are magisterial, the drawing perfect and the colouring vivid and fresh.

Oudry, Juan Bautista. *A French painter, born in Paris, 1685,*
and died in Beauvais, 1755. A disciple of his father and of Serre.

Num. **2793**, *Lady María Josefa Drumond, Countess of Castilblanco.*
Daughter of Lord John Drumond, she was the second wife of don
José de Rozas y Meléndez de la Cueva, who was born in Loma and
obtained the title of Count of Castilblanco on 1709. The Countess
has her hand placed on the head of a puppy, under which appears
the coat-of-arms. It is a very French portrait of the XVIII century
in which flowered Boucher, Largilliere, Quintin de la Tour, dedicated
exclusively to praise the beauty of woman.

Num. **2794**, *Don José de Rozas y Meléndez de la Cueva, I Conde*
de Castilblanco. Husband of the former, The Count, who served the
pretender James II, had as his heir doña María Teresa de Vallabriga
y Rozas, the morganatic wife of the Infante don Luis de Borbón.
The portrait shows the badge of the Order of Alcántara.

Ferro, Gregorio. *A Spanish painter, born in Santa María de*
Lamas (La Coruña) in 1742 and died in Madrid in 1812.

Num. **2780**, *The Count of Floridablanca*, appears as a protector

of Commerce, represented by Mercury and Pluton. It shows the
Order of Carlos III. Although it bears the half erased signature of
Goya, it is apocrypha.

Two small pictures of the class of Carnicero and two landscapes
by Vollardt constitute the rest of the signed section. Amongst the
anonymous, perhaps the most interesting is num. **2791**, a canvas
by a French painter which shows Catherine the Great of Rusia,
with a low-cut dress, carrying the mantel of ermine and the sash
of the Order of Saint Andrew.

Room XCV.—(Continuation)

Toledo, el Capitán Juan de. *Born in Lorca, 1611 and died in
Madrid, 1665. A soldier in Italy, he served in the Spanish campaigns,
fond of battle themes. He painted the larger series of pictures of the
nuns of D. Juan de Alarcón, in the street of Puebla of Madrid. He
married Catalina de Amós and died in the greatest poverty, being
buried at the expense of a footman of the Queen.*

Numbers **2775** and **2776**, *Battles*. Two paintings of twin proportions each with combats as the author himself had been able to
see them, being reminiscent of ther paintings of similar subjects
contemplated in Italy.

Joris van Son. *Joris, or George, was born and died in Antwerp
(1623-1667). He was received as master in the Guild of Saint Lucas
in 1643. He was dedicated almost exclusively to the painting of fruits
and flowers.*

Num. **2728**, *The Virgin and Child in a garland*. In effect, inside
a garland of flowers and fruit, the group of the Virgin and Child is
in monochrome as if the importance of the composition lay in the
vegetal circle which surrounds them.

Wildens, Juan. *Was born and died in Amberes (1586-1653). He
was the disciple of P. Verhulse and friend of Rubens and Van Dyck.
The best engravers of Antwerp, Hollar, Hondius, Matham, etc., engraved
his best paintings. He had one son, Jeremías, also a painter.*

Num. **2773**, *Landscape with Flora. Mercury and nynphs*. It is
a canvas of greater width than depth with miniaturised figures,
very fresh with colour.

Boulogne, Juan de. *Commonly called «El Valentín». He was
born in Coulommiers (Brie), 1594 and died in Rome, 1632. He was
probably called Valentín de Boullogne, a direct descendent of the branch
of this illustrious name. The resemblance of his art with that of Vouet,
aroused the thought that he might be his disciple; today this hypothesis
has been discarded. He studied Caravaggio and was a friend of Poussin*

*and it is even said that the latter imitated him on some occasions. A cold
bath that he took was the cause of his death at the age of thirty six.*

Num. **2788**, *St. Peter's denial.* A large and broad painting, very
vigorous. To the left, St. Peter before the questions of a servant
and soldier, denies knowledge of Jesus. To the left soldiers play
with coins. In the treatment of the light and shade, the influence
of Caravaggio is seen immediately.

Anonymous Italian. Num. **2760**, *Garden.* It is an alehouse.
Two are still considered to be of **J. Pillement** números **2795** and
2796, of landscape with soldiers.

Room XCVI.—(End of Legacy)

No less than twelve coppers of **Franck** «el Mozo» the
son of Franck «the Old», hang in this Room. He was born
and died in Amberes (1581-1642). The dynasty of Franck
was very extensive which has occasioned not a few doubts
in the attribution of his works. This one «the Young», came
to be dean or deacon of the Guild of St. Lucas. He went to
Venice to study the ancients. On the death of his father,
and when he commenced painting his sovereign Francis III,
he also adopted the name of «Den ouden», that is «the Old»
which ledd to even greater confusion between the works
of father and son.

The coppers refer for the most part to episodes from the
Old Testament.

There are also *Alehouses* by **Frans Ikens** (1601-1693), a
painter of Anrwerp, and **Willem Klaesz Heda** (1594-1681),
a painter from Haarlem (Holland).

Caracciolo, Juan Bautista. *He was born and died in Naples
(1570-1637). A disciple of Caravaggio, he also received lessons from
Imparato, Francisco, a disciple in his time of Pierino da Vaga and
of Titian. Having arrived at a mature age with only mediocre works
behind him, he grew fond of the art of Anibal Cárracci; he went to Rome
and returned to Partenope and attained the recongnition of his good art.*

Num. **2759**, *The doctor saints Cosme and Damian.* Cosme, who
was writing, raises his head to question Damian, who also has a
pen in his right hand. The canvas was painted by artificial light.
in the «Caravaggiesco» fashion, to obtain strong contrasts of light
and shade. The two figures have noble and pensive faces.

The other painters of this last Room of the Fernández-Durán
Legacy are already known to us and add nothing to that which has
already been written.

Room XCVII.—FRENCH PAINTERS

Juan de Boullogne, «the Valentín». (See tha data for this
painter in the description of Room XCV.)

Num. **2346,** *The Martyrdom of Saint Laurence.* The executioner
puts the naked saint on the grating; soldiers, spectators and a woman
with a child. A beautiful large-size canvas with chiaroscuros which
are reminiscent of Caravaggio. The naked figure of the saint is
admirably sculptured. While it was in the Alcázar, it was attributed
to Mosu Pusin, that is to say, Monsieur Poussin; but Voss has
restored it to its real artist, recognising that it is an important work.

Houasse, Miguel Angel. Numbers **2267** and **2268,** two *Bac-
chanalia* with Bacchus, naked figures, followers of Bacchus, fauns a
priest sacrificing before the altar... Delirous scenes, showing a lot of
action, with beautiful fore-shortenings and landscape frescoes. The
two canvases are signed, one in 1719 and the other in 1720. (In La
Granja, collection of Philip V.)

Gobert, Pedro. Num. **2274,** The Second Mademoiselle of Blois,
in the shape of Leda. Surrounded by maid-servants and cupids.
Leda is placed at the edge of the pool. A large-size canvas, superficial,
decorative, «nice», very much to the taste of the times in which it
was painted. Mlle. of Blois was called Francisca María, and was a
legitimate daughter of Louis XIV and Madame Montespan. It is to be
noted that the heads are superposed. (In 1747 it was in the Palace.)

Coypel, Antonio. *Was born and died in Paris (1661-1722). Son
and pupil of Noel, whom he accompanied to Rome. On his return to
Paris he was named «painter of gentlemen», at the age of twenty, at
which age also he entered the Academy, of which he later became Director.
In 1716 he had already become painter to the King, who made him a
noble in the following year. The Regent also made him his painter and
heaped him with honours. He is reproached for having introduced bad
taste in Paris due to his excessive pompousness, the blame for which
is given to Bernini, with whom he was very friendly in Rome and by
whom he allowed himself to be influenced too much.*

Num. **2247,** *The Indictment of Susannah.* She is dramatically
accused by the ancients. It may be that there is an excess of show
and that the sumptuous architecture is exaggerated: but it cannot
be denied that the composition is beautiful and well-balanced. (The
picture was bought at Kelly; in 1772 it was already in the Palace.)

Drouais, Francisco Huberto. *French painter, he was born and died in Paris (1727-1775). Pupil of his father Huberto and later of Largilliere for five years. On the occasion of the coming to Paris of Peter the Great, of Russia, Drouais's portraits were seen by the king who commissiones Drouais to paint his own. He wanted to take him back to Russia with him, but the artist declined the invitation. For his cynegetic themes he grew to be the favourite painter of Louis XV, who lodged him in the Louvre. He secured the appointment of superintendent of the Gobelin factory, and for this reason summoned Boucher and Natoire to collaborate with him. He illustrated the Fables of Lafontaine.*

Num. **2467,** Madame Pompadour. Oval-shaped canvas. Head and shoulders; a bow at her breats exactly the same as the one which secures her lace headdress. Her name was Juana Antonia Poisson and she was educated as a courtesan by her mother. She married Guillermo Lenormant. Louis XV met her on a hunting expedition, and when his favourite, the Duchess of Chateauroux, died, he made her his mistress. She used up real fortunes organising festivities in the palace to entertain the bored monarch; she made herself mistress of his will, managed, with him as arbiter, the State's affairs, some of which she mismanaged with disastrous results. Received the title of Duchess of Pompadour and that of Lady-in-waiting to the Queen, and was a great patroness of poets and artists. The most beautiful portraits of were executed by Quintin de la Tour, When he got tired at length of his mistress, the king substituted her for Mlle. de la Romana. A little later, she died. (A donation by the Duchess of Pastrana, in 1889.)

Num. **2488,** *Madame du Barry.* By name, María Juana de Vauvernier, illegitimate daughter of Ana Becu, she was educated in a convent by nuns. She was employed in a fashion shop and her youth was one long scandal. The Duke of Richelieu and M. du Barry gave her in marriage to a brother of the latter, Guillaume by name, they introduced her at the Palace and presented her to Louis XV as a lady gifted with great talents and exceptional qualities. In 1770 the King made her his official mistress, and thus she received the greatest dignities of the State in the Palace. On the death of Louis XV, she was exiled by his son Louis XVI, though Marie Antonielte made her live in the palace at Luciennes where she installed a salon for admirers, among which there were some notabilities of the epoque. When the Revolution exploded, she went to London, but was aware that her duty lay in being beside the one who had protected her, and returned in order not to conceal that she embraced the cause of the Royal Family. This event led her to being condemned to death. She went to the guillotine in the Place de la Concorde, on the orders of the Tribunal of the Revolution. The portrait we have before us is an oval-shaped one; in it she is shown crowned with roses and carrying a garland in her hands. Really beautiful, it makes a pair with the preceding picture. (Also donated by the Duchess of Pastrana.)

Dorigny, Miguel. *There were various painters related to each other, of the same name. He was born in St. Quentin, 1617, and died in Paris, 1665. Pupil and son in-law of Simon Vouet, he was a teacher at the Academy.*

Num. **2249,** *The Triumph of Prudence;* it is in praise of Prudence. In the clouds and in front of a portal, Justice, Charity, Strength, or Hercules and Temperance; two winged spirits, in the centre, a sun surrounded by five stars, with the label: «Solio Prudentia, Sol ets». It deals with an allegory which appears to be painted for a ceiling. It was formerly held that this canvas was by Bourdon. From 1876 onwards it has been attributed to Miguel Dorigny.

Beaubrun, Enrique. *Also a member of a large family of painters Was baptised in Amboise, 1603, and died in Paris, 1677. Nephew of Louis Beaubrun, painter; but he spent more time with his brother, Charles, to such an extent that the picture which one began was finished by the other.*

Num. **2231,** *Ana of Bourbon.* More than half-size portrait, in a plain white dress adorned with pearls and aquamarines. She was the daughter of Gaston, grand-daughter of Enrique IV, the Bearnese, born in the Louvre in 1627. First, she was known as «Mademoiselle of Orleans», later «the great Mademoiselle» and finally «Mademoiselle of Montpensier». She died in Paris at the age of sixty-six. At the beginning the canvas was signed; later the signature disappeared, perhaps when the canvas was lined. (It comes from the Retiro.)

Poussin. Num. **2315,** *Roman Gladiators fighting.* On the right, on his throne, is the Emperor; between the columns, the Patricians; in the lower part, on the left, the crowd. In the arena, three gladiators lying dead and a fourth fighting with his sword. It is a group of blackened, naked figures, due to the careless conservation of the canvas. (In 1772 it was in the Retiro.)

Room XCVIII.—SPANISH PORTRAIT-PAINTERS OF THE 19th CENTURY

This Room, only recently completed, forms a gallery of portraits of members of the aristocracy —or mostly— of the nineteenth century, executed by famous artists who belonged to the same century. They are portraits which are beautifully made within the traditional tonic of the age: academic, adornment in detail, and very true to life. The drawing is in every case very correct and the colouring fresh and succulent.

The most valuable painters are the **Madrazo,** a dynasty of painters who filled almost a century of our Spanish painting. They are **José de Madrazo,** born in 1781; **Federico** and **Luis,** sons of the previous mentioned, the first born in 1815 and the second in 1825, and **Raimundo,** born in 1841. Also to be mentioned are **Vicente López, Zacarías González, J. M. Fernández Cruzado,** etc.

Num. **2603,** *The Marquess of Manzanedo*, by R. de Madrazo. The Marquess was Cuban and became by her marriage Duchess of Santoña.

Num. **2495,** *Don Antonio González Velázquez*, by Zacarías González Velázquez. Half-size portrait, with palette and brush, it is the artist's father, who was also a painter.

Num. **863,** *María Isabel de Braganza*, by Bernardo López Piquer, son and pupil of Vicente López. She is pointing to the building to the Prado with her right hand. María Isabel, the daughter of Juan IV of Portugal and of Carlota Joaquina of Bourbon, married her uncle the king Ferdinand VII, in 1816.

Num. **2826,** *Portrait of a Bishop*, by Vicente López. Half-size portrait, he appears with a sheet of paper in his hand. (Legacy of Mariano Lanuza.)

Num. **2813,** *Jaime Girona*, by F. de Madrazo. He formed a part of the Financial Board and the Queen Regent made him Count of Eleta. (Bequeathed by the son of the subject of the painting.)

Num. **2814,** *Saturnina Canaleto of Girona*, by F. de Madrazo. Wife of the former.

Num. **2879,** *Don Gonzalo of Vilches*, by J. de Madrazo. Was the first Count of Vilches, official attaché to the Legation of His Catholic Majesty in Rome and secretary at the Embassy. (Bequeathed by the Count of la Cimera.)

Num. **2878,** *The Countess of Vilches*, by F. de Madrazo. She was formerly Amalia de Llano y Dotres, married the first Count of Vilches; was a writer, authoress of the novels «Berta» and «Lidia». (Bequeathed by the Count of Vilches.)

Num. **2560,** *Lady in the low-cut Dress*, by Joaquín Manuel Fernández Cruzado, born in Jerez de la Frontera, 1781, and died in Cádiz, 1856. It is a half-size portrait of the lady, who is seated: her

hair is dressed «de tres potencias»; with shell comb and a fan in her
hand. (Bequeathed by the Count of Pradere.)

Num: **2559,** *Doña Piedad Jandiola;* by Antonio Esquivel, born in
Sevilla, 1806, and died in Madrid, 1857. The subject of the portrait
was the grandmother of the Count of Pradere, who bequeathed the
picture to the Museum.

Num. **2848,** *Lady with a Fan,* by Gutiérrez de la Vega.

There are other portraits, up to now unnumbered, such as that
of *José Gutiérrez de los Ríos,* by Vicente López, and the one of *Lady of
Delicado,* by the same painter, both Puncel legacies; the one of the
lady of Creux (oval-shaped), by Luis de Madrazo, bequeathed by
María de la Cuesta; that of *Isabel Aragón Escolar,* by Luis Ferrant,
bequeathed by Carlos Escolar; that of *Mrs. Alice Lolita Muth Ben
Maacha,* by Ignacio Zuloaga, bequeathed by the subject of the portrait; that of *Manuela de Erraztu Urureta-Goyena,* by R. de Madrazo,
bequeathed by Joaquín Irureta-Goyena; and finally, the one of the
Marchioness of San Carlos de Pedroso, by Felix Henri Giacomotti,
bequeathed by the Count of San Esteban de Cañongo.

Room XCIX.—(Stairs)

The section of the staircase is adorned with twelve small
pictures by *Teniers*-popular, genre scenes.

Both, Juan. *Dutch painter, was born and died in Utrecht (1618-
1652).*
Num. **2062,** *The Aldobrandini Garden in Frascati.*

English anonymous. Num. **2457,** *Charles II of England.* More
than half-size portrait; is armed, his helmet under his right arm.
He was the son of Charles I; was born in London in 1630, reigned
from 1660, and died in 1685. (Acquired by Philip V.)

Paul van Somer, *«the Old». Was born in Antwerp, 1576, and died
in London, 1621. After having set up in Amsterdam, he removed to
England, where he painted the portraits of many important figures,
until he became Court painter.*
Num. **1954,** *Jacob I of England.* Grey suit and green cape pro-
fusely adorned with pearls. He wears badges of the Order of the
Garter. He was the son of Mary Stuart and Lord Darnley, was
born in 1566, succeeded Elizabeth of England and died in 1625. Was
painted about 1600. (Comes from the Museum of the Trinity.)

English anonymous. Num. **2410,** *Jacob II of England.* More
than half-size portrait, armed, cane in his left hand, pointing to a

trench with the right hand. He was the son of Charles I, was born in 1633, succeeded his brother Charles in 1685, was dethroned in 1688 and died in 1701. (Acquired by Philip V.)

Room C.—PICTURES BY ENGLISH PAINTERS

Reynolds, Joshua. *Was born in Plymton-Earl's (Devonshire) in 1723, and died in London in 1792. Son of a Protestant minister, who seconded, his son's vocation, he was apprentice to Hudson. At the age of twenty three, he was already established in Plymouth and had gained an outstanding reputation. On his way to Italy he passed through Spain where, perhaps he was introduced to Goya's art. Apparently he did not like Rafael, nor Michaelangelo, nor the Florentine painters in general; but on the other hand, the Venetians satisfied him completely, so much so that he appropriated a great deal from their luminous palette. On his return to London, he was sought out as an artist by all the gentry. His «cachets» were much exalted, a fact which contributed to the selectness of his clientele and the prestige he gained. He set up a house in Leicester Square; he was to be seen frequently with the Duque and Duchess of Devonshire, was a friend of Lord Hamilton and sat at the table of George III. He had only one weakness; a stifled hatred for his rival, Thomas Gainsborough, though, summoned by the latter a short time before he died, he was reconciled with him.*

It is without doubt that Reynolds has been the most «complete» artist England has produced. His palette is brilliant and solid and his drawing impeccable. Preoccupied by the effects of colour, however, he conceived the idea of an obtained fermentable bitumens which have ill-treated a good part of his work. He exhibited until two years before his death. His remains are buried in St. Paul's Cathedral, London.

Num. **2858**, *Portrait of a Minister*. Neither its drawing nor its colouring give any idea of Reynolds' art, although it has been verified as one of his works. It is one of those pictures of no real interest which are painted during every artist's life. (Acquired by the Ministry of National Education privately in 1943.)

The *Portrait of Mr. James Bourdien*, which displays a better technique than the preceding one, is also by Reynolds.

Romney, George. *Was born in Dalton-le-Furness (Lancashire), in 1734, and died in Kendal, in 1802. A wretched neurotic, he played the part of a musician in some places, mechanic in others and sketcher in others; he went round from fair to fair, painting bust portraits for two and a half guineas, and full-size portraits for six. He got married in*

Kendal, had two sons and left home to live a Bohemian existence together with Ozias Humphrey, a painter of miniature. He left for Italy, was absent for two years, and on his return installed himself in luxury in Hampstead and Cavendish Square. His success was assured by the famous Emma Lyon, the beautiful, libertine girl, who, from being the hostess in an unsavoury «joint», finally became Lady Hamilton. Romney painted many portraits of her, giving her the shape of figures from Art or Mythology; Saffus, Bacchus, Magdalene, Serena, Joan of Arc, Odalisque, Alope, etc. And these renderings were received so well that the haughtiest ladies in London waited their turn to have their portraits painted in such' a way. Compared with the stiffness of Reynolds's, Romney's feminine portraits are graceful and full of feline flexibility.

Disconsolate at the loss of Emma Lyon, to whom he had given all the love he had denied his own, flattered by the aristocracy and steeped in riches and honours, there came a moment in which he felt old and ill. Thus it was that he thought about his forgotten wife and the children he had abandoned, whom he had never seen during all those years of separation. And in 1799 he gave up his brushes and returned to Kendal. His wife put aside the past and received him with opened arms, and it was in her arms that he died shortly afterwards.

Num. **2584,** *An English Gentleman.* As was the case with the other picture, by Reynolds, this portrait is not a faithful reflection of Romney's art, which justly distinguished itself in his portraits of women, vaporous and full of grace. This gentleman, in dress coat and with his hat under his arm, has definite mien, and as a pictorial piece is superior to the two by Reynolds. (Bequeathed by the Duke of Arcos, it arrived at the Museum in 1935.)

Hoppner, John. *Was born in Whitechapel in the year of 1758, and died in London, 1810. Son of a German musician father established in England. He dedicated himself to music, and finally became a singer in the Royal Chapel. Attracted by painting, he entered the Academy of which Reynolds was Director, and did so well that he was awarded the Golden Medal for his picture* King Lear. *Patronised by the Prince of Wales, he made contact with the English aristocracy, among whom he gained quite a reputation. First an imitator of Reynolds and later, of Lawrence, he at length discovered his own personality as an artist. He painted some very good portraits, and perhaps the one that brought him most fame was that of the Countess of Oxford.*

Num. **2474,** *Am Unknown Woman.* A very English portrait; very delicate, with touches of real grace. It cannot be denied that there are more than a few retouches; but, in spite of everything, the easy handling of the original painting is disclosed. (From the Errazu legacy.)

Gainsborough, Thomas. *The son of a humble shopkeeper esta-*

*blished in the county of Suffolk, he was born in 1727, and died in London
in 1788. He had to struggle hard with wants and he made himself conspicuous by his painting of landscapes, so much so that when Reynolds
saw his pictures, he said he was «the best landscape painter of our time».
Later he began to work at the portrait, and was soon among the best
portrait painters, much to the extreme jealousy of Reynolds, whom he
finally surpassed with his portrait of the great tragedy actress Mrs. Sid-
dons. At the hour of Gainsborough's death, the two made their peace.*

Portrait of Dr. Isaac Sequeira. It is a good example of the work
of this English artist, although his feminine figures were always
more successful. His second picture is the *Portrait of Robert Butcher*,
inferior to the other.

Lawrence, Thomas. *(1769-1830). He was a real child prodigy.
At the age of nine he was already painting admirable portraits. Pupil
of the Academy, he received Reynolds's counsels and was patronised
by George III, until whose death he was the King's official painter.
He travelled widely and was always received with praises. He is considered one of the most elegant painters England has known.*

Portrait of the 10th Count of Wesfmorland. This is a marvellous,
full-size portrait, worthy indeed of Lawrence's palette, as much for
its excellence as for the brilliant palette which this great artist boasted.

There are other canvases by various artists, of minor interest,
with the exception of a *Portrait of a Gentleman*, by Sir **John Watson
Gordon** (1790-1864), which is one of the best paintings in this
English Room.

Room CI

Dughet, Gaspar, *also called «el Pusino». Was born and died in
Rome (1613-1675). He was the pupil and brother-in-law of Poussin.
To observe nature more carefully, he bought four houses in Rome, two
in the most elevated places of the City, the third in Rivoli and the fourth
in Frascati. He worked a great deal in the main cities of Italy.*

This Room has several not very large picture, the landscape
predominating among them, by Dughet. His easy way of painting
can be observed in his pleasant works.

There are also works by **Bramer, Alsloot** and **Monper.**

Mirevelt, Miguel. *Was born and died in Delft (Holland), 1567-
1641.*

Num. **2106,** Dutch Lady, almost full-size, with coif and vandyck
collar in white and dressed in black. (In 1794 it was in the Quinta of
the Duke of Arco.)

Herb, Guillermo van. *Flemish painter, was born and died in Amberes, 1614-1677.*

Num. **1986,** *The Liberation of Prisoners.* Two groups of prisoners in a prison: in the doorway, the warden followed by a soldier with a halberd. It was formerly attributed to Stefano de la Bella. (In the Retiro.)

Pourbus, Francis *«the Young».* *Flemish painter, was born in Antwerp, 1569, and died in Paris, 1622. The son of Francis Pourbus, «the Old», it is not known whose disciple he was. He was only ten when his father died. He painted in Brussels for Isabel Clara Eugenia and Archduke Albert; in Paris he received the title of «Painter of Maria of Medici», wife of Enrique IV, «the Bearnese»; he painted for Vicente I of Gonzaga, in Mantua, and finally in Paris painted the portrait of Louis XIII, as a child.*

Num. **2293,** *Episcopal Blessing.* The inside of a temple. The dishop is blessing a kneeling family, probably conversion of protestants. An audience of the faithful. (Acquired by Charles IV.)

Also hanging here are some *Seascapes,* by **Willaerts.**

Room CII

Backer, Adrián. *Dutch painter, was born and died in Amsterdam, 1636-1684.*

Num. **2557,** *A General.* More than half-size, armed and with cane. On the left, a tent; on the right, the helmet, adorned with plumes. (Bequeathed by the Count of Pradera.)

Van der Neer, *born in Amsterdam in 1634, and died in Dusseldorf, in 1703. Dutch painter.*

Num. **2120,** *Cavalry Skirmish.*

Dutch, Anonymous. Num. **2167,** *Portrait of J. van Oldenburnevelt.* The subject of the painting was born in Amersloot, in 1547; he was a rival of Maurice of Orange, signed the «Twelve-year Truce» with Spinola, and was beheaded in the Hague in 1619. (Acquired by Charles IV.)

Stomer, Mateo. *Flemish painter, it is known that he was born at the end of the sixteenth century, that he was a pupil of Honthorst in Rome, and that he died in Messina some time after 1650. Nagler holds that he was the second master of Juan van Houbracken.*

Num. **127,** *Roman Charity.* The scene refers to a text of Valerio Máximo, in which he says that Cimon, a Roman citizen, was condemned to death from hunger in a gloomy prison, and that his daughter. Pera kept him alive by breast-feeding him. The attribution is made by Longhi. In the Budapest Museum there is a similar picture, attributed somewhat doubtfully to Stomer. (From the collection of Elizabeth Farnesio, in La Granja.)

Harlem, Cornelis Cornelisz van. *Dutch painter, was born and died in Harlem, 1562-1636.*

Num. **2088,** *Apollo before the Tribunal of the Gods.* Apollo is being judged by Jupiter, Mercury, Bacchus, Neptune (with his back turned), Mars (also with his back turned), etc. Signed on the stone on which Apollo is sitting. (In 1827 it was brought from the Academy of San Fernando.) The naked figures, painted in various tones, in miniature, are exquisite.

Lamen, Cristóbal van der. *Flemish painter, was born about 1615 in Brussels or Antwerp, where he died some time before 1652.*

Num. **1555,** *Banquet for Soldiers and Courtesans.* Six people, four men and two women; one of the men is playing the flute. The meats are on the table. (Collection of Elizabeth Farnesio, in La Granja.)

INDEX OF PAINTERS

(The numbers in bold type indicate the page where the painter's biography may be found.)

INDEX OF ILLUSTRATIONS

INDEX OF THE NUMBERS
OF CANVASES

(See NOTE page 15)

INDEX

ENTRANCE → LII

LII

FERNÁNDEZ DURÁN BEQUEST

XCV   XCVI

XCIV

XCIII

XCII

XCI

NO